Biology and Human Behavior: The Neurological Origins of Individuality, 2nd Edition

Part I

Professor Robert Sapolsky

THE TEACHING COMPANY ®

PUBLISHED BY:

THE TEACHING COMPANY
4151 Lafayette Center Drive, Suite 100
Chantilly, Virginia 20151-1232
1-800-TEACH-12
Fax—703-378-3819
www.teach12.com

ISBN 1-59803-081-7

Robert Sapolsky, Ph.D.
Professor of Neurology and Neurosurgery, Stanford University

Robert Sapolsky holds the John A. and Cynthia Fry Gunn Professorship of Biological Sciences at Stanford University, where he is also professor of Neurology and Neurosurgery. His laboratory focuses on the mechanisms by which stress and stress hormones can damage the brain and on the development of gene therapy strategies to save neurons from neurological insults. In addition, Professor Sapolsky has spent his summers since the late 1970s studying a population of wild baboons in East Africa, examining what social rank, personality, and patterns of sociality have to do with vulnerability to stress-related diseases.

Professor Sapolsky writes regularly for nonscientists in such publications as *Scientific American, Discover, Natural History,* and *The New Yorker.* He is also the author of five books, including four nontechnical publications for the general public: *Why Zebras Don't Get Ulcers: A Guide to Stress, Stress-Related Diseases and Coping,* 3rd edition (2004, Henry Holt); *The Trouble with Testosterone and Other Essays on the Biology of the Human Predicament* (Scribner, 1997); *A Primate's Memoir* (Scribner, 2001); and *Monkeyluv and Other Essays on Our Lives as Animals* (Scribner, 2005).

Table of Contents

Biology and Human Behavior:
The Neurological Origins of Individuality
2nd Edition
Part I

Biology and Human Behavior:
The Neurological Origins of Individuality
2nd Edition

Scope:

From time immemorial, the more philosophical among us have pondered: "What is the essence of who I am? What is it that has made me who I am?" Behavioral biology is the science of trying to figure this out, with the guiding assumption that an understanding of who and why we are cannot be achieved without considering our biology.

Now, a human asking these sorts of questions is more complicated, for a myriad of reasons, than a wildebeest asking, "Why is it in my essence to ovulate during one short period of time each year?" or a migratory bird wondering, "Why is it that each year I wish to fly from Tierra del Fuego to Alaska?" Tackling the biology of behavior is particularly daunting when considering humans and their social behaviors.

These challenges are even more extreme when considering an aspect of our behavior that is often the most interesting and important to study: What is the behavioral biology of our *abnormal* human behaviors? Because of the intrinsic intellectual challenge of a subject such as this, and because of its implication, when we ask a question about the biology of abnormal human behavior, we are often, de facto, asking: Whose *fault* is it that this has occurred; who should be held *accountable*? Multiple murderer: damaged frontal cortex or tainted soul? Spouse unable to get out of bed or go to work: victim of the neurochemistry of depression or self-indulgent slacker? Child failing at school: learning disabled or lazy?

This course is an introduction to the biology of human behavior, often of abnormal human behavior, with an emphasis on the brain. The purpose of the course is twofold: first, to teach the contemporary science of how our brains regulate our thoughts, emotions, and feelings—how our brains make us the individuals that we are—and second, to teach how our brains are regulated—sculpted by evolution, constrained or freed by genes, shaped by early experience, modulated by hormones. In this framework, the view is not of the brain as the be-all and end-all of what makes us individuals but, rather, the brain as the final common pathway, the conduit by which our individuality is shaped by biology that started anywhere from seconds to millions of years ago.

After an introductory lecture presenting this framework, a quarter of the course (Modules I and II) will be devoted to the functions of the nervous system. These lectures are updated versions of those in the first edition of this Teaching Company course and will start at the level of how a single neuron functions, building upward until we examine how millions of neurons in a particular region of the brain operate. The focus will be on the regions of the brain most pertinent to emotion and behavior, rather than, say, to regulation of kidney function.

The middle portion of the course (Modules III, IV, and V) will explore how the brain and behavior are regulated. First, we will cover how the brain regulates hormones and how hormones influence brain function and behavior. Then, we will examine how both the brain and behavior evolved, covering contemporary thinking about how natural selection has sculpted and optimized behavior and how that optimization is mediated by brain function. We will then focus on a bridge between evolution and the brain, namely, what genes at the molecular level have to do with brain function and how those genes have evolved.

Hormones, evolution, genes, and behavior, however, do not work in vacuo but, instead, are extremely sensitive to environment. The next section of the course (Module VI) examines *ethology*, which is the study of the behavior of animals in their natural habitats (rather than, for example, in a laboratory cage).

With these various approaches in hand, the final quarter of the course (Module VII) will examine how each approach helps explain an actual set of behaviors. Among a number of possible topics, we will focus on aggression, both because of the extensive information available and the importance of the subject.

The facts of this subject are not intrinsically difficult, even for the nonscientist. The implications, however, should seem far from simple. Yet this is a subject that each of us must master, because all of us are, de facto, behavioral biologists. We serve on juries, deciding whom to incarcerate, whom to put to death. We vote for elected officials who have stances regarding gun control and whether violence is inevitable, who determine whether certain types of love between consenting adults should be consecrated by the government imprimatur of marriage, who help decide whether a certain social problem can be fixed by government expenditures or is biologically irrevocable. And many of us will have to be behavioral biologists when confronting loved ones whose behaviors have changed them to an unrecognizable extent and deciding whether it is "them" or "their disease."

The final lecture of this course will consider issues such as these: What are the societal and philosophical consequences of knowledge about the biology of our behaviors, the biology of what makes us the individuals that we are?

Lecture One
Biology and Behavior—An Introduction

Scope:

The purpose of this course is to explain the biology of what makes us who we are, the biology of our individual differences, the biology of our behaviors. This introductory lecture presents the framework of the course: that there is a neurobiology of who we are, that it is vital to learn about it, and that it can best be understood with the interdisciplinary approach of this course. Throughout the subsequent sections, the constant themes will be the interactions of the various disciplines in their effects upon the brain and how all this helps us to understand individual behavioral differences.

Outline

I. Biology must be considered as a possible factor in human behavior and individuality.

    A. Examples of changes of behavior in two adult males illustrate this factor.

        1. Chuck has always been an extrovert—charismatic, confident, and flirtatious. Recently, though, he has been getting more introverted and more withdrawn.

        2. Arthur, on the other hand, has always been obsessive, rigidly ethical, and extremely reliable at work. But recently, he has started to tell inappropriate sexual jokes, and he has even taken to stalking women.

    B. Could such changes of behavior, often explained as a midlife crisis, actually be the result of a mutation in a single gene? In these two cases, the answer is yes.

    C. There is a biology to our sexual choices, the extent and type of our religiosity, and everything else about us.

II. How do we tend to approach the challenge of understanding our behavior?

    A. Typically, we think categorically, as with colors, coming up with labels and explanations, but categorical thinking has its advantages and its limits. (Figure 1a)

        1. Categorical thinking helps our memory.

2. But categorical boundaries distort our ability to see the differences and similarities between two different facts.

3. If you pay too much attention to the boundaries, you have trouble seeing the big picture.

B. This course's goal of noncategorical thinking about behavior is critical. Little can be explained by merely thinking about genes alone, or brain chemicals, or hormones, or early experience, or any other single factor.

C. Our blueprint for the entire course is to start off looking at what a behavior is in a particular category and a particular class, then to begin to ask biologically, where did that behavior come from? (Figure 1b)

1. We start off by studying the brain and the nervous system.

2. Beginning to work back in time, we then try to understand further the things that modulate the nervous system, such as environmental triggers, hormones, and perinatal and fetal development.

3. Then working further back, we look at the genetic attributes of the population that an individual comes from.

4. This approach pushes us all the way back to examine what the pressures are of natural selection that sculpted that species.

D. Isn't this approach obvious to everyone? Perhaps it is now, but in the not-too-distant past, many prominent scientists in this field were unable to think of the biology of our behavior in such a subtle way and, thus, often became damaging ideologues.

III. What are the special challenges of thinking about the biology of behavior in humans versus behavior in other animals?

A. In some ways, human behave just like any other animal, as with the synchronization of female reproductive cycles.

B. In other ways, humans have a physiology very similar to that of other animals, but they utilize the physiology in unique ways.

C. In still other ways, human behavior is utterly unique in the animal world, as with aspects of human sexual behavior for nonreproductive purposes.

IV. The general strategy for this course is to see how behavior can be understood in the context of everything from milliseconds of brain activity to millions of years of evolution.

    A. We start with how the brain works and how the brain produces behavior.

        1. We first study a single brain cell, a neuron, and then move on to understand how one neuron communicates with another.

        2. We work our way up to large networks of neurons, then to how the nervous system can regulate how all of our cells work.

        3. In the section on neurobiology, we will focus on two themes: first, understanding why one individual's nervous system works differently from another's and, second, understanding how this function can change over time (*plasticity*).

    B. The subsequent lectures explore what it is that changes how the nervous system works, whether the environment, hormones, early experience, fetal life, genetics, or evolution.

    C. Finally, we approach a set of human behaviors with this set of strategic ideas, focusing on a contentious and important area of human behavior: aggression.

Further Reading:

For the most nuanced and insightful book written concerning the biology of human behavior, by an eminent scientist/physician:

M. Konner, *The Tangled Wing: Biological Constraints on the Human Spirit.*

Questions to Consider:

1. What are the most substantive differences between humans and other animals?

2. What are the most substantive similarities?

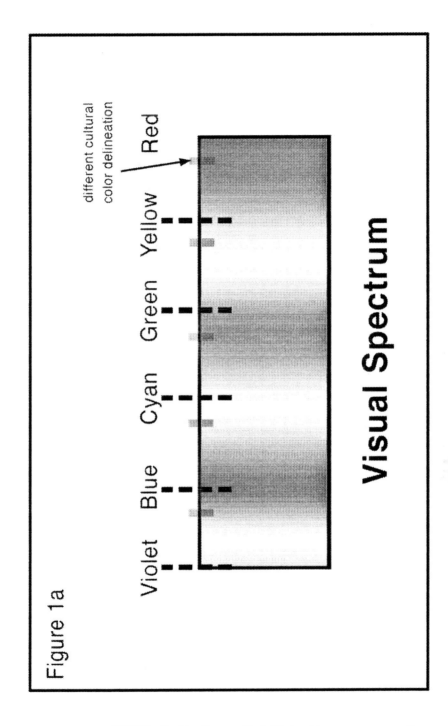

Figure 1a

different cultural color delineation

Violet | Blue | Cyan | Green | Yellow | Red

Visual Spectrum

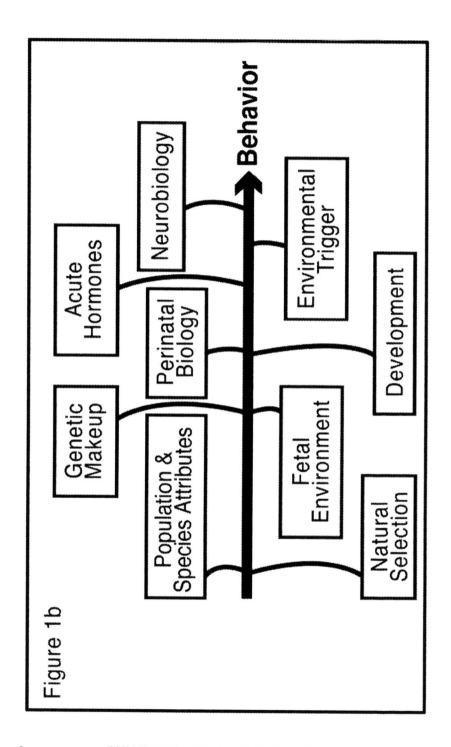

Figure 1b

Lecture One—Transcript
Biology and Behavior—An Introduction

Hello. My name is Robert Sapolsky. I'm a professor of neurobiology at Stanford University, and I'm very pleased to be doing this course because, not surprisingly, I think this is a subject that is so important that every child and adult in America should be forced to learn about this. Basically, it's trying to understand the biology of what makes us who we are; the biology of our individual differences; the biology of our behaviors; what I believe is an incredibly important subject for every one of us to study.

Okay, to begin with, let me give you a scenario that should catch your attention. It involves two hypothetical individuals. The first one is Chuck: Chuck is in marketing; Chuck is extraverted, charismatic, life of the party in this superficial sort of way; he's confident; he's flirtatious; he's having some fidelity problems with his third marriage right now. In contrast, we've got Arthur: Arthur is down in marketing; he's obsessive; he's rigidly ethical, sufficiently so that the people at the IRS wonder what's up with this guy; he's extremely reliable at work, and as a result, he is regularly exploited by his co-workers; he lives alone; he spends his evenings making model ships and airplanes.

However, there have been some changes in Chuck and Arthur recently. Chuck, bizarrely, is suddenly getting more introverted; he's getting more withdrawn; he's getting less talkative—long periods of silence that are beginning to make his customers uncomfortable— and within a few months is going to cost him his job. Most bizarre, from out of nowhere, he's developed this obsession with painting. He is now painting every spare moment, and these are dark, brooding canvasses that he can't begin to explain. Meanwhile, Arthur has been having some changes as well. He's starting to tell sexual jokes, and this is initially sort of puzzling and amusing to his co-workers, but lately they've been getting a little bit beyond the edge, a little bit inappropriate. He is taking to stalking women; within a month or so it is going to get him into trouble with the law for the first time when he exposes himself.

What is remarkable is that within a year or so, both of these men are going to be institutionalized. What is going on here? Are they having horrendous mid-life crises? Is there satanic possession? Are they psychiatrically disturbed? Remarkably, each one of these men has a mutation, a single gene mutation, giving rise to a neurological disorder, where these are among the first symptoms. And most amazingly, they've got the exact same mutation.

So, we're suddenly stuck with this major puzzle. Where's this coming from? What do we make of the fact that we can be so determined by our genes that this could change these men's personalities? What do we make of the fact that we are so free from our genes that the same exact mutation could produce such incredibly different changes in these two men? What do we make of the fact that we're beginning to understand the biology of what goes wrong in a case like this? And, we're beginning to understand the biology of even far more subtle states; we're beginning to grasp something about the brain anatomy that may have something to do with our sexual orientation. Amazingly there is a type of neurological disorder where one of the most consistent side effects is you develop this passionate interest in philosophy and religion. What do we do about the fact that recently scientists have figured out a way to change the brain chemistry of a male rodent and turn him from being polygamous into monogamous? It's not clear if this counts as an intervention, or if this counts as a therapeutic sort of issue that we should be trying in our human males. What do we make of the fact that we are beginning to develop a biology that explains our taste, our personalities, how we vote, what foods we like, who we love and how faithful we are to them? What do we do with the fact that we are beginning to get a biology of what makes us who we are?

Now in trying to think about this here in this course, we are taking this on in a very particularly challenging way. It is trivial, relatively, to figure out how some migratory bird figures out how to get to Tierra del Fuego at a certain time of year with the biology of migration. Sort of, how come, biologically, all the wildebeests in the Serengeti ovulate the same week. That's easy. That's easy in comparison to what we're trying to figure out here, which is the biology of human behavior, the biology of why some humans behave differently than others, and most challenging, the biology of where some of our most damaging, most frightening, most inappropriate behaviors come from.

Now this is not easy to go after. We tend to have a way to deal with a complex subject like this: What is the biology of our behavior? We tend to think about it, to approach the subject with a certain cognitive style. Essentially, what we do is, we think categorically. We try to come up with labels, we try to come up with buckets of explanation: here is a genetic explanation, here is an environmental one, here is a hormonal one, here is a.... And we hang onto that bucket as our explanatory model. It's not surprising we think that way for a very simple reason: categorical thinking helps our memory in certain realms.

Let me give you an example here. Here we have a diagram of the visual spectrum—visual spectrum, the colors we can see, starting at violet one end, red at the other, classic sort of rainbow—this continuum of color where there's no obvious transition, where you go from yellow to orange or orange to red. There's no obvious transition, but there's something we do in every single language on earth, which is we impose an artificial boundary. We say, okay, here's a category, here's another category; break it up from this to this point. We suddenly change color terms; everything in here, we call one color, everything in here another. And what's most important is, from one language to the next, the boundaries that are put in different places for these color terms. Why do we put these color terms with boundaries? It turns out it helps our memory. Classic sort of studies: you show somebody a color, and if that color comes from right in the middle of their color category, versus right on the boundary between two different colors, people remember the colors better from the middle of their category. "Yes, they showed me that red before, I'm not sure if I saw that yellowish-green thing or not." When we think categorically, it helps our memory.

But, there is a downside to it in a couple of ways. The first one—as was shown in the same classic studies—back to this diagram: what do you do in this case is you show somebody a pair of colors, and in one case, the two colors come within the color term in their language, in the other case it comes across the boundary. In terms of the visual spectrum, these two pairs are equally different, but you ask somebody how similar are these two colors on a scale of one to ten, and what you see consistently are two things: if the two colors come within a color category in that language, people tend to underestimate how different they are; and if they come across a boundary, people tend to overestimate how different they are. Categorical boundaries distort our ability to see the similarities or differences between two different facts.

There's another downside to thinking categorically in this way, and for this one I need to give you an example and you need to think this through on your own. What you need to do is, I'm going to tell you an imaginary word in English and what you should do is just think in your head, don't write it down, just think about how you would pronounce this imaginary word, just using the rules of English phonics. C-H-O-P-H- O-U-S-E. If you're like 90% of the people out there—including me—what you've just come up with is the imaginary word "cho-po-use." What you should do when you have a chance is write down that word and see what it actually is, and what you see here now is our third lesson of all of the problems with categorical thinking, which is if you pay too much attention to the boundaries, you have trouble seeing the big picture, a picture as a whole. So we've got this tendency, and what the purpose of this course is, is to try to fight that tendency, instead of thinking categorically, to think in a much broader way.

Okay, what do I mean about this when we look at the biology of our behavior? What would count as categorical thinking? You've got some chicken, some male chicken. You see some female chicken on the side of some street, and the female chicken does some sexually solicitive thing with her wings, or whatever it is female chickens do, and he, very excited, goes running over to her, and thus we have this behavioral biology question: Why did this chicken cross the road? You could answer this as an anatomous, and you can say, well because the musculature in the legs of the chicken has a certain fulcrum and all of that. Or you can answer it like an endocrinologist: a-ha, if and only if this chicken has certain levels of circulating hormones…. Or you could answer it like an evolutionary biologist: over the course of millennia, male chickens who didn't respond to this solicitive gesture left fewer copies of their genes. And you could respond to it in a categorical way.

The challenge of this course is to avoid that categorical thinking. What we'll be doing instead—as shown on this chart, which is basically our blueprint for the entire course—is to start off looking at what a behavior is in a particular category and a particular class— sexual behavior, aggressive behavior, parental behavior—and then begin to ask biologically, where did that behavior come from? Well, what we will start off with is a whole bunch of time on the brain, the nervous system, which is in a sense a way of asking: what went on in that person's brain two second before that parental behavior, that aggressive act occurred? What is the neurobiology of where that behavior came from? For someone thinking categorically in the realm of the brain as a bucket, that's where you stop. This is how you explain behavior, the brain basis of behavior. That's not what we're going to do.

What we will then start doing—as shown on this chart, working back in time—is to then ask an environmental question: what in the environment triggered that brain to produce that behavior? What sound, what smell, what pain, what frustration, beginning to work back in time. Then trying to understand further the things that modulate the nervous system. One step further back: what about the hormones in the bloodstream that day of that individual? How do those hormones make that individual more or less sensitive to that environmental trigger, which causes the brain to produce that behavior?

And then—working to the left on this chart, all the way back in time—what are the early experiences of that organism? What are the hormones—not the hormones that day, that week, but hormones back in childhood—during fetal life? What was the nutritional environment, the stress environment of that fetus back when? And then working further back, what are the genetic attributes of the population that individual comes from, which pushes us all the way back to this evolutionary set of questions: what are the pressures of natural selection that sculpted that species, that population, to have a certain biology, played out in fetal life, played out in hormones this week, making you more or less sensitive to this environmental trigger of the brain producing this behavior?

That's going to be our general strategy, and the critical concept of this entire course is to go one step beyond saying, "Oh, it's important as we look at this chart to not only know something about the neurobiology, the endocrinology, the early experience, etc." The most subtle point of this entire course is, at any given stage, whatever of these boxes, whatever of these categorical buckets you are sitting in, it is simply a way of saying this is where we are in describing all of the biological influences that have come before, from one second before in the nervous system, to millions of years back in natural selection. At any given point, it is merely a way of describing it. If you talk about evolution, natural selection, you are talking about genes. If you are talking about genes and their effect on behavior, you are talking about a brain that works one way versus the other. All of these are ways of pulling these pieces together.

Okay, so that's great. Officially, we are going to think in a complex subtle way. Hooray for us. You might sit there and say, well yes, this is a whole lot of verbiage, essentially getting to the point of saying this is a complicated subject and we've got to think in a complicated way, and obviously any serious scientist out there knows to do the same.

Let me read three quotes to you to show you the extent to which all sorts of card-carrying scientists out there have not thought this way; instead have thought in very, very demarcated categorical buckets. Okay, first quote.

> Give me a dozen healthy infants, well formed, and my own specified world to bring them up in, and I'll guarantee to take anyone at random and train him to become any type of specialist I might select: doctor, lawyer, artist, merchant-chief, and yes, even beggar man thief, regardless of his talents, pensions, tendencies, abilities, vocations, and the race of his ancestors.

This is someone categorically stuck, pathologically stuck in the notion that environment, reward, punishment, positive/negative reinforcement can control the entire world; and we know that's not true. We know that certain individuals have certain biological constraints that no matter what the environment is, you cannot turn them into anything you wish them to be. Where is this quote from? A scientist named John Watson early in the last century. This was the founding father of a field of psychology called "behaviorism." This is a whole view that you explain all behavior within one of these buckets having to do with the environment. Very interestingly, a few years after this quote, Watson left science completely and became an extremely successful advertising executive—I do not think this is by chance.

Okay, next quote—this one is even worse—as follows: "Normal psychic life depends upon the good functioning of brain synapses, and mental disorders appear as a result of synaptic derangements. Synaptic adjustments will then modify the corresponding ideas and force thought into different channels. We obtain cures and improvements, but no failures." Now, in a couple of lectures we'll learn what these brain synapses are, but the main point here is, we've got a problem. We've got these synaptic derangements, and then go in with these synaptic adjustments. What do you think these synaptic adjustments are? Some sort of drug? Some sort of pharmacy? No, you wish it were that gentle. What we have here is a synaptic adjustment, which is go in with a big old knife and cut out the front part of the brain, a frontal lobotomy. And this is a person pathologically caught up in the notion that one of our buckets—that of the "brain explains the entire world." "We obtain cures and improvement, but no failures." Who is this? This was a Portuguese neurologist, Egas Moniz, upon the occasion of his receiving the noble prize for inventing frontal lobotomies.

Final quote, and this is the worst one yet. "The immensely high reproduction rate in the moral imbecile has long been established. This phenomenon leads everywhere to the fact that socially inferior human material is enabled to penetrate and finally to annihilate the healthy nation. The selection for toughness, heroism, social utility, must be accomplished by some human institution if mankind is not to be ruined by domestication-induced degeneracy. The racial idea as the basis of our state has already accomplished much in this respect, in the extermination of elements of the population loaded with dregs." Who was this? Was this Hitler? No, Hitler was a little bit busy with other things. This was one of the scientists who supported Hitler; this was a scientist who we all know from those Time Life specials, a scientist named Konrad Lorenz. Konrad Lorenz, we all know from those pictures—this cherubic Austrian guy with his little suspenders and shorts and the little duckies following him around. Konrad Lorenz, who was also in Nazi propagandas, served time as a war prisoner afterward for doing so. This is a man pathologically stuck in a different bucket of explaining behavior, one that happens to be built around the notion of saying that something's broken that isn't broken, and coming up with the most appalling possible fix.

These are not obscure scientists. These are not marginalized individuals. These are some of the most influential humans of the last century. They have shaped how we educate people, how we medicalize people, how we institutionalize them; they have an influence on 9-12 million people being vaporized by war. These are people who were pathologically unable to think about the biology of our behavior in a subtle way, and that is what we are going to try to avoid doing here.

Now when we think about this issue, again, it is not trivial to try to approach this subject looking at the biology of human social behavior; and there's a bunch of challenges intrinsic in this. Some of the time, the challenge of making sense of humans is recognizing that we are exactly like every other kid on the block, every other animal out there when it comes to the biology of our behavior.

One example of this: okay, you are a hamster, you are a female hamster, and as is the tendency as a female hamster, what you do is, you ovulate every 4 days; that's the ovulatory cycle of a female hamster, every four days, except under a certain circumstance. Somebody has taken another female hamster and put her in the cage with you, and over the next couple of weeks, what happens is, you both begin to extend your cycles and you synchronize them. Within three cycles or so, you are ovulating at the exact same time. This is this amazing phenomenon.

What's even more amazing about it is, it's done entirely with odors. The odor of one of the females synchronizes the cycle of the other one. How can you demonstrate this? You can use the famed nose clip test: if you simply close up the hamster's nose, it doesn't happen anymore; or you damage the olfactory system; or in the most elegant version, you don't put the second female in the same cage as the first, you just pump the air from one cage into the next one and they synchronize their cycles. It's absolutely extraordinary. What is really striking is, it's not random which female synchronizes which. The female who is more socially dominant synchronizes the other one there. This is really wild, and this is very wide spread. You can show this in hamsters, you can show this in all sorts of other rodents; and primate species, you can show this in pigs.

Apparently, if you were some farm kid out in Iowa or something, you can go down to the local 7-Eleven and buy some product—apparently it's called Matrix—and what it is, is some big old can of spray, and you go back home and you spray it all over your pigs and they all synchronize their cycle. I have no idea why you should want to do this. I grew up in New York City and we never attempted to do this to our farmyard animals. But for some reason, there's a reason to do this, and you go out and you can synchronize pig ovulatory cycles by taking advantage of these odorance, these pheromone things. It's remarkable.

What the most remarkable thing is, it works exactly the same way in humans. It's called the Wellesley Effect, named after Wellesley College, an all-women's college, where in the early 70s a scientist named Martha McClintock showed this, and showed that women who wind up in the dorm together, within about three cycles or so, close roommates are beginning to synchronize their cycles—except for one exception, and this is the same thing you see in the hamsters; take a male hamster and plunk him down into the cage with these two synchronized females and their cycles scramble and desynchronize.

The same thing happens in humans. All of these roommates had their cycles tending to synchronize except for the ones who had boyfriends, close intimate relations. This was then followed up with some really high-tech science where you would get women volunteers, and they would take little gauze pads and get their armpits and show that just the smell of one of these things could do the synchronizing instead; and unless you had a nose cold, once again, it was non-random. There are hints in the literature that women who are more socially extraverted, more socially dominant, synchronize the other one to this. This is well enough understood that when I was in college, people would sit around the table and say, bragging, when we roomed together this summer, "I had her synchronized by August 1st." This is a problem with living with biologists, but this is very well understood, and the most striking here is, we are just like every other animal out there. The big challenge often is recognizing that and accepting that.

Now some of the time the challenge takes a second form, which is recognizing we have the exact same physiology as any other animal out there. We have our bodies working in the same way, except we use that physiology in circumstances that are recognizable elsewhere in the animal world.

Let me give you an example of that. You take two humans and they are involved in this strange human ritual: they sit at a table, they're silent, they make no eye contact with each other, and just every now and then one of them virtualistically picks up their hand and moves a little piece of wood on the table. And if these were the right humans and the right circumstance—two grand master chess players in a tournament—their bodies are doing the exact same thing as some male baboon, which just savaged his opponent and ripped open his stomach on the Serengeti at dawn. The physiology of people during grand master chess tournaments approach that of people running marathons in terms of blood pressure and heart rate, in terms of how many extra thousands of calories their bodies go through each day— and they're doing nothing more than thinking.

Some of the time what is remarkable about us as humans is, we could turn on classical physiology, the type you would get running for your life, and all you're doing then is thinking about the fact that you know, my heart's going to stop beating. Poof—sudden stress response there. We can turn on classical boring mammalian physiology with the most abstract of cognitive states.

That begins to explain some of our propensity towards stress related disease—for example, a stress response system designed to sprint you away from a predator—and we turn it on for 30 year mortgages; we turn it on thinking about tragic events on the other side of the globe; we turn it on at abstract state. Some of the time what makes us challenging humans is the fact that we have boring typical physiology used in the most extraordinary ways.

Finally, some of the time, the challenge is going to be to make sense of our biology, recognizing stuff that we do that simply has no precedent at all out there in the animal world. Let me give you an example of this, a very shocking example form the standpoint of any other species.

Okay, we've got this human couple: they're together; they come home at the end of the day, their work day; they talk about how their day was, they have dinner, they talk some more, they go to bed, they make love, they talk some more, they fall asleep. They then do the same exact thing the next day: they come home from work, they talk, they have dinner, they talk some more, they go to bed, they have sex, they talk some more. They do this every single day for a month running. A giraffe would be disgusted by this. There are hardly any other species out there that have sex for non-reproductive reasons day after day, and we're the only species that talks about it afterward.

And when you look at that, when you look at linguistic use, language use, when you look at certain aspects of our sexual behavior, when you look at this very pathological propensity of some humans to confuse sexuality and aggression, you are on turf there that is completely novel, there are no other species out there doing stuff like that.

So as we begin to approach this course, what we will have to do is expand our notion as what counts as normal human behavior. How sometimes it is just like any other animal out there, sometimes this unique way in which we use typical physiology, sometimes the ways in which we behave for which there is no precedent out there at all. These will be our challenges.

And over and over in this course, we will approach this exactly as shown here on this chart, beginning with a whole bunch of lectures looking at how the brain works and how the brain produces behavior. We will start off in the level of how one single brain cell, a neuron, goes about its business, how one neuron communicates with another one; a pair of neurons. And then beginning to work our way up, how do small clusters of neurons work, how do large networks, networks in the part of the brain very relevant to emotion, to behavior, and then finally expanding from there into our nervous system, can regulate how every cell, down to our big toe, works in our bodies.

Throughout that section of neurobiology, we will have two themes. The first one is to understand why one individual's nervous system works differently from another's—individual differences. The other will be to study how all of this function can change over time—*plasticity*, that's the jargon used in the field—how very little of this neurobiology is set in stone.

What that sets us up for are all the subsequent lectures, asking what are the things that change how that nervous system works? What are the things working our way back in time on this chart, things in the environment? How do hormones affect the nervous system, early experience, fetal life, genetics, and evolution? How do all of those wind up producing behaviors coming out at the other end?

That will take us through the first 19 lectures. What we will then do is try to approach an actual set of human behaviors, try to approach it with this whole set of strategic sort of ideas here, this business of looking at the behavior. And then moving backwards, what's the neurobiology bit? What are the environmental factors that change the neurobiology, all the way back to where do these behaviors evolve from?

What we will focus on is an immensely contentious area of human behavior, and arguable the single most important one to understand biologically, where does violence come from? Where does aggression come from? This will both be a vehicle for understanding how to integrate these different approaches, as well as give us insight into an area of behavioral biology, which we better get a whole lot of insight into if we want to survive as a species.

So, that will be our general strategy for the course—and probably now finishing up, before we start, we should probably all raid the refrigerator. So given that, we will pick up in the next lecture starting off with, how does a single brain cell go about its business?

Module I

The Neurobiology of Behavior at the Cellular Level

Module Scope:

This module, which covers the next three lectures, begins with an overview of how a single neuron works. This study will then be expanded to see how two neurons communicate with each other through the use of neurotransmitters—chemical messengers in the brain. Finally, there is an overview of the critical topic of how such intercellular communication can change over time, that is, how the brain, at the level of pairs of neurons, learns and changes in response to the environment.

Lecture Two
The Basic Cells of the Nervous System

Scope:

This lecture covers the basic building blocks of neurobiology, beginning with an overview of the neuron, its various parts, and how each part functions and communicates with other neurons. We will come to understand the difference between the quiescent state, or *resting potential*, of neurons and the excited state, or *action potential*, of neurons. We will also go over the two types of brain cells, *neurons* and *glial cells*.

Outline

I. The basic constituent of the nervous system is the brain cell. (Figure 2a)

    A. The main brain cell is the *neuron.* The other type of brain cell is the *glial cell*, which we will discuss later in this lecture.

        1. All neurons go from left to right, at least in diagrams.

        2. On the far left, we have the dendrites, the ears of the neuron, which create chemical excitation in the neuron.

        3. To the right of the dendrite is the cell body, the centerpiece of the cell, where energy is produced.

    B. A wave of chemical excitation passes from the dendritic end through the cell body down a long cable called the *axon.*

        1. Axons are very long projections of neurons.

        2. The *axon hillock* is the transitional point between the end of the cell body and the start of the axon.

        3. At the end of the axon is the *axon terminal* that connects to the dendrites of the next neuron.

II. Neuronal communication includes both *resting potentials* and *action potentials*.

    A. To be prepared to communicate clearly, neurons must concentrate on contrasts during resting potentials. (Figure 2b)

       ©2005 The Teaching Company Limited Partnership

1. In a state of equilibrium, neurons create chemical contrasts.

2. Neurons expend a great deal of energy redistributing ions during the resting potentials.

B. When new information is transmitted by a single dendritic spine, channels open and ions begin to move, causing a change in the electrical state of the neuron.

1. No single neuronal input triggers an action potential; there is not enough power for the flow of electrical information to continue.

2. Integration at the neuronal level occurs because of a process called *summation*.

   a. *Temporal summation* occurs when the same input is triggered over and over so that it finally moves down the axon.

   b. *Spatial summation* occurs when enough different dendritic spines are being stimulated at once so that information moves down the axon.

   c. A neuron cell body is an integrator of the inputs of all the different neurons around it.

C. When there is enough of a wave of depolarization to reach the axon hillock, the axon hillock integrates the various inputs and decides whether or not to act.

1. When the axon hillock is triggered to act, neurons are in action potential.

2. Action potential does not decrement over space and time; it regenerates and continues passing information through the axon terminals to the next neurons.

3. The axon hillock is a critical feature of the nervous system.

III. Glial cells, which were once thought to be unimportant, can wrap around the axon and form a myelin sheath.

A. Myelin sheaths create an insulation that increases the speed with which electrical waves move down the axon.

B. People are not born with myelin sheaths but develop them after birth. As myelin sheaths form, new skills are possible, including comprehension and production of language and regulation of behavior.

C. Multiple sclerosis is a disease in which the immune system attacks and destroys myelin.

IV. Neurons are a complex, integrated network with interesting implications.

A. The numbers of dendrites, neurons, and connectors vary from individual to individual and can change at different points of the life cycle because of environmental stimulation.

B. Axon hillocks can also change over time and under different circumstances.

C. These neurological differences and changes affect individuality.

Further Reading:

For a good broad introduction to the nervous system:

E. Widmaier, H. Raff, and K. Strang, *Vander, Sherman, and Luciano's Human Physiology*, 9th ed.

For a somewhat more advanced treatment:

J. Nicholls, R. Martin, B. Wallace, and P. Fuchs, *From Neuron to Brain*, 4th ed.

For the best (although more advanced) textbook in the field:

E. Kandel, J. Schwartz, and T. Jessell, *The Foundations of Neural Science*, 4th ed.

Questions to Consider:

1. How have neurons evolved so that they exhibit a huge contrast between being silent and being excited?

2. What are ways in which a typical neuron might differ between two individuals?

Figure 2a

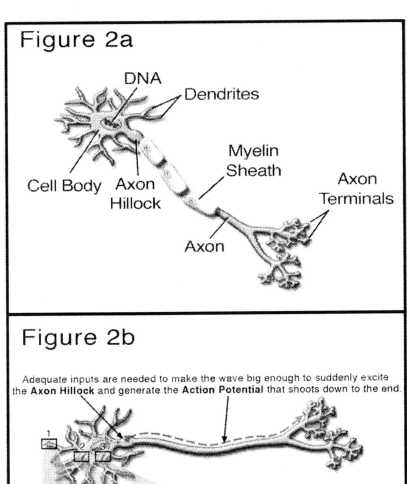

DNA

Dendrites

Cell Body   Axon
Hillock

Myelin
Sheath

Axon
Terminals

Axon

Figure 2b

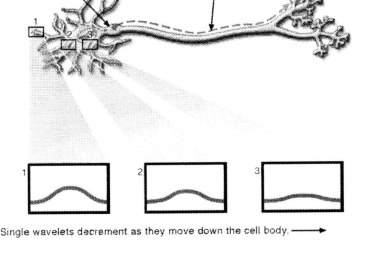

Adequate inputs are needed to make the wave big enough to suddenly excite the **Axon Hillock** and generate the **Action Potential** that shoots down to the end.

1

1   2   3

Single wavelets decrement as they move down the cell body. ⟶

Lecture Two—Transcript
The Basic Cells of the Nervous System

Welcome back. Let's see, hopefully we are all stoked up now on Rocky Road ice-cream from the last break and ready to learn about neurobiology.

Okay, what was the main point of the last lecture, the introductory lecture? We want to understand behavior; we want to understand human behavior, where it's coming from; we want to understand the biological basis of it and where all of those influences, starting with evolution a gazillion years ago are going to funnel eventually into the nervous system. How do all of those things influence the functioning of the nervous system, and how does the nervous system in turn produce behavior? What we'd be doing in the next half dozen lectures is starting off the introduction to the nervous system—how does one neuron work, how do a pair of neurons work—working our way out until getting a sense of how the nervous system controls every outpost in the body, how it produces behavior.

So, we start off here with the single cells making up the nervous system. And there are two different types, one of which gets most of the attention—your basic off-the-rack brain cell is a neuron. Neuron, that's the work horse of the nervous system; that's the type that sends the messages down your spine, that remembers somebody's birthday, that tells you to shake hands at the right moment; the part of your brain that's really central on the level of single cells. There's another type of cell in there called *glial cells*, and the general take over the years has been that they're utterly boring and that you should pay no attention to glials. There are all sorts of neuroscientists who stab you for believing something like that. We'll see where glial cells fit into this picture. For our purposes for the moment, they have a supporting role in getting neurons to work.

Okay, so we switch over here to looking at our prototypical neuron, here in this diagram. And this neuron, this is exactly what all neurons look like, identical. And remarkably enough, they all from left to right; it's required if you're going to be a neurobiologist to always draw your neurons from left to right. Here we have the classic pieces of the neuron. Starting on the far left we have *dendrites,* what are called dendrites; also termed dendritic spines. Metaphorically, these are the ears of the neuron; this is where information flows into, as we'll see, information from other neurons coming in there—dendrites.

Sitting next to the dendrite is a basic part of a neuron that you find in every cell out there, the *cell body*, this is where energy is mostly produced; this is where your nucleus full of your DNA is; this is sort of the centerpiece of the cell. Then, heading towards the right is, metaphorically, the mouth of the neuron, the means by which the neuron communicates to the next neuron in line. Beginning with something called the *axon*—and you can think of an axon just as the long cable reaching out towards the next outpost in the brain—and reasonably enough, the axon terminating in axon terminals, a whole bunch of little fibrils, each of which reaches out to the dendritic spine of the next neuron. As we'll see, the end of the axon terminal and this dendritic spine don't actually touch, that's the subject in the next lecture.

So this is the basic neuron, and despite my stating they all look exactly the same, they all look completely different. You've got some neurons that are a thousandth-of-an inch long, absolutely tiny, very local little neurons. Then amazingly, you've got neurons that are feet long. If you are a blue whale, you've got neurons that are sixty feet long going down your spinal cord. I don't mean one neuron, sending a message to the next one, the next one; I mean sixty feet worth of one single cell. This is outlandish from the standpoint of cell biology. A big challenge in understanding how these cells work is dealing with that they have these long, long cables; this is a special challenge for any cell from a standpoint of energy.

Okay, so we switch back to the diagram, and the basic thing that happens in a neuron when it's got something to say to the world is there's a *wave of excitation*. And we'll see in a bit what excitation means in this case. For the moment, the most important thing is the excitation starts at the dendritic end. From there, it flows to the right. Where does that excitation come from? That's as a result of the previous neuron in line sending an excitatory message, causes this wave of excitation in the dendrites.

This wave then spreads over the cell body, and from there spreads onto the axon. There is this transitional point between the end of the cell body, the start of the axon, called the *axon hillock*—we will see in great detail what's happening there—reaching the axon, shooting down the axon all the way to the end, out to every single one of those axon terminals and the wave of excitation, then sweeping on to the next neuron in line.

Now the whole point here is that this flow of information is not guaranteed. Just because you have excitation of a dendritic end, it doesn't guarantee it's going to get all the way to the axon terminal. What we will need to see now is how does this occur? How do the various inputs into a neuron, how do the various neurons upstream yelling messages at this neuron turn in some cases to this neuron passing on the information? How does this game of "telephone" work in this case? In this case, the challenge isn't one neuron saying something to the next one, to the next one—the traditional telephone game—but a hundred different neurons saying something to this neuron, and this neuron sorting it out and deciding whether the message goes on.

Now to begin to make sense of the functioning of neurons in these ways, the most important thing to keep straight is neurons do very dramatic things; what they are all about is contrasts. Let me give you an example. Okay, think back to the day that you reached puberty, the day that there was sudden change. Your parents had been preparing you for this for months and giving you these boring books to read about cows and babies and who knows what, and finally that morning came and this was a big event and your mother baked waffles and you were carried around town on a sedan-chair by your neighbors and they slaughtered a goat in your honor and all of that. This was a big event biologically; however, would it have made all that much of a difference if you had reached puberty 24 hours later? Probably not.

Second scenario, you are suddenly finding yourself confronted with a saber tooth tiger. You are running for your life. What do you need to do with your nervous system at that point? You need to tell your heart to beat faster, increase your blood pressure, and do something or other effective with your thigh muscles. What would happen if your brain did that to you 24 hours later? You would be consumed.

What we see here is a critical thing, all sorts of parts of your body do what they do, and if they do it right now, if they do it minute from now, if they do it a day from now, it's not that big of a deal. Growth can start tomorrow. Hormones don't have that much of a time pressure. Your nervous system is all about incredibly rapid, incredibly synchronized behaviors, your nervous system is about being very quiet when it has nothing to say, and screaming its head off when this sort of message comes along.

You can see this in all sorts of settings. Okay, let me give you an example here. Watch very carefully, because I'm only going to do this one. Watch this... okay. An ameba would kill to get to do something like that; and you can't do this unless you have a nervous system to get that sort of amazing coordination. The only way you're going to do this is to have very special cells. And what neurons are about is the specialty of being very silent when there's nothing happening, and then exploding into our mysterious process of excitation when they're excited.

So we start off with how they do this silence business; how they are so quiet. The term that's given for this is the *resting potential*. And the resting potential, reasonably enough, is about the neuron resting, and everything that's going on there is about a neuron that is quiescent. What this is about is, you have a whole bunch of thingies floating around outside the neuron and others inside—we step here for just a second into dread ninth-grade chemistry—the whole notion that there are ions—okay, don't panic—things like sodium and chloride, which together makes salts and other things, potassium—do not panic. The only point of all of this is they're not evenly distributed within the neuron and outside the neuron; there's not the same exact amount of sodium inside and outside or chloride inside and outside that's utterly boring, that's just even distribution.

What you need instead is a contrast. When you are being a quiet neuron, you want all of the sodium outside the neuron; and as soon as you are screaming your head off, you want all of the sodium inside. When the neuron's being quiet, you want to keep all the potassium inside; when it's getting excited, you want it to go outside. The main point here is contrasts. Contrasts, that's the way you tell the difference between a quiet neuron and a hysterically screaming one. The neuron has to work a whole lot to keep these ions separated, to keep charge separated, and to keep an unequal distribution. During the resting potential, you've got a profile of unequal distribution—and I'm not even going to torture you with telling you which way it goes—a whole bunch of the sodium is on one side of the picture, a whole bunch of potassium is on the other side; outside the neuron, inside. The main point here is this is a very clear-cut state, there's no missing the fact that this is a neuron that's being silent.

Very importantly, you want to just have your ions evenly distributed; the same exact amount outside and inside. You don't have to spend any energy on it. If you want to set up this huge sort of dam to keep all of one bunch of ions outside and all of one bunch inside during this resting stage, that costs you a fortune. Amazingly enough, neurons spend almost half of their energy just keeping these ions separated under resting circumstances. And what that begins to tell you, just sort of as an aside, is when you get nervous systems that don't have enough energy, you begin to get all sorts of chaotic changes in those resting potential. A lot of neurological diseases involve that.

Okay, so we've got the resting potential. And the main point there is, there is no mistaking the fact that is a neuron that has something missing; this is a neuron that's spending a fortune being quiet. And, that's a hallmark of the nervous system. So what we have to transition to now is what happens when the neuron gets excited. You already know on an ionic level what happens, contrast all of those ions, the sodium that's kept outside the neuron is going to come pouring in; eventually the potassium you're spending a fortune to keep inside is coming out. Major, major change in your state, you are moving from a resting potential, this quiescent state, to a state of excitation.

The way this happens is, we start back at the dendrites, back at our diagram, something or other—next lecture—something or other happens to those dendrites, which causes this ionic change to begin to happen, which causes those dendrites to switch from a resting state to an excited state. That's the excitation: a wave of ionic change occurring at these dendrites, and is shown in the diagram. What is going to happen now is that wave of ions suddenly going from their resting state into their excited state; this wave now sweeping down the cell membrane, sweeping to the cell body, all the way down to the axon. That's the chemical basis of this excitation we've been hearing about.

What we have to focus on here is a very important feature of this excitation. You remember what I said, you get one little dendritic spine—as is drawn here—there's a whole bunch of these little fibrils; you get this excitation going on at one little dendritic spine. Does that mean this ionic wave of excitation is going to sweep over the cell body and the axon hillock and the axon down to the axon terminals? No, we already heard any given input is not going to necessarily produce excitation all the way down the line. And the reason for this has to do with how that dendritic excitation works.

Switching here in the next diagram, what we have is our prototypical neuron, once again, and we have some of that excitation, some of that leaving the resting state, some of that ionic change, some of that excitation occurring out at one little dendritic spine. And what we've got in this hypothetical case is we've stuck in an electrode that could measure these ionic changes. We've stuck in this electrode right at that dendritic spine. And, as shown in the diagram, right there in that neighborhood, you suddenly get a wave of excitation. This excitation occurs, the wave is over with, and what we've seen already is the wave now moves down, further down the membrane heading towards the axon.

You want a metaphor? What you've got is this pond, and you've just taken a rock and thrown it in the middle of the pond, and the ripple you produce is the wave of excitation. That metaphor is real useful for what happens next. Now we've stuck the electrode just over on the cell body, a little bit away from the dendrite. And then we've stuck another electrode even further down, and what you'll notice is that wave of excitation that was this huge dramatic ionic event out of that dendritic spine is a little bit smaller when you get further out, and even smaller further out; and this ripple eventually decrements down to nothing. You throw that pebble into that pond and you are not going to see the same size wave, it heads outward and it dissipates. How come? Because that same amount of water displacement is spreading further and further out a larger perimeter, it eventually decays. And that's exactly what you wind up seeing here. You have this local ionic event in this little patch of dendritic spine, and that wave of ionic perturbation, this wave of excitation, and it decrements, it disappears.

By the time you've gotten out to this corner of the cell body, it is long forgotten. There is no way excitation at this dendritic spine is going to get you all the way down to the other end. What you get instead is a very set bunch of rules where you essentially need a whole bunch of neurons talking to this one at once. No given dendritic input, no given excitation at any single dendritic spine is going to be enough to send a message shooting all the way down to the axon terminal; instead, you've got to have *summation*—a jargony term in the field.

You've got to have either the one neuron sending this excitatory message to the dendritic spine, you've got to have it firing over and over and over again—what is called temporal summation—so that you get enough of a wave going here that it finally gets all the way down; or, you need to have a whole bunch of neurons having inputs all at once, a whole bunch of little dendritic spines starting their little wavelets, which combine together; in this case, spatial summation. You've got to have a whole bunch of neurons agreeing all at once, or one neuron talking over and over. What you wind up having then is an implication that no given single input is enough to pass on the message; you've got to have a whole bunch of signaling going in there all at once. So that's great.

Eventually, what you have with one neuron going over and over—temporal summation—or a whole bunch of neurons having their input at once—spatial summation—eventually what you have is enough of a wave, enough of this ionic chemical wave, enough of it happening that it reaches the axon hillock. And this is where something very important occurs.

Back to the axon hillock on the diagram, it's the very first piece of the axon; it's that transitional point from the cell body to the axon itself. The axon hillock is real important, because what is does is sit there and count on its fingers and toes how many inputs are we getting per second, how many inputs, how much of a wave; it's the threshold, it's the thing in the neuron that decides whether to pass on that signal. Metaphorically, again, you've got that pond, you've thrown in that pebble, and you've made this wavelet, and the axon hillock is this wall down at the end. As long as that wavelet doesn't get over the top, the message doesn't go on. If and only if there is enough of a wavelet, enough of a wave of excitation that you finally get something going over the top, that's the signal, that's the threshold for now passing the signal down the axon. And it's when that happens that something very different occurs.

We see at the dendritic end what's called a *decrementing signal*. You get some excitation and you get this wave and it goes a little bit further and it disappears and no given input is all that exciting. You get the axon hillock suddenly excited and something very different occurs; you get this explosion of excitation, this massive influx of ions and outflow, this tremendously excited event, called the *action potential*. And the main point of the action potential is—we're not talking pebbles being thrown into ponds and wavelets that decrement—the action potential shoots down the axon and it doesn't lose force over time, it gets *propagated* again and again—that's the term that's used—it has an "all or none" property.

If you manage to get an action potential by getting two little droplets over threshold at the axon hillock, or getting a tidal wave over it, it doesn't matter. At that point you initiate the same exact massive action potential, which goes shooting down the axon with the exact same strength that keeps getting regenerated—it doesn't decrement—and that thing goes hurdling down the axon, down to the axon terminal, and triggers this neuron to talk to the next neurons in line.

So we have from an engineering standpoint a very interesting system: we have an analog/digital system, analog at the dendritic end—a wave could be of all sorts of different sizes, and over space and time the wave decrements—and the second you get the axon hillock in on the scene, you've got this digital, this all or none property. Either nothing's happened in the axon, or everything is happening there; this wildly excited action potential. And you've got this wonderful mechanism on a cellular level for integrating inputs into the neuron.

Just to give you a sense of what we're up against here, your average neuron has ten thousand dendritic spines, and your average neuron has ten thousand axon terminals. Your average neuron could be getting input from ten thousand other brain cells and be talking to ten thousand other ones in line. What's the implication of that? No single neuron talking to this guy is going to have much influence, no single dendritic spine carries that big of a wavelet, an amazing amount of information coming in, and it's the axon hillock that sits there deciding what the threshold is.

One additional piece of the system, one additional wave making sense of how a neuron works: we have here on the diagram—I'm drawing something which looks not at all what it looks like in real life—but what it is, is a solution to a big problem you've got in these neurons—back to cell biology. Cells are things that fit on the period at the end of a sentence, and here you've got this neuron with this three foot long axon going down your spine. From the world of cell biology, you get some action potential starting right by the axon hillock, and you've got a three foot long neuron, and it's going to take a week and a half to get the message down to the end; and your brain thinks, what a clever time it would be to take my foot out of the fire here, and three weeks later you manage to do that. You need some sort of mechanism to send that action potential shooting down the axon even faster; and that's something a neuron had to evolve, simply because you've got these outlandishly long cells.

What it comes up with, as drawn here, is essentially a form of insulation. It's something that's called the *myelin sheath*. What's that? You remember we talked about those boring glial cells. What they serve here is they're basically insulation around your wire, and for extremely complex reasons that I barely understand, it causes the action potential to shoot down even faster. It's a way to accelerate the action potential so that you can get a message from your brain down to your toe in some reasonable amount of time.

This myelin, this axonal wrapping, this insulation, is real important stuff; and you can see two measures of why that is the case. The first one is when you were born you didn't have a lot of myelin in your nervous system—and you can see there's all these developmental landmarks right around when some behavior starts occurring; that's when the relevant part of the brain has myelinated. The part of the baby's brain that comprehends language for example, myelinates fully about two months before the part of the brain that produces language, aspects of motor pathways.

Here the most amazing thing of all: there's a part of the brain which we are going go hear about over and over again in this course, a region called the *frontal cortex*, and it's got something to do with regulating your behavior—gratification postponement—and this part of the brain does not fully myelinate until somewhere in your mid-twenties. It is the last part of the brain to fully come on line, this myelination process is extremely important.

The other way of appreciating how important this myelin is, is what happens if you have a disease that destroys the myelin. That's the disease MS, multiple sclerosis. You've got your immune system for some bizarre reason attacking your myelin, and that's not a nervous system that works very well afterward.

So we've got this basic picture here, excitation at the dendritic and these decrementing little wavelets, if and only if you have enough inputs into there to get the axon hillock suddenly excited; you generate your action potential, it goes shooting down to the end— really fast thanks to your myelin—gets to the end there and causes all of your axon terminals to release its message on to the next neurons in line. This is the basic flow of information. It is of staggering complexity when you think about the ten thousand inputs, the ten thousand outputs; that's why our brain can write poetry and our spleens can't, that's where the complexity comes from.

Now as promised, the two things we will focus on in every one of these lectures is, number one, where do individual differences come from at that level of the biology; number two, how could that function change over time?

In terms of the individual differences, all you need to do is come up with a whole list of suspects here. We differ in our brains as to just how many dendritic spines we have; just how many axon terminals we have. We differ as to just how quiet our resting potentials are, just how big that dendritic wavelet is. We differ as to how excitable our axon hillock is. We differ as to how fast the action potential goes. We differ in all those realms, and put that together with a couple of hundred billion neurons and you begin to see a very subtle, enough array of ways in which one nervous system can work differently than another.

And just as one example from an extreme. There are certain neurons, and thus certain nervous systems that are markedly more excitable than others. What's that about? That's what epilepsy is. That's what a nervous system is that has uncontrolled synchronous action potentials in certain areas. All you need to go is from that sledge hammer—one subtle example—to everybody else's brains with these subtle differences. That's where these individual differences come from.

The other thing we need to explain here, to take at least a first pass at, is *plasticity*. How could the functioning change over time? In lots of different ways, but the one I'll concentrate on here in these last few minutes is the axon hillock. Axon hillock is important. Big news, it's the one that's sitting there deciding, "Am I impressed enough with all this dendritic mumbling, and all this dendritic whispering in my ears to finally pass on and form an action potential? What is my threshold? Of those ten thousand dendritic spines there, do I need to have nine thousand of them get excited to cause an action potential, or do I need nine of them to get excited? What's my threshold?"

And critically, that threshold could change over time. Let me give one wonderful example of this. Once again, you are a female hamster, and female hamsters have this reflex. Reflex—the doctor hits you on the knee, out goes your leg. Female hamsters have a reflex called the *lordosis reflex*. If there is pressure placed on your flanks, you suddenly get this reflex where the female arches her back; you get a lordotic reflex. What's that about? Who's normally pressing on the flanks of a female hamster? A male hamster. This is when mating is going on, and by arching her back, she exposes her genitals, increases the ease with which mating occurs. We've got some evolutionary song and dance; female hamsters have evolved the capacity for load. Lordosis left more copies of their genes, etc. What we have here is a reflex. And you could illicit the lordosis reflex with a male hamster, or you could illicit the lordosis reflex with some poor graduate student having to pressing the flanks of the female in order to get a "doctorate" at the other end of it. You can illicit the lordosis reflex out of a female hamster, if and only if she is ovulating at the time.

And what you have is a rule, the axon hillocks of the neurons, the relevant neurons in the spinal pathways of the female hamster, are sensitive to estrogen levels. Estrogen comes along and changes the threshold of that axon hillock. In the absence of estrogen, you could be pressing the flanks of that female hamster with the entire Encyclopedia Britannica and you're not going to get a lordosis reflex. The threshold, the axon hillock's threshold, is way too high. Along comes the right hormone at the right levels and literally what you change is the chemical composition of some of those sensors at the axon hillock. Here we have the environment in the form of this neuron's environment, what sort of hormones it's marinating in, changing how excitable that neuron is.

This is a first pass at plasticity of the nervous system—how readily a neuron functions. In our terms in this lecture, how readily a neuron responds to input by forming an action potential that sends an output out the other end changes in response to the world around us.

Okay, so this gives us a first pass at how a single neuron functions. How a single neuron functions differently in you versus me. How it could be functioning differently today versus last week. What we now need to see in the next lecture is how is that single neuron, when it finally has that action potential, is going to pass on the excitation to the next neuron in line. And, as we're going to see, it needs to use a very different language than the ionic wave of excitation we've seen already. It's going to have to find a way to send a chemical messenger to the next neuron.

So that will be the topic of the next tape, looking at how two neurons communicate with each other.

Lecture Three
How Two Neurons Communicate

Scope:

This lecture moves from how the brain works on the level of a single neuron to how information moves across the synapse from one neuron to the next. Exploring how electrical signals are changed to chemical messages in the brain provides a critical foundation for understanding how the brain works, the effects of certain drugs on the brain, and the neurological origins of individuality.

Outline

I.   In order for information to move from one neuron to the next, information must cross the synapse. (Figure 3a)

    A. An electrical signal cannot pass through the synapse; thus, a neuron must translate its excitation into a different "language."

    B. The release of neurotransmitters translates an electrical signal to a chemical signal.

        1. Neurotransmitters are packaged in vesicles attached to the membrane wall.

        2. During action potential, vesicles release neurotransmitters into the synapse.

    C. The neurotransmitters bind to their receptors.

        1. The shape of the neurotransmitter and its receptor must be complementary—the classic notion of key and lock.

        2. The binding of the neurotransmitter to its receptor changes the excitability of the next neuron in line.

        3. Multiple receptor types exist for the same neurotransmitter.

    D. Upon deactivation, neurotransmitters either are recycled back into the next vesicle being formed or they float into the synapse, where they are eventually broken down by enzymes.

    E. There are multiple types of neurotransmitters and not all are *excitatory.*

1. How many types of neurotransmitters exist? A limited number, but we have multiple uses of the same messenger.

2. *Inhibitory* transmitters cause a decrease in excitability of the postsynaptic neuron.

3. Not all neurotransmitters are equal; there are subtle graduations of the effects among both the excitatory and inhibitory transmitters.

II. The construction of neurotransmitters is less intimidating than you might think.

A. They are constructed from cheap and plentiful precursors—simple amino acids that you get in your diet in huge amounts.

B. A small number of biosynthetic steps are required in their construction; thus, they are produced quickly.

C. Multiple messengers can be squeezed out of a single synthetic pathway.

D. Neurotransmitters are also easily recycled.

III. What criteria are used to determine what constitutes a neurotransmitter? (Figure 3b)

A. It is located in the axon terminal.

B. It is released during the action potential.

C. It floats across the synapse and binds with receptors on the postsynaptic neuron.

D. Any interference with the neurotransmitter will alter the neurochemical events in a predictable manner.

IV. Now we can better understand how the nervous system changes over time and how individual differences have consequences for behavior.

A. Changes in the amount of neurotransmitter released can change the strength of signaling across a synapse.

B. Changes in the number and sensitivity of receptors can change the strength of signaling across a synapse.

V. Neuropharmacology manipulates the neurochemistry of the

synapse to better understand the workings of the neurotransmission process.

A. Research with drugs that alter brain function is an important tool for studying normal and diseased states.

B. Some drugs so closely resemble a naturally occurring neurotransmitter that the receptors are fooled by it.

    1. An ingested drug can get into the bloodstream, enter the brain, get into a synapse, and very effectively bind to the receptor because that drug has a chemical structure almost identical to that of an actual neurotransmitter.

    2. For example, hallucinogens, such as LSD, mescaline, and psilocybin, are able to artificially stimulate the serotonin receptor.

C. Other drugs block the access of a neurotransmitter to its receptor, halting communication across the synapse.

    1. Curare can block the acetylcholine receptor in the diaphragm, causing breathing to cease.

    2. Antipsychotic drugs can block the dopamine receptor, lessening symptoms of schizophrenia.

D. Some drugs cause the inappropriate release of neurotransmitters.

    1. Amphetamines and cocaine trigger the premature release of dopamine transmitters.

    2. Because the release of dopamine makes a person feel pleasure in at least one part of the brain, artificially releasing more of it makes such drugs as cocaine highly addictive.

    3. Drugs that release dopamine can trigger schizophrenic behavior, while drugs that block dopamine are used to halt schizophrenic behavior.

E. Some drugs alter the breakdown and recycling of neurotransmitters or can be used to destroy particular neurotransmitters completely.

    1. The neurotransmitter norepinephrine can be destroyed to lower blood pressure.

2. Antidepressants, including Prozac, cause amplification in the neurotransmitter's signal by blocking its degradation.

F. Another manipulation is to increase the amount of precursors for certain neurotransmitters, for example, increasing the L-DOPA level for patients with Parkinson's disease.

G. Manipulation of chemicals always has the risk of side effects, primarily because each neurotransmitter has multiple jobs in different parts of the brain.

VI. An example of how neurochemistry influences individuality can be seen in the neurotransmitter endogenous benzodiazepine, which is a compound similar to the drugs Valium and Librium.

A. Endogenous benzodiazepine receptors influence anxiety levels.

B. How much benzodiazepine an individual makes, releases, and breaks down will determine his or her anxiety level.

C. Tranquilizers, such as Valium and Librium, are used to decrease a person's anxiety level.

Further Reading:

For the best introductory book specifically about neurotransmission:

J. Cooper, F. Bloom, and R. Roth, *The Biochemical Basis of Neuropharmacology*, 8th ed.

For a more difficult text:

G. Siegel and B. Agranoff, *Basic Neurochemistry: Molecular, Cellular, and Medical Aspects*, 6th ed.

For a particularly good overview of what neurotransmitters have to do with mental illness:

S. Barondes, *Molecules and Mental Illness*, 2nd ed.

Questions to Consider:

1. What is the chemical nature of neurotransmitters, and how can drugs alter their function?

2. What are the ways in which the neurochemistry of two individual brains might differ?

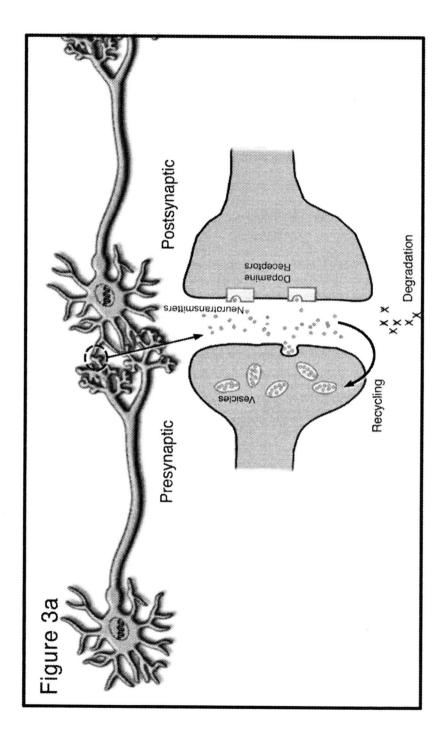

Figure 3a

Postsynaptic

Presynaptic

Dopamine
Receptors

Neurotransmitters

Vesicles

Degradation

Recycling

Figure 3b

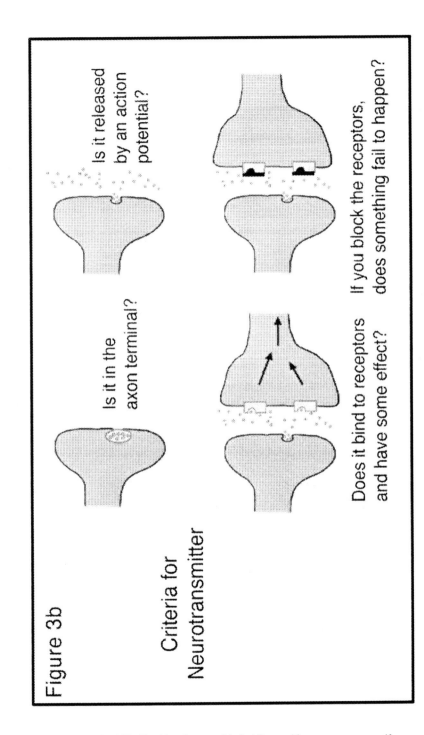

Criteria for Neurotransmitter

Is it in the axon terminal?

Is it released by an action potential?

Does it bind to receptors and have some effect?

If you block the receptors, does something fail to happen?

Lecture Three—Transcript
How Two Neurons Communicate

Hi. We are back and ready to resume our quest to understand the nervous system and how it produces behavior, and how everything on earth that came before that nervous system can regulate its function. What had we got to in the last lecture?

We've looked how one neuron gets excited, how a neuron pays a fortune to be quiet, when it has nothing to say—the resting potential—how excitation comes in at the dendritic end, how very importantly that wave of excitation is going to dissipate over time. If and only if a whole bunch of neurons are screaming at this one simultaneously, the axon hillock has its threshold passed to degenerate the action potential, goes shooting down extra fast because of that myelin and gets down to the axon terminal, and then we've got a problem. And that problem is today's lecture.

As we have drawn here, we've now made a very important transition. We've now gotten to step number two of being a neurobiologist, which is to now draw the neurons in this much more schematic way. We've got one neuron talking to another; we're now up to two neurons in our diagram. And you will note there, right at the point where the axon terminal of the first neuron is reaching out to the second, something is happening there; and that is expanded in the diagram below. What you see highly magnified is the two neurons don't actually touch each other. They don't touch. Instead there's this yawning microscopic river of extra cellular fluid in between the two of them, something called the *synapse*.

The synapse is the space between two neurons, and the synapse is basically the subject of today's lecture. Now the whole key thing is people didn't used to know that synapses existed. Back when, in the 19th century, the basic view was each neuron connected with the next one, and thus this neuron sent its ten thousand axon terminal projections merging into the next, forming this huge net throughout the brain. And there was always this sort of cadre, this lunatic fringe of scientists who said instead, no they don't actually touch, there's a space in between. So there were the neural people, and there were the synapse people, and their conflict was actually sort of the central, sociopolitical sort of debacle of the 19th century—thousands of peasants slaughtered, violent brother pitted against brother—and finally what happened was the whole debate got resolved because somebody invented a microscope that was powerful enough to see there's actually a space between the two.

And thus the synapse was confirmed; and thus an entire problem was generated, because we've just made this action potential in the last neuron shooting down the line, gets to the axon terminal, and that electrical wave, that electrical signal is not able to jump across the synapse. This huge ocean of extra cellular fluid makes it impossible for an electrical signal to get across. If that first neuron, if that presynaptic neuron, is going to talk to the postsynaptic one, it has to translate its electrical message into a different language. It translates it into a chemical one.

And, as shown here on the diagram, sitting in this axon terminal on the left in the presynaptic neuron, there are these little packets, these little balloons filled up with chemical messengers. Along comes the action potential, and this causes these little balloons, tethered to the very end of the axon terminal, to get pulled into that membrane. They merge with the membrane and they dump their chemical messengers out into the synapse. What do they do at that point? They float across the synapse, where they have an effect on the postsynaptic neuron.

And as shown in the diagram on this postsynaptic neuron, there is a receptor; a receptor for this chemical messenger. Now it's absolutely required to be a neurobiologist, you have to use the following cliché; the chemical messenger that comes floating out, fits into the receptor—here's the cliché, get ready—it fits like a "key into a lock." The particular shape of the messenger and the particular shape of the receptor, they are complimentary, and if and only if this right messenger fits into the receptor, that causes this dendritic spine to get excited.

We have just found a means by which we go from one neuron to the next and then initiate all that electrical excitation stuff from the last lecture. These chemical messengers that go floating across the synapse are called *neurotransmitters*. And what you wind up having is, when a neuron gets excited to the point of having action potential, action potential sweeps to the end and out of all of its axon terminals. It releases neurotransmitters that float across the synapse and have their message heard in the next neuron.

Now the one additional piece we need to do here, in making sense of this flow of information, is in the diagram at the bottom. What happens to your neurotransmitters after they bind like a key into the lock of the receptor? They come floating off. And there's a critical final step there which becomes very relevant later on. What you do with the neurotransmitter then? Two options: you could be ecologically minded; you can recycle your neurotransmitter, and it is taken back up into the presynaptic axon terminal, repackaged again in those little balloons, these vessels, these *vesicles*—that's the term for them—you can recycle your neurotransmitter; or, you can be ecologically unminded, you can have some enzyme you can throw out your neurotransmitter, an enzyme sitting there in the synapse, which rips your neurotransmitter up into little pieces, flushes it down the toilet.

What's your brain's toilet? Your cerebral spinal fluid, where it gets into your bloodstream and eventually into your bladder. You can have either recycling of neurotransmitter or their degradation, their breakdown, tossing them out.

Okay, so now we come to this question: How many different types of neurotransmitters do you need? If you want to do something very boring with your nervous system, you don't need a whole lot of neurotransmitters. You've got your arm and you want to pull it up, you want to activate a flexor muscle. All you need is one type of neurotransmitter that goes from your spine to this muscle telling you to pull it up. Okay, one neurotransmitter.

Suppose you want to do something more complicated; you've got your heart and sometimes you want to speed it up and sometimes you want to slow it down, two different directions of messages. You're up to needing two different kinds of neurotransmitters. Get into the brain and start writing symphonies and start filling out your tax forms and stuff like that—two neurotransmitters aren't going to do it. Remember, we've got hundreds of billions of neurons, each one making ten thousand synaptic connections; we've got a gazillion synapses there. Does that mean we have a gazillion different kinds of neurotransmitters? Not at all.

All you need to do to appreciate that is think about the fact that we can generate virtually an infinite number of messages having only 26 letters in the alphabet. All you need are rules for how you combine them. All you need is some sort of rule that when you take one of those letters that has sort of two lines that are angled like this in a horizontal lane, you're talking about a letter which, if you put it, sort of imbedded in a C and a T you're talking about things with whiskers, and imbedded in some other combination, you're talking about existentialism; we learn rules for using the letter A in different context.

In the same exact way, neurotransmitter A in one part of the brain means, remember to turn the lights off before you go out; and another part of the brain it makes your pancreas do its thing. You've got multiple uses for the same neurotransmitter in different parts of the brain. All you need are conventions in this part of the brain, this presynaptic neuron and this postsynaptic one have worked out; this is what releasing the neurotransmitter means here. Meanwhile, four counties over, in another part of the brain, it has a completely different use. There are multiple forms of neurotransmitters.

What you then wind up seeing is an important elaboration, which is different neurotransmitters have different powers, different strengths in what they do in the postsynaptic neuron. There are some types that are highly excitatory. What does that mean in ionic terms? What does that mean back to the last lecture? They cause a huge wavelet of excitation; they're one big boulder that you've tossed into the pond. There are other neurotransmitters that are only weakly excitatory. You've got a whole range of the strength of the message.

Likewise, you've got neurotransmitters that are termed *inhibitor neurotransmitters* that make the postsynaptic neuron less excitable, lock it in more strongly in its resting state. So you've got a whole bunch of neurotransmitters that are yelling at the neuron, some of them saying get really excited, some are saying get only moderate excited, some are saying get really inhibited. And once again, we've got the axon hillock there integrating all those excitatory and inhibitory inputs. So we've seen the need here for a bunch of different neurotransmitters, and the best estimates are there are a couple of hundred out there. As they are used in multiple ways, they can service your brain with its trillions of synapses.

So now what we need to look at is, how do you construct these neurotransmitters? What are these chemical messengers like? And right at this point, if you're a first year medical student, the entire point of the lecture now is to completely overwhelm and demoralize you with these horrendous multi-syllabic terms and these awful biosynthetic pathways; and despite that, all of the neurotransmitters are made, or synthesized, with some very simple rules and they make perfect sense.

Once again, you want to use your neurotransmitters in the next hundredth-of-a-second to run you away from the saber tooth tiger, you don't want to spend the next three weeks constructing this wonderful molecule that's going to be the most gorgeous neurotransmitter on earth, and you're long dead. They're used quickly, they are obsolete an instant afterward. As a result, you see a whole bunch of rules about their synthesis built around being as cheap as possible.

Today's newspaper is obsolete tomorrow, and all it's good for is paper training the dog. You don't want to put a whole lot of energy into a messenger that is almost immediately obsolete; and you see this played out in a number of ways, a number of rules.

First off, what do you build your neurotransmitters from? What are the building blocks, the precursors? And what you wind up seeing is they are all built from very simple, boring, plentiful molecules that you get in your diet in huge amounts, very simple amino acids, very simple constituents of fat, so that you are never, ever up the creek in trying to run for your life from the saber tooth tiger and—oops, bad luck—you've run out of the critical neurotransmitter, because you haven't had enough precursor on hand there, there's a shortage this year. Very plentiful, cheap precursors.

Shown here on the diagram, what you see is the next step, which is you make your neurotransmitter out of this precursor Just a couple of biosynthetic steps; nothing fancy. You just make a couple of changes here and there, just so you know this isn't an amino acid anymore, this is one of those fancy specialized neurotransmitters. Just a couple of steps. Nothing terribly exotic. You need to do it quickly, very cheaply.

So you've gotten that far. The next trick you find is, for the same precursor, depending on where you are in the nervous system, depending on which type of neuron, you could generate different neurotransmitters. In other words, you can squeeze multiple messengers out of one precursor.

Another way to be really cheap, to be really efficient about your system—what's the fourth way of being efficient, we saw it a few minutes ago—which is whenever possible, recycle your neurotransmitters. Use them over and over again, and that's a great way to make the whole system very cheap. So you've got these enormously fancy chemicals, which nonetheless are very simple in their principles. They are really easy to make, they're made out of cheap precursors, you squeeze a lot of different types of messengers out of one precursor and you recycle them. That's exactly the system you would have to see where you're using neurotransmitters 20, 30, 50 times in a second across a synapse. These are not fancy molecules; they've got to be cheap, functional ones.

So that's a whole lot about their biosynthesis. What you then ask is, okay, there's a gazillion different chemicals you find in a neuron, maybe in this axon terminal. How do you decide is this thing a neurotransmitter? What are the criteria that are used? They make perfect sense, and there are four classical ones.

The first one, as shown on this diagram, is no surprise. It's something that's going to be a neurotransmitter, you've got to show it's in the axon terminal, and the axon terminal contained in one of those balloons, one of those vesicles, it's got to be there. The next thing you have to show is that you've got to release it. Along comes an action potential and you've got to show that this vesicle full of this putative neurotransmitter merges with the wall, with the membrane, and dumps out the chemical messenger. You send it into the synapse.

The next thing you have to show is perfectly logical as well. It gets to the other side of the synapse and lock and keyish into the receptor there, and it does something or other now to the neuron, the next one in line as shown here in the diagram. The neurotransmitter is released, floats across the synapse, binds to receptors in the postsynaptic neuron, and some excitatory event changes in that neuron.

Those first three criteria show you that something could be a neurotransmitter. The final criteria shown in the diagram is a critical one. If you mess with the system, things don't work normally afterward. If you throw in some drug which blocks the receptor, which makes it impossible for that key to fit into the lock, something important now no longer occurs in that postsynaptic neuron. What you've shown is, normally it serves a function; block that function and something doesn't work anymore. You've now shown this thing as a messenger.

So it's got to be there, it's got to be released, it's got to have an effect on the postsynaptic neuron, and if you block that effect from occurring, something is mighty wrong at that point—that's how you show something's a neurotransmitter. At this point, there's maybe 20, 25 different chemicals that have met all of those criteria, and there's close to a hundred others that meet a few of those criteria. You go away for a long holiday weekend, you come back the next Monday morning and seven new things are now putative neurotransmitters. It's a very rapidly changing field identifying these messengers. And, as we'll see in later lectures, some of these neurotransmitters violate all the rules we just set up. But these are your basic, off the rack neurotransmitters.

Now what you begin to see as the next question is: How do you wind up manipulating the system? How do you wind up beginning to see how the system can change over time? And that will actually be the subject of the next lecture: how does synaptic communication change? You can begin to see exactly what this is about. You change the amount of neurotransmitter being released. You change the amount of receptor; you change the sensitivity of the receptor. You change how easily you do the recycling; you change how readily you have the enzyme ripping up the neurotransmitter, degrading it afterward. This is where we begin to see all those individual differences out there. We all differ in how readily we make those neurotransmitters, how readily we make the receptors. We have different versions of those receptors from one person to the next, and we're beginning to understand where those differences have consequence for behavior. We can readily see where these individual differences come from, as we will just as readily see in the next lecture how you can change the functioning over time. We'll see it in the special "K's," the change of synaptic function that we call learning and memory.

Now, what we focus on here is one additional important piece of how these synapses work. And this one's real important because it is relevant to the lives of a lot of us: how you can use drugs to change the functioning of synapses. *Neuropharmacology*: the ability of having pharmaceuticals change neural function. And this is relevant to understanding certain drugs of abuse, and this is relevant to understanding a huge number of medications out there. What you have essentially is an array of ways in which you can manipulate the nervous system, manipulate synaptic communication with drugs.

First example—and this is one out of the realm of substances of abuse—here we have a synapse in this diagram, and we've got all our usual components: we've got the neurotransmitters and the vesicles, we've got the synapse, we've got the receptors, we've got the reuptake mechanisms, we've got the degradative mechanisms. It just happens that this synapse is completely silent. There's nothing happening there. The presynaptic neuron hasn't had a creative thought in its head for weeks; it has nothing to say. There's no action potential, there's no neurotransmitters coming out; the synapse is completely quiet.

It just so happens, this individual has ingested a drug, and the drug has a certain chemical structure to it. The drug gets into your net, it gets into your bloodstream; it eventually gets into the brain and gets into synapses all over the place. And the critical feature is that drug has a chemical structure that is almost identical to the actual neurotransmitter. And what does it do? As shown here on the diagram, it comes floating into the synapse from out of left field, gets into the synapse and binds to the receptor. It binds so effectively and looks so much like the real thing that it fakes out the receptor. The receptor believes it has just bound the actual neurotransmitter released by the presynaptic neuron.

The second neuron gets excited, gets a wavelet of ionic changes. What's going on? That second neuron is hearing voices. It's hearing voices that aren't there. This is how hallucinogens work. And there's a particular class of neurotransmitter called *serotonin*, and all of the major hallucinogens, chemically they're structures are just like serotonin, almost identical. That's the case for LSD, mescaline, psilocybin—all of those artificially activate serotonin receptors when there's no serotonin being released. As a result, you've got pathways that are getting excited when your brain had no intention of doing it. That's what a hallucination is.

Why hallucinations take certain forms and have certain coherent, visual aspects to them so on, why you hear voices instead of random sounds, nobody really understands. But that's one way of chemically manipulating the synapse; send a message when it isn't really there.

What's the next thing you can do? Potentially, exactly the opposite. Now put in a drug that binds to the receptor, except in this case, it doesn't bind in a way to activate the receptor, it just gums things; it blocks it. You block the receptor. Two examples of this: one of them blocks a bunch of neurotransmitter receptors that have something to do with your diaphragm, and suddenly your brain is not able to send a message telling you to breathe and this proves to be fatal. That's the drug curare; this is how curare winds up being a poison. It blocks a class of neurotransmitter receptors, and your diaphragm doesn't work anymore and you are up the creek.

Here's a more interesting example straight out of clinical medicine. This is a drug that blocks a different class of receptors; a class of receptors for a neurotransmitter that we're going to hear a lot about; a neurotransmitter called *dopamine*. Now where does this become relevant? In one part of the brain it seems as if dopamine has something to do with coherent, logical, linear thinking. And if the levels of dopamine are incorrect, you've got a person with a great deal of trouble with coherent, logical, linear thinking. What are we describing? This is the psychiatric disorder schizophrenia; a pattern of very dramatic thought disorder. During the mid 1950s it was discovered, throw in any of the class of drugs that block dopamine receptors and schizophrenics get better.

These are drugs that are called *anti-psychotics*, also termed *neuroleptics*—haldol, thorazine. Any time in some made-for-TV movie where somebody has their psychotic break, and the orderlies come down and wrestle the guy down and they get the syringe into him to calm him down, this is most typically a dopamine receptor blocker that's being used.

Okay, so you look at this and you say, here we have this florid psychiatric disorder of abnormal thinking, of disordered thinking; throw in a drug that blocks dopamine receptors in this person's brain and suddenly they get less psychotic. I bet you there was too much dopamine in the first place. And that's the leading hypothesis as to the neurochemistry of schizophrenia: too much dopamine release. So that's a way of manipulating the system.

Then there are other drugs that you can throw in. What they will do here—as shown in this diagram—is you can be releasing neurotransmitters when you had no intention of, you can trigger the release of neurotransmitters. That's another version of something vaguely resembling a hallucination; you're forcing the neuron, the presynaptic neuron to send a message, when it has no intention of.

Other ways of manipulating the system—in this case what you can do is change aspects of the recycling of the use of a neurotransmitter after it's done its thing; after it has bound to a receptor there. What were the two things that happened at that point? One of two choices that we've heard: you can recycle your neurotransmitter, some pump in the presynaptic neuron grabs onto the neurotransmitter, pulls it in, and sticks it back in a vesicle; or, you can have an enzyme floating around the synapse that grabs onto the neurotransmitter and tears it into little pieces and flushes it out to sea. So you can use drugs that manipulate either of those steps. One version of it.

Now we manipulate that enzyme that tears up the neurotransmitter. And this is a neurotransmitter called *neuroepinephrine*, and it's an enzyme that rips it apart called MAO, *monoamine oxydaze;* and during the early 60s, people developed a drug which inhibited MAO; an MAO inhibitor. What does an MAO inhibitor do? It inhibits this enzyme from ripping up the neurotransmitter neuroepinephrine. You don't rip up the neuroepinephrine, it stays there longer. And what does it do at that point, for a lack of anything else to do? It hits the receptor a second time, a third time, and a 40th time; you boost up the neuroepinephrine signaling in the system.

What you see then, and what people discovered in the early 60s was, you take somebody who is clinically depressed and give them an MAO inhibitor and they start feeling better. Ah ha! What does your theory have to be at that point? If you take a drug that blocks the breakdown of neuroepinephrine, that causes neuroepinephrine to have more of an oomph, to send more signaling than it used to, and depressions get better, I bet you there wasn't enough neuroepinephrine in the first place. And, this is one of the leading theories as to what's wrong with that disease.

Now the other thing we could do there in manipulating, as mentioned, is you can stop the recycling, the reuptake of the neurotransmitter. And there is a drug, which these days is probably the most heavily prescribed in this country, which blocks the reuptake of a certain type of neurotransmitter, blocks the reuptake of serotonin, and only serotonin. What are these things called? *Selective serotonin reuptake inhibitors*; SSRIs. What's the most famous version of this? Prozac. Prozac, another antidepressant; and that causes a whole bunch of people to now think about serotonin. Ah ha! You take somebody who's depressed and you make it impossible for them to remove the serotonin from the synapse, and as a result, serotonin stays around longer and works more. I bet there wasn't enough serotonin in the first place.

And those are the two leading hypotheses of depression these days: a shortage of neuroepinephrine and/or a shortage of serotonin; in both cases, shown with a chemical manipulation of the system.

Now there's another manipulation you can do there, which is quite interesting. How about you change the amount of neurotransmitter that you make? How about you boost up the synthesis of neurotransmitter? And this is shown in another disease. Unfortunately, one that's becoming increasingly common, neurological disease of aging, Parkinson's disease. Parkinson's, motoric disease, you have trouble initiating movements; you can have a very florid Parkinsonian tremor. The best evidence since the early 1960s is Parkinson's is due to degeneration in one area of the brain that makes tremendous use of the neurotransmitter dopamine.

Dopamine? Wait a second, I just heard about dopamine with schizophrenia. This is a completely different area of the brain. In this part of the brain, dopamine is about smooth movements. And what you see there is a massive loss of dopamine; for reasons we're beginning to understand, the neurons there die.

So what do you think? What's a good way of boosting up dopamine levels in the remaining neurons? Give them more dopamine to release. It's hard to put dopamine into somebody's gut and get into the brain. You use a precursor, something called L-DOPA. L-DOPA is a couple of steps before dopamine. Stoke up somebody on L-DOPA and they make more dopamine in that part of the brain, and some of the Parkinsonian symptoms calm down at that point. That's been one of the leading therapies since the early 60s. So you manipulate the system, you boost up the levels of the neurotransmitter.

Okay, if you were watching closely here and skeptically, you should notice there's a problem. Schizophrenia—too much dopamine. You throw in a drug that blocks dopamine receptors, schizophrenia gets better. Parkinson's—too little dopamine in a different part of the brain. You throw in a drug to boost up the dopamine levels.

Where are you putting those drugs in? You're not spritzing them into this one area of the brain. You're putting it in the gut, it gets into the blood work, it gets all over the brain and suddenly, you should be having this... "Ah ha, what's going on here?" In Parkinson's disease, too little dopamine; so you give the person L-DOPA, and in this part of the brain there's not enough dopamine, and you correct it and the Parkinsonian symptoms get better. Meanwhile, in the other parts of the brain with normal dopamine levels, you push things above normal. What should you see? One of the most common side effects if you overshoot your L-DOPA level is the patient gets psychotic.

Some of you will have seen the movie *Awakenings*, based on Oliver Sacks; and what you have there is a very rare neurological disease, "Stiff-man Syndrome, which has something to do with Parkinson's. And what you saw there was these people who have so much of a tremor that they are frozen. And what you got there was treating people with L-DOPA, and you had these miraculous awakenings; people moving for the first time in years. What you also saw with the Robert DeNiro character there is when you overdo it you get this florid paranoid psychosis. So try to fix up Parkinson's, and a possible side effect is inadvertently generating something that looks like schizophrenia.

Meanwhile, over in the other corner, you've got the schizophrenic and you give them antipsychotic to block their dopamine signaling. And in this part of the brain where there's too much, you bring it back down to normal. And in the other parts of the brain, you depress dopamine signaling. What's the side effect of too much anti-psychotics? You start getting Parkinsonian tremors. And there's a special name for it in psychiatry, it's called tardive dyskinesia— Kinesia, kinetics, body move; and dyskinesia, abnormal movements. And you go to some state hospital and you go to the back ward, and you find somebody trembling there like that; and this is somebody who's been taking anti-psychotics for a long time.

So what we see here inevitably is there is no free lunch, built around the fact that the same neurotransmitter is being used in very different parts of the brain.

So that gives us a sense of the workings of this. The last thing we need to do is, as usual, look at the individual differences. We've already heard about it. We differ as to the amount of neurotransmitter release, the amount of receptors, etc. There's increasing evidence of a type of neurotransmitter system very closely related to a class of drugs that decrease anxiety, drugs like Valium and Librium; and we have our own versions of those inside our brains. It's been identified that certain rodent strains, rat strains that differ in their levels of anxiety, differ genetically as to how well the receptor binds to this Valium-like compound, which begins to explain those individual differences.

Okay, so what have we gotten to at this point? We have now graduated from one neuron. We're up to two neurons, and how they talk to each other. Our other theme here, plasticity, how these neuronal functions change over time, will be the subject of the next lecture.

What I see now is the big hand is approaching the six, so it's time for us to shut down. What we will see after this is how synaptic communication changes in response to experience—the biology of learning.

Lecture Four
Learning and Synaptic Plasticity

Scope:

This lecture examines how communication within and between neurons changes as a result of experience. Particular emphasis is placed on *long-term potentiation* (LTP), including an explanation of how the process occurs in two different parts of the brain: first, in the hippocampus, with implications for learning and memory, and second, in the amygdala, with implications for fear and anxiety. Ways that the LTP process is enhanced and disrupted, both naturally and artificially, are also investigated.

Outline

I. Changing the strength of synaptic communication is the basis for learning.

    A. The dominant paradigm is that learning is the process of making certain pathways work more readily than they did before.

    B. In earlier times, it was believed that whenever something new was learned, a new neuron or a new synapse was formed; this may actually be true.

    C. The cortex and hippocampus are the main regions of the brain responsible for learning and memory.

        1. Problems in the hippocampus may result in such diseases as Alzheimer's disease.

        2. The famous case of H.M., who had his hippocampus removed, shows the importance of the hippocampus to memory.

II. *Long-term potentiation* (LTP), a synaptic model for learning, is the process of stimulating a dendritic spine in a dense cluster of rapid action potentials, resulting in that synapse becoming hyperresponsive or *potentiated*. (Figure 4a)

    A. After potentiation has occurred, the pathway is stronger.

    B. Potentiation increases the likelihood that a single neuron can cause an action potential.

C. These changes are long lasting.

III. How does the initial phase of LTP work?

    A. LTP is the result of glutamate being released into synapses throughout the hippocampus.

        1. Glutamate is a simple neurotransmitter made from an amino acid.

        2. Glutamate is the most excitatory neuron with two receptor systems, each of which is differentially excitable.

    B. The workings of the two receptors explain the "Ah ha!" of learning. With repeated stimulation, enough glutamate is dumped into the synapses to open the second receptor, which allows a wave of excitatory calcium to pour in, causing great potentiation.

IV. How does LTP become long term? (Figure 4b)

    A. As LTP occurs, calcium enters the neuron.

        1. Calcium triggers an increase in the number of glutamate receptors in the relevant dendritic spine.

        2. Calcium causes the receptors to stay open and activated longer once they are excited.

        3. Calcium changes how readily the electrical wave spreads once there is some excitation.

    B. Once calcium rushes in, it causes the synthesis of a neurotransmitter that floats back to the presynaptic neuron.

        1. These retrograde neurotransmitters increase the amount of glutamate being synthesized by the presynaptic neuron.

        2. Some of these new transmitters are made from gases and, therefore, do not need vesicles.

V. The vulnerability of *glutamatergic* pathways to neurological insults is relevant to a number of neurological diseases and disorders.

    A. If glutamate levels get too high (a condition called *excitotoxicity*), the postsynaptic neuron can be excited to death. This condition can occur in stroke, seizure, and cardiac arrest.

B. Monosodium glutamate (MSG) and other dietary constituents that resemble glutamate may be worth worrying about.

VI. How do you forget anything?

    A. This is an important topic in the field of neurobiology, and it is still under study.

    B. In some manner, however, forgetting is thought to be a reversal of all the steps that we have just covered regarding LTP.

VII. Several factors influence how readily LTP occurs.

    A. Some factors are known to enhance LTP.

        1. Abundant energy—lots of glucose in your blood that translates into neurons with more energy—facilitates LTP.

        2. Short-term stress (stimulation) causes stress hormones to be released on a short-term basis, and these hormones enhance memory.

    B. Some factors are known to disrupt LTP.

        1. Energy depletion makes LTP less likely to occur. When you run out of energy, the whole transport of neurotransmitters is disrupted.

        2. Chronic stress, unlike short-term stress, disturbs many types of memory consolidation and memory retrieval.

        3. Alcohol in sufficient amounts dramatically disrupts LTP.

VIII. Individual differences in the area of LTP can manifest themselves in a number of ways.

    A. The amount and functions of neurotransmitters, receptors, and so on can vary greatly from person to person.

    B. An experiment at Princeton provides an interesting view on this subject.

        1. Scientists at Princeton developed Doogie mice, genetically engineered rodents that had better than average LTP and demonstrated better than average learning.

2. Then, the scientists developed their less heralded cousins, mice with an impaired capacity for LTP and learning.
3. They then raised the impaired mice in an extremely stimulating environment, which overcame their deficit.
4. This experiment shows that even something as seemingly deterministic as a major genetic defect can still be subject to important environmental modulation.

Further Reading:

For a good, although by now somewhat dated, introduction to the neurobiology of learning and memory, including LTP:

L. Squire, *Memory and Brain.*

For an excellent neuroscience textbook that covers LTP in some detail:

L. Squire, *Fundamental Neuroscience,* 2nd ed.

Questions to Consider:

1. What are the ways in which synaptic function can change in response to experience?
2. How might neurons differ in the ease with which those changes occur?

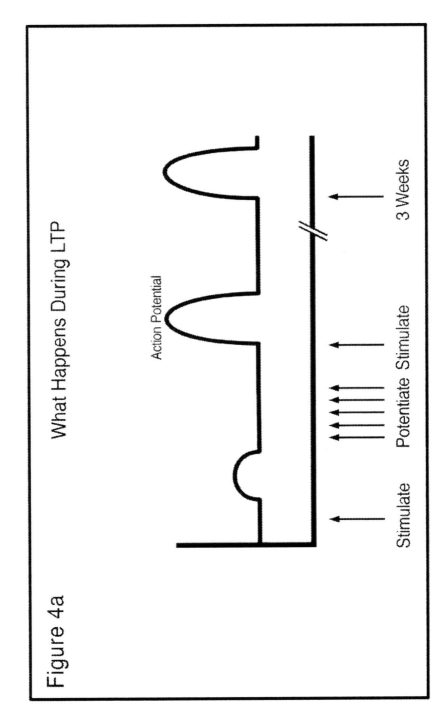

Figure 4a

What Happens During LTP

Figure 4b

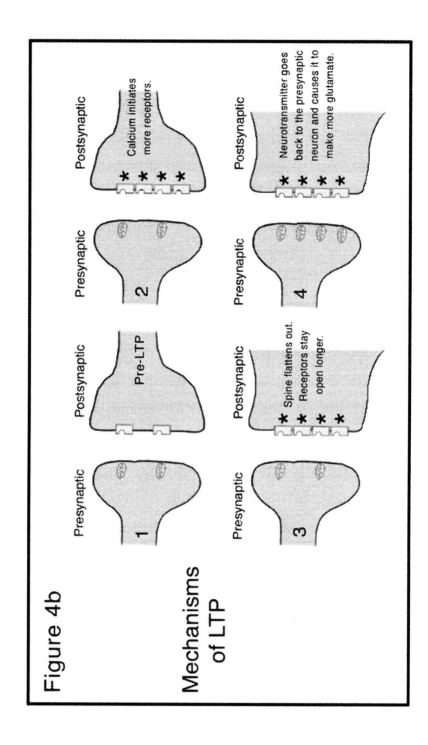

Mechanisms of LTP

©2005 The Teaching Company Limited Partnership

Lecture Four—Transcript
Learning and Synaptic Plasticity

We are back for more, back for more in our goal to understand how biology works in shaping our behavior; and, as we've started in these lectures, trying to understand that from a standpoint of how the brain works. We've looked at how one, single neuron works; how it integrates an incredible number of inputs from all sorts of other neurons; how it, in turn, talks to the next neuron in line. Last lecture was the world of neurotransmitters, transsynaptic communication—communication across the synapse—and finished up with a sense of individual differences, of how one person's synapse may work differently from another.

Now our theme has been at the end of each lecture, two-fold: one is looking at plasticity, how things change over time, individual differences, and when it comes to plasticity in the synapse, how it functions differently in response to experience. That's such an important topic that gets an entire lecture today.

What plasticity means in this case is learning. How do you learn something new? How do you remember it? Remarkably enough, or maybe not so remarkable when you think about it, your brain works differently when you have learned a fact, and what we now know is somewhere in your brain your synapses work differently. Learning is about changes in synaptic communication. Memory is about those changes lasting a long time.

Now people have not always understood learning to involve changes in synapses, mainly because earlier on in neurobiology people didn't even know synapses existed. What was the first notion? This quaint, charming idea that any time you learned a new fact, you made a new neuron; and then people figured out, adult brains don't make new neurons. That can't explain it.

So the next version of charming incorrect theories was the notion that when you learn a new fact, you form a new synapse. Either an axon terminal and a dendritic spine that weren't connected now connect to form a synapse; or, you actually grow a new axon terminal. People figured out that was ridiculous and was some charming, outdated idea. What people came to realize instead was that synapses that were already there work differently.

Naturally, in the last decade, what people have learned, revolutions in this field, is the adult brain actually does make new neurons and they may have something to do with forming memories. The adult brain actually forms new synapses. That completely overturned some of the dogma in the field. Nevertheless, what still remains the dominant paradigm for how learning occurs is synapses work differently.

The official jargon in the field is what learning is about is you strengthen pre-existing synapses. What does strengthen a pre-existing synapse mean? If the first neuron, the presynaptic neuron has an action potential, and talks to the second neuron, it is now more likely that that second neuron will have an action potential. You have strengthened the communication between the two.

This was a notion which came up by a guy named Donald Hebb, this famous neuroscientist in the 1950s. Hebb—basically, if you're a neuroscientist, you are not able to talk about any subject without someone in there saying Hebb—and it was in the 1950s that Hebb first predicted that this is how the brain was going to work. This guy predicted the next 80 years work of neuroscience. He was the first one to say, it's not about new neurons, it's not about synapse forming anew; it's about synapses that are already there, working differently, working stronger. Learning is the strengthening of synaptic connections.

Now what people have realized is your brain is not this undifferentiated mass of tofu. There're different parts of your brain and different parts do different things. And there're two areas that from day one have been implicated in learning and memory, as shown in the diagram here—we now get into our first anatomy of the entire brain—it's these two regions, one called the *hippocampus*. Latin fans will recognize hippocampus means "seahorse" in Latin, and presumably some neuroscientist who didn't go anywhere near the seashore often enough decided this part of the brain looks like a seahorse. It actually to me looks more like a jelly roll, but nobody knew the Latin name for it. It's this curving structure underneath the surface of the brain. It's very involved in learning and memory.

The other region at the top of the list is the surface of the brain called the *cortex*, and in this diagram what we see is that all across the top we have the cortex. The hippocampus is buried underneath a sub-cortical structure. These are two really important areas for making sense of learning and memory.

What's the best evidence for it? Two-fold, the first one is a horrendous disease, the disease that probably collectively we are most afraid of out there, disease that most polls show is more frightening to us than cancer, than HIV, than heart disease—Alzheimer's disease. Alzheimer's disease, which melts away your brain, melts away your capacity to learn new things, access memory; and, overwhelmingly, Alzheimer's disease is a disease of the hippocampus and the cortex.

The other strongest bit of evidence comes from a man who's probably the most famous patient in the history of neurology. This is a guy who is only known by his initials, H.M., and he winds up in every single textbook. H.M. had an extremely rare type of epilepsy when he was a kid, before any of the modern drugs existed. The epilepsy, the seizures, tended to begin in his hippocampus. He was having multiple seizures per day, and in an extremely desperate and radical move, his hippocampuses were surgically removed—the only time this has been done to a human—and emotionally solved his epilepsy. Since then H.M. has had a 30-second memory capacity, and then everything is gone. An amazing story in and of itself, but this is some of the evidence, along with Alzheimer's, that shows hippocampus and cortex are what learning and memory are centered in. These are the parts of the brain where experience causes synapses to be strengthened.

The particular jargon used in the field is you *potentiate* the synapse; you make it work more strongly. This potentiation is long term, that's what the memory is. Thus the jargon is *long-term potentiation*, LTP. That's the jargony term for synapses working stronger in response to experience and remembering it.

Now here we see sort of on a schematic-sized version of what happens during LTP in this diagram. We are regarding from some dendritic spine, and an arrow here represents a point where you stimulate it. You dump some neurotransmitter on, and as we know by now, we get our little wave of excitation. Now what you do is you potentiate that synapse. You stimulate it over and over and over and over, 20 times a second for a certain number of seconds, even faster—this cluster of arrows—you stimulate that synapse like crazy.

Then you wait a bit and you stimulate it again, and something amazing has occurred. As shown here, that little wavelet of excitation is a lot bigger than the previous time. You have potentiated that wave of excitation. This is now a more excitable synapse. The signal coming out of the presynaptic neuron makes the second, postsynaptic neuron more excitable than it used to be. You get a greater likelihood of an actual potential occurring.

Now the really amazing thing is, you take a break from your experiment and you go out and you take a nap for three weeks, and you come back after that and you check out that synapse, and it is still potentiated. The potentiation is long term, LTP, and for lots of people out there, this is the nearest thing to what's going on during learning and memory. At first it was thought this is a great model for strengthening a presynaptic and pre-existing synapses. What is now pretty much accepted is this is no model. This is what goes on during learning.

What's come to be realized is, even though LTP was first identified in the hippocampus, then the cortex—that's ground zero for learning and memory—it occurs all over the place in the nervous system. One example, there's another part of the brain called the *amygdala*, and we will hear about that in later lectures. The amygdala has something to do with fear, with trauma, and the right type of stimulation, the right type of trauma, and you get long-term potentiation in the amygdala. What do you get then? You have just conditioned a phobia. You have just conditioned something like post traumatic stress disorder. You have an amygdala that's hyper excitable.

There're parts of your spine that undergo LTP in chronic pain syndrome so that you're left with the slightest touch in that area, a hypersensitivity causes pain. LTP seems to be common throughout the nervous system—how different parts of your brain become more responsive, remember it.

So how does LTP work? This has consumed the careers of gazillion scientists over recent decades, trying to sort it out. People actually by now have a pretty good sense of it, and it is built around a neurotransmitter that is pretty studied at this point. It is interesting for two reasons. A neurotransmitter called *glutamate*, glutamate is the most excitatory neurotransmitter ever discovered. What do we mean by that? For the same amount of glutamate coming out as any other neurotransmitter, you get a bigger wave of excitation in that postsynaptic neuron than is provoked by any other neurotransmitter out there. It's the most excitatory neurotransmitter. The second thing about it that is really interesting, that's real important, is glutamate has not one receptor, it's got two types of receptors, and it's this transition to a dual receptor system that begins to explain where you get learning and memory from.

So what happens? You release glutamate. What's the most glutamatergic part of the brain? What's the part of the brain where the greatest percentages of synapses use glutamate to speak? You guessed it—hippocampus and cortex. So we're sitting there in the hippocampus and out comes some glutamate and it binds to the first type of receptor. And you get your little wavelet of excitation in the postsynaptic neuron. Nothing's happening with the second receptor. So you dump a little bit more glutamate out and you fill up the first receptor; the second receptor doesn't fill up as readily. Fill up the first one, you get another little wavelet. It's not until you get enough glutamate coming in there, it's not until you buzz that first receptor enough times, that there's a certain chemical coupling between it and the second receptor. Pass a threshold and the second receptor suddenly responds with a tidal wave of excitation, and suddenly you've got the biggest burst of wavelets going on in that postsynaptic neuron that you ever see in the nervous system.

So what have we got? We've got a nonlinear system. You get a little bit of glutamate, nothing's happening with the second receptor. You got a moderate, nothing's happening. You get a whole lot, nothing's happening. You get a real whole lot and suddenly it explodes, opens up with excitation; you've got a nonlinear system, and this is what learning is. You sit there, a lecturer says something; it goes in one ear and out the other. The lecturer drones on, says it again, goes in one ear and out the other. Says it over and over and suddenly you get this "ah ha"; suddenly the light bulb goes on. That's the moment when there's been enough stimulation in this pathway that you switch over to the second receptor system; you get that explosion coming in.

What that explosion is about is an entirely new ion, one we haven't mentioned before. You remember back a couple of lectures, we're dealing with sodium and chloride and potassium changing directions. It's the ion that's critical now, that comes pouring in and is called *calcium*—calcium, the same thing that's good for your bones. A little bit of calcium is used up in your brain for this sort of excitation stuff, and when that second receptor gets excited, it allows this tidal wave of calcium to pour in and that causes tremendous excitation.

That's the potentiation, that's that sudden burst, as shown on the chart here. What you've done with this repeated stimulation, repeated stimulation, is finally dump enough glutamate into the synapses to kick open that second receptor, this calcium-gated receptor, and in goes the tidal wave of enormously excitatory calcium. And you've potentiated this pathway. Hooray for you. So this event has made an impression on you, and what people have shown is repeated stimulation, not stimulation with an electrode in there, with stimulation, a fact coming in over and over, drives those neurons enough to finally cause that calcium influx.

So you've just explained the learning part. You've explained how you potentiate this pathway with repeated stimulation. So that's great, but most of us would like to remember the things we've learned for more than 30 seconds. How do you turn it into long-term potentiation? How do you turn it into a memory that will be there an hour from now? By definition, long-term memory, or that will be there in your old age, remembering your childhood, language, things of that sort? How do you turn it into a change of synaptic strength that will persist for three quarters of a century? An enormous amount of work has gone into understanding where the long term comes from in long-term potentiation.

What we see on this diagram, very schematically, is what goes on, and there's a whole bunch of mechanisms. What I've put down here are four of the more common ones, and what you see is, in different parts of the brain, LTP involved different of these mechanisms, other ones as well. People make entire careers sniping at each other as to whose mechanism is most important in their part of the brain, and whether their version of LTP is the real gold standard LTP. A bunch of things happen and they make sense.

Here what we see on top is our usual synapse, pre LTP, and we got the presynaptic neuron with its neurotransmitter and the vesicles, and we got the receptors on the postsynaptic side, and everybody's happy there, going about its business. How does that influx of calcium now become a long-term signal, a persistent signal? What comes close to being a permanent signal? The calcium does it in a bunch of ways.

First thing that happens, calcium comes rushing in, and you see an interesting thing. It turns out neurons have a whole bunch of spare receptors around. They have them mothballed, in storage. Sitting there just underneath the surface of that dendritic spine, there are these little bubblet things, these little sorts of spheres of membrane that's got all sorts of receptors stuck in there. Do these receptors do anything? No, they're in storage. What calcium dose is initiate a pathway by which some of those receptors are pulled out of storage and put onto the surface, put onto that dendritic spine, and what have you got now? More receptors; metaphorically, you got more ears. Actually that's a terrible metaphor, but you have more ears at that point. Instead of listening to the presynaptic neuron with two receptors, you're now listening with four. You've increased the sensitivity of that postsynaptic neuron to a signal.

The next thing you do, in addition to changing the number of those receptors, is you change their function. Specifically what's done, as shown here by these asterisks in the diagram, is you make a chemical modification in these receptors. For those of you who care about such things, you do something that's called *phosphorilation*. You basically throw a switch on those receptors so they work differently. How do they work differently? They stay open, activated for a longer time. So for the same amount of glutamate buzzing the system, you not only have more receptors to act upon, the receptors allow more excitation, more of those ions to flow in and out of the neuron. So you've got the postsynaptic neuron listening better, more receptors, more receptor sensitivity.

A third thing happens, and this was actually the first mechanism uncovered to explain LTP. What you could see in this diagram, what may look arbitrary at first, but is quite intentional, the shape of the dendritic spine changes. In the top picture we've got the dendritic spine as this very sort of constrained little out-pocking, and literally what happens with LTP is the spine flattens out a little bit. For extremely complex, biophysics reasons what that means is each little wavelet of excitation spreads further than it used to. Technical term, there's less *resistance* in the membrane. Just like in electrical systems, the same wavelet spreads further, and why was this, the first mechanism discovered? Because this was before fancy biochemistry, this was before molecular biology. You just need a microscope and you see, ah ha, neurons from brains that have undergone LTP in the hippocampus; the dendrites have a different shape.

As it turns out, when calcium comes in, it causes all sorts of restructuring in that dendrite. You disassemble this whole scaffolding, this superstructure of proteins; the term is the cytoskeleton. You undo the whole super structure there and rebuild it in a way so that the shape's a little bit different. So now what have you got? You've got a dendritic spine with more receptors that stay open longer, and the wave of excitation sweeps further.

One last step, and this one boggled people when this first became clear. When the dendritic spine is stimulated enough, when that calcium wave comes in, what does it do? It releases a neurotransmitter that goes back to the presynaptic neuron and causes it to make more glutamate, causes it now to release more glutamate. Okay, you should be leaping out of your chair in offense and finding your receipt for this course. What's going on? You got neurotransmitters in the dendritic spine being released, going backwards across the synapse. This is heretical; this is a whole new area that people have discovered. Neurotransmitter, unconventional neurotransmitters, these ones are called retrograde neurotransmitters. They go in the wrong direction.

There's a way of signaling. What do you know? It turns out the nervous system can communicate in both directions across the synapse. There's a whole bunch of these weirdo neurotransmitters that are made in dendritic spines and they go backwards. Not only are they weird for where they're found and what direction they go, turns out they're weird in terms of their structure. Some of these are made of gas.

For example, there's a neurotransmitter called nitric oxide. Others are made of all sorts of unlikely materials that are made out of the membrane. These are really weird messengers, they go backwards, they go in the wrong direction; they're made out of conventional things, but what do they do? They go back and they stimulate the presynaptic neuron to start making more glutamate.

So what have you got here? Four very effective steps; you are now releasing more neurotransmitter out of the presynaptic neurons. There's more glutamate on board, so you're yelling louder, and the postsynaptic neuron is listening more effectively, more receptors stay open longer, more and more of the spread of that wavelet of excitation; this is what LTP is. This is what a potentiated synapse is about.

Now what's very interesting is, from out of nowhere, this turns out to be very relevant to a bunch of neurological diseases. Now if you talk about glutamate and calcium influx and multiple glutamate receptors, and you're doing this at a meeting of scientists who think about learning and memory. Glutamate is your friend; it's the greatest neurotransmitter on earth. It gets you better SAT scores. Meanwhile, over in the next auditorium, if you're sitting with a whole bunch of neurologists and you're talking about glutamate and calcium, it is at the centerpiece of some of the most common of neurological diseases, and this makes sense.

What's going on here? So you've got glutamate coming out, and what have we already heard is the most excitatory neurotransmitter in the brain? What if glutamate levels get too high? And there is a jargony term in the field given for it, when levels get high enough. You transition from glutamate being an excitatory neurotransmitter to what is called an *excito toxin*.

If you get too much of this stuff on the scene, you can excite the postsynaptic neuron to death through a number of mechanisms, but one that is readily appreciated, how about you do regular old LTP, you get a big wave of calcium but nothing and say, What did we see you undo, part of the scaffolding there in the dendritic spine, and you change the shape a little bit. What if you get a massive amount of calcium coming in, because of a massive excito toxic amount of glutamate? You don't just remodel this little dendritic spine, you blow apart the scaffolding in the entire neuron, and it collapses on you, and you got a dead neuron at that point.

When does this occur? This is what happens during a stroke. This is what happens during epilepsy. During epilepsy, you've got so much glutamate coming out by this repeated stimulation that you get glutamatergic toxicity. In a stroke, your brain is running out of energy and doesn't have the energy to remove the glutamate from the synapse anymore, and you excite the second neuron to death. This whole world of glutamate excitotoxicity is at the centerpiece of understanding these neurological diseases.

Two quick disturbing "uh ohs;" one is, glutamate, some dietary thing that's resembling MSG, monosodium glutamate. MSG does not get into the adult brain very well, it just gives some of us a headache, but it doesn't get into the adult brain. It gets into baby's brains very well, where it could potentially be cytotoxic, and the FDA long ago banned MSG from baby's food. I grew up in the era of eating MSG, no doubt, three times a day, and that was probably not a good thing to happen to my brain. Currently it is recognized that you don't want MSG in the brains of babies. You increase the risk of some excito toxicity.

The other thing, and hopefully I won't get sued for this, is pointing out a compound that structurally is pretty close to glutamate, and this is aspartame; NutraSweet. When it is broken down, it generates a neurotransmitter a lot like glutamate. Nobody can tell you whether consuming a lot of food with NutraSweet is causing brain damage, but enough in a lab rat can. It's something to be a little bit worried about.

Okay, so we've got the basic workings of the system; and we've got the basic ways in which the system can go awry, can be too excited. Somewhere in there you have to ask the reasonable question, how do you ever forget anything? Big topic in the field, not at all clear how it works, but in some manner, you need to reverse all the steps we've just seen.

So now we see how LTP works. What we begin to look at now is how external factors in your environment can regulate LTP, can make it more likely to occur, can make it less likely. There're at least two things that are now recognized that enhance LTP, and they both make sense.

The first one is lots of energy. If you've got a lot of food in your gut, that translates into a lot of glucose in your bloodstream, which translates into neurons with a lot more energy. Energized neurons are happy neurons and they can pull off LTP more readily. I mean think about this massive project. You're dumping glutamate over and over and over, and you got to get it out of the synapse so you don't get excited toxicity. That reuptake pump is extremely expensive. Lots of energy facilitates LTP. That's a good thing.

The next thing is, there's a class of hormones which you secrete during stress, and during the first few minutes of stress, these stress hormones make LTP work better. They enhance LTP, and that makes perfect sense. What do we call short- term stress? We call it stimulation, and stimulation enhances memory. That's the whole business that you don't learn very well when you're semi-comatose. You've got to be alert, you've got to be sharp; and that's this whole flashbulb memory phenomenon. Where were you when you heard …? I'm willing to bet, like most anyone watching this, most will remember exactly where they were when they heard the news about which actress had some truly hideous outfit at this year's Oscars. We need a mechanism for remembering the really important stuff in life. These short-term exciting stimulatory stressful events sharpen LTP. So that's great.

Meanwhile, there's a bunch of things that disrupt LTP, and they're exactly the flip sides of these. Energy depletion makes LTP less likely to occur. What do you know—being severely hyperglycemic is not a good time to take a final exam in college. LTP synapses don't work as well when you're running out of energy; the whole transport of neurotransmitters, the whole resting potential is disrupted.

The next thing is, what if there're great stress hormones that enhance memory short term? What if it becomes chronic stress? Anything more than a couple of hours, those same stress hormones now disrupt LTP, and that's why severe stress does very bad things to memory consolidation, memory retrieval.

I will just briefly mention a third thing that disrupts LTP, and need to no more than merely mention it, because it's obvious and the take-home lesson is clear there. Another thing that messes with LTP dramatically is alcohol. No surprise; get enough alcohol in your system, and you are not LTP-ing anything. The next morning you don't remember a thing; alcohol is not very good for it either.

Okay, so now we've got an enormous range of ways in which there's plasticity, and in synapse, a number of different mechanisms by which the synapse works differently—learns, remembers, a number of outside factors that modulate such plasticity energy, stress—some of the things you consume. The last issue, the one we always need to look at, this point is how does LTP differ from one person to the next. You know immediately what the usual suspects will be. How much glutamate do you release? How many glutamate receptors and what are the ratios of the two types of glutamate receptors—how much calcium, how much you phosophorilate those receptors—all those sorts of things—a couple of really striking examples of how this can work.

About ten years ago, a bunch of scientists at Princeton made a transgenic mouse, a mouse that they manipulated its genes to express more of one type of glutamate receptor. These mice were the smartest mice anyone had ever seen on earth; these were brilliant, philosophical, introspective mice. These were mice that they quickly—the scientists sensing a fabulous public relations opportunity—gave a name to; they called this the "Doogie mouse," named after some television character, Doogie Howser, who is, I think, like a 6 year old going to medical school. This was a genetically engineered mouse which had better than average LTP and better than average learning This was all over the media—Time Magazine, the cover—manipulate LTP, manipulate the building blocks of it, and you manipulate the ability to learn.

Now at that point, these scientists sat down and did what, in retrospect, was an even more interesting study. They made a different type of genetically engineered mouse. This is one where they knocked out the glutamate receptor, removed the gene for it, so that these were mice that could release glutamate until it was coming out of their ears, and they would not excite that postsynaptic neuron. These mice were not the sharpest ones on the block; these were very impaired mice. They were so impaired that they didn't even get some flashy, irresistible name. These were mice with impaired capacity for LTP and learning.

So what seems to be the punch line there? Look at this, you manipulate one single gene, and you dramatically change the learning abilities in an organism—genetic control of cognition, genetic control of intelligence, genes as destiny—not so fast. Then these guys did a really interesting follow up, showing that these were more than just some mindless molecular biologists futzing with genes. They then took these glutamate-receptor impaired mice that couldn't learn anything and they raised them in an extremely stimulating environment. And you know what? It completely overcame their deficit.

So what initially looked like one big win for nature over nurture, and genetic destiny and genetic control over brain function and intelligence—get those mice in the right environment, and you overcome that genetic deficit. In other words, if it can happen in a mouse, we've got no excuse to talk about genetic destiny and brain function.

Okay, so what have we gotten to here, just in time for all of us to take a nap now? We all see the functioning of one neuron, how it talks to another one, and most importantly, how that is not set in stone. How our brains, our synapses, function differently in response to experience.

What this sets us up now for, in the next lecture, is the huge leap now from the functioning of two neurons to networks of neurons. How do networks operate and give us much more complex functioning?

Module II

The Neurobiology of Behavior at the Systems Level

Module Scope:

This portion of the course expands the scale beyond that of cellular neurobiology to look at the functioning of networks of neurons. Lecture Five is an introduction to the computational potential of neuronal networks. Lecture Six is an examination of how millions of neurons—entire subregions of the brain—function. That lecture will specifically focus on the part of the brain called the *limbic system*, which is vitally concerned with emotion. Finally, Lecture Seven examines how the limbic system regulates the function of the body by way of the autonomic nervous system.

Lecture Five
The Dynamics of Interacting Neurons

Scope:

The next integrative level of neuron function examines how networks of neurons carry out complex processes. We will study how neurons sharpen detection signals through inhibition and how layers of neurons that overlap and form networks directly impact individual memory, pain, and creativity.

Outline

I. The brain consists of networks of neurons.

  A. The brain has far more than patterns of single neurons in line.

  B. Instead, neurons send axons to many other neurons, sending branches off, even back to themselves, forming networks.

II. Neurons sharpen the detection of signals by inhibiting themselves and other neurons.

  A. Neurons communicate with themselves. (Figure 5a)

    1. The ability of neurons to have projections coming off the axon and sending projections back onto themselves (called *recurrent collateral projections*) allows them to inhibit themselves and sharpen their signals over time.

    2. This communication creates individual action potentials, followed by resting potentials.

    3. Recurrent collateral projections are seen in many neurons.

  B. Through lateral inhibition, neurons sharpen their signals over space. (Figure 5b)

    1. The excitation of one neuron leads to the delayed inhibition of other neurons.

    2. This lateral inhibition helps to enhance the precise localization of information.

III. The work of Hubel and Wiesel helped to explain the wiring of neural networks. (Figures 5c, 5d, and 5e)

    A. By studying how each section of the cortex processed visual information, they were able to show that each layer of the cortex became increasingly sophisticated.

        1. Point-for-point mapping at the first layer indicated that these neurons "know" about dots of light.

        2. The neurons in the second layer of the cortex "know" about straight lines of light.

        3. The neurons in the third layer of the cortex "know" about moving lines, while the neurons in the fourth layer "know" about angles.

    B. Following this logic, it was believed that one could continue through the layers and find even more super-specialized neurons that recognize more specific information (for example, "the grandmother neuron" that could recognize a grandmother's face).

        1. This finding was not possible because there could not possibly be enough neurons for each to contain a single piece of information.

        2. It is not single neurons that contain information but patterns of neuronal excitation.

    C. A neural network is a series of neurons that interact among themselves and with neurons from other networks.

        1. Neurons from different networks can overlap and be used in different settings.

        2. Memory retrieval is the result of tapping into many networks and integrating all those inputs.

        3. Mild neuron loss, including that associated with early-stage dementia and Alzheimer's disease, does not destroy memories as much as it makes it harder to retrieve memory.

IV. Neural networks also influence how the human body feels and responds to pain. (Figure 5f)

    A. In instances of sharp pain, the neurons directly affected "turn on" pain, and through inhibition, the pain is "turned off."

B. In instances of dull pain, those neurons directly affected "turn on" pain; however, the lack of self-inhibition causes the throbbing to continue.

C. The loss of the more "expensive" pain pathways helps explain chronic pain in diabetes.

D. Stimulating adjacent pathways shuts down the pain (for example, back rubs and scratching around a maddeningly itchy mosquito bite).

V. It is the individual differences that exist in the overlapping projections of networks that cause people to know different information and to make different connections with that information. That is what creativity is about. On a simplistic level, creative people have broader networks than most other people, resulting in their ability to make unique associations.

Further Reading:

All of the following neuroscience textbooks have good sections on this subject:

E. Kandel, J. Schwartz, and T. Jessell, *The Foundations of Neural Science*, 4th ed.

J. Nicholls, R. Martin, B. Wallace, and P. Fuchs, *From Neuron to Brain*, 4th ed.

L. Squire, *Fundamental Neuroscience*, 2nd ed.

L. Squire, *Memory and Brain.*

Questions to Consider:

1. How might the "wiring" of networks differ between individuals and, thus, explain differences in their functioning?

2. How might wiring networks develop in the fetal brain?

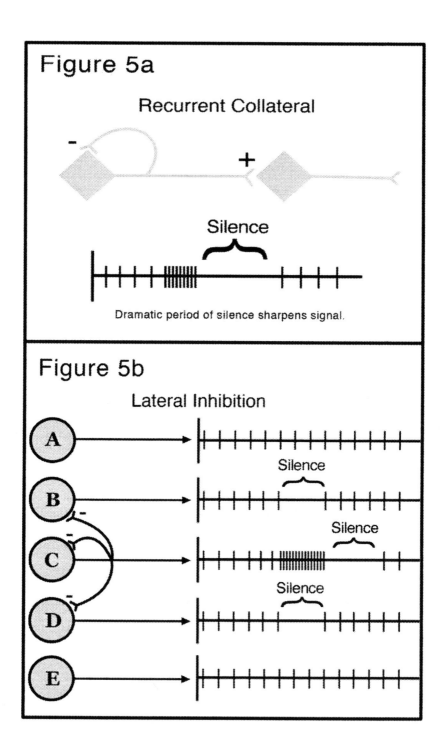

Figure 5a

Recurrent Collateral

Silence

Dramatic period of silence sharpens signal.

Figure 5b

Lateral Inhibition

A

B

Silence

C

Silence

D

Silence

E

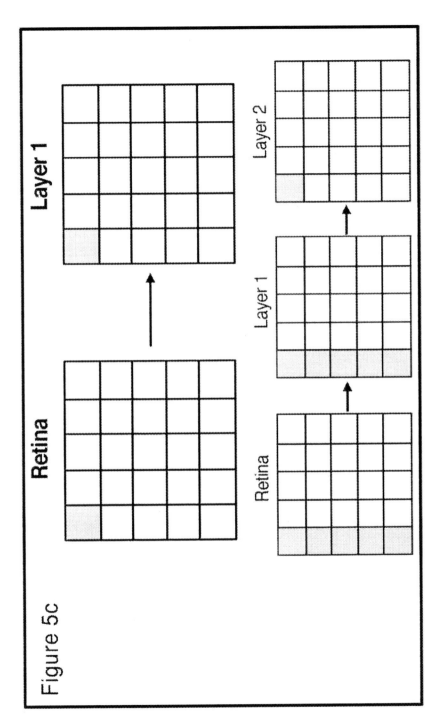

Figure 5c

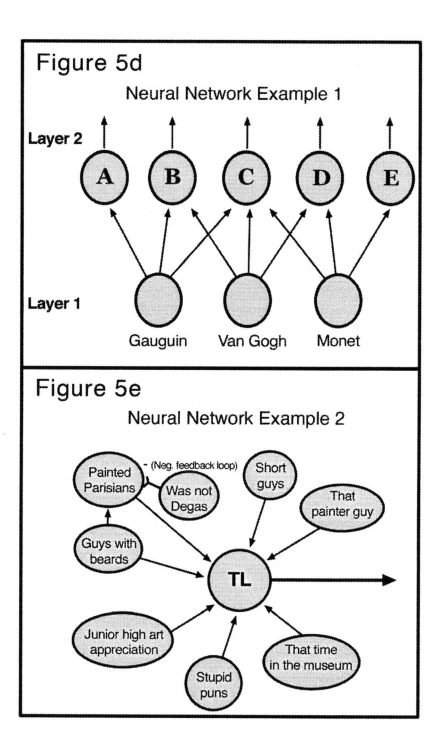

Figure 5d

Neural Network Example 1

Layer 2

A B C D E

Layer 1

Gauguin   Van Gogh   Monet

Figure 5e

Neural Network Example 2

Painted Parisians

− (Neg. feedback loop)

Was not Degas

Short guys

That painter guy

Guys with beards

TL

Junior high art appreciation

Stupid puns

That time in the museum

Figure 5f

Pain Pathway

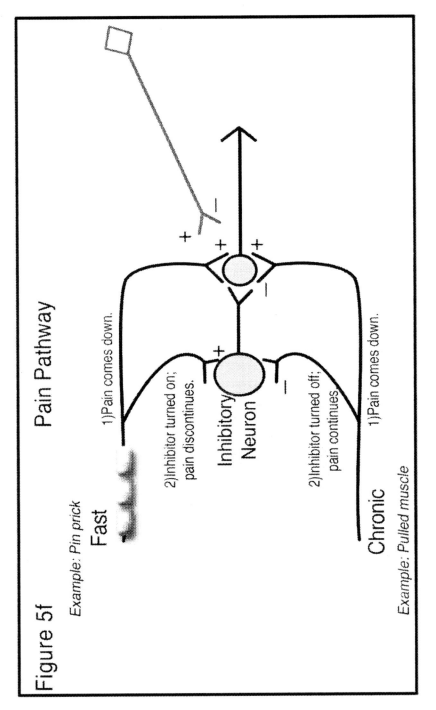

Example: Pin prick

Fast

1) Pain comes down.

2) Inhibitor turned on; pain discontinues.

Inhibitory Neuron

2) Inhibitor turned off; pain continues.

Chronic

1) Pain comes down.

Example: Pulled muscle

Lecture Five—Transcript
The Dynamics of Interacting Neurons

We are back and ready for more riveting, edge-of-your-seat neuroscience, because we are leaving the limited pedestrian world of two neurons behind us, and moving up to three today, maybe even more than that. We are now accomplishing this ever-expanding view of how the nervous system works. Now, having moved from one neuron getting excited, two neurons talking to each other, two neurons changing, they're talking to each other over time, potentiating a synapse; now expanding to begin to see how networks of neurons work.

Essentially the reason why we have to do that is we've been dealing with a very simplistic picture so far. What we have on the top of this diagram is one neuron sending all of its projections to the next neuron in line. And that neuron, in turn, sending all of its projections, all ten thousand axon terminals, to all ten thousand dendritic spines, of the next neuron, just a straight line, a straight cable. This is boring; this is incredibly limited. And, this what goes on in your spinal cord. This is the reason why your spinal cord can't lecture for you. This is a very simple aspect of wiring.

Once you get into the brain, once you get into an area where much more complicated things are happening, you don't have this network pattern of single neurons in line. Instead, you've got neurons sending projection, sending axon to a bunch of other neurons, which send to a bunch of others and back to itself, and you begin to get networks. And out of these networks you can get very, very complex processes. What we'll see in this lecture is how some aspects of wiring, how some of these networks are put together; how you can begin to get function coming out the other side.

Okay, we start with a first example and we go back to our limited world of the past, back to two neurons; but, we introduce new element into this, which is a new thing that the axons can do. You'll note here we've got our typical old neuron sending its axon to the next neuron in line—that old world of ours—but you will notice something different with this axon in the first neuron, which is it branches off. It branches off and sends a big projection coursing backwards to, of all places, itself. It sends a projection back onto itself and as diagrammed here; the neurotransmitter, it's releasing onto the receptors of the next neuron, the postsynaptic one. The neurotransmitters there are excitatory. This projection back onto itself is inhibitory.

This is what would be termed a *recurrent collateral*, a collateral of branching off, of the axon sending a projection back onto itself. Why on earth would a neuron that's excited want to send a signal back to itself that's inhibitory, that turns itself off? What you have here essentially is a mechanism, a feedback loop, a mechanism to sharpen the signal.

What do I mean by this? Here we see on the right of the diagram showing when that neuron has action potentials. And what you'll see is, in the absence of any sort of external stimulus, every now and then the neuron has a hiccup, has an action potential, that's something very different than what I was telling you before. Ooh, neurons spend a fortune in this very resting, restful state and being absolutely silent. It doesn't work perfectly; every now and then there are these spontaneous little action potentials.

But along comes the arrow here, some major stimulus on the system, and the neuron starts firing like crazy. What you see is, after a delay, finally that recurrent collateral kicks in and inhibits that neuron. What happens is, after that burst of action potential, you get a period of dramatic silence. What have you done? This is the same principle we heard a few lectures ago: enhancing the contrast between a neuron being silent and a neuron being excited. What you impose here is the silent period afterward. That neuron has just told the world, I am done with this period of hyper excitation. It's a way of sharpening the signal over time. It's a way of getting more certainty that you're done with your signal.

Now this property turns out to be one that occurs all over the nervous system: neurons sending recurrent collaterals back on themselves. What you then see is an elaboration on this, so that you can sharpen a signal, not only over time, but over space. And here we have in this diagram, a version of it. These neurons, we've got a line of these— A, B, C, D, E—these five neurons which then send their axons in parallel; these are some sort of sensory neurons. These are five photoreceptors in the eye sitting next to each other. Or, these are five neurons in your cochlea, hair receptive cells responsive to sound. Or, these are five neurons that respond to tactile information right next to each other.

So what happens? You stimulate one of them. You stimulate the middle one, neuron C, right in the middle of the stretch, somewhere in the eye, whichever sensory system. You stimulate that neuron C. It gets excited, it starts getting its action potentials. We've already seen what it does to itself. It's got a recurrent collateral back onto itself, which means, as we saw before, it gets this period of screaming its head off, and then imposes that negative feedback loop, that period of silence. You know exactly when that neuron has stopped its excitation.

But meanwhile, we have an additional piece of wiring. And what we see here is it also sends collaterals off to the neighbors, on either side; neuron C inhibiting neurons B and D. Inhibitory neurotransmitter—what is it doing there? It's turning off the neighbors, the folks immediately to the side of it. The term given for this is *lateral inhibition*. What are you doing? You are sharpening the signal in space. Neuron C, by shutting down B and D, makes it absolutely clear it's this spot, not one a little bit over; it's this spot of light, not one a little bit over. As shown in the diagram here, on the right, as we record from neurons A through E, you see the little bit of spontaneous action potentials now and then. Neuron C suddenly gets very excited, and by shutting off B and D, you are sharpening the signal, you are making clearer where the local signal is coming through. It's a way to sharpen over space and time. So here we have no mistaking the fact that it's neuron C, not B or D that's getting excited, and no mistaking the fact that neuron C has ended its message. Self-inhibition and lateral inhibition, both of these are fabulous ways of sharpening a signal.

Okay. So that's one general property of all sorts of networks, this business of sharpening signals. We move now to another version of networks. This, as you'll see, is a far more complicated one. This is, in lots of ways, the most exciting piece of neuroscience that was done in the third quarter of the 20th century. Amazing work; it is canonical. It is in every neuroscience textbook. All of us neuroscientists love this work. We worship the people who came up with it. This was a fabulous piece of work showing how your cortex processes sensory information.

This was work done by a pair of neuroscientists at Harvard at the time named Hubel and Wiesel. You cannot disconnect those names, they are like peanut butter and jelly: Hubel and Wiesel, Hubel and Wiesel. And this is just an amazing piece of work that goes together with these two names. These guys figured out how the cortex processes sensory information—or at least everybody thought they did.

Here's what they showed. Okay, we start off on the top of this diagram with a grid of neurons. It just happens this grid is in the retina. These are photoreceptors; these are cells in the retina that respond to light. The way it works is, in this grid, you can stimulate this neuron that will see this dot of light, or stimulate the next one over, which sees the next dot of light. You can do this as Hubel and Wiesel did, with a very controlled pinpoint of light, stimulate one single photoreceptor.

What they found up in the cortex was the very first layer of the visual cortex that got information from the eye. Information from the eye—we know what that means by now, which is the eye sends its projections, its photoreceptors have its axons projecting up a couple of synapses away and gets into this first layer of the cortex. What Hubel and Wiesel saw was something marvelous. They would stimulate one photoreceptor as shown here—this one up in the left corner—and one single neuron in that first layer of the visual cortex would get excited, a point-for-point connection.

They would then shift the light over a little bit and stimulate the next photoreceptor; over in the next layer, one neuron would get excited, move over, move over, point-for-point parallelism. What is it that neurons in this layer of one know about for a living? They know how to recognize dots of light, and they are organized in these columns, so that these neurons respond to this moving line; and the next column over, the next moving line; these neurons are specialized to recognize little points of light.

Great. Hubel and Wiesel take the weekend off. Monday morning they come in and now they start stimulating from layer two in the visual cortex. In other words, layer one sends all of its axons into layer two. What's going on up there? And here it's something very different.

Back to the retina. They stimulate one single photoreceptor, and one single neuron in the first layer, gets excited. Nothing's happening in the second layer. Now they shift over, they shift down to the next one and the next layer, one neuron gets excited. Nothing's happening in the second layer. Next one, next one, down, down, down, and only when they've done a whole bunch of these, and a whole bunch of layer one neurons in succession, suddenly one of the layer two neurons gets excited. What do layer two neurons know about for a living? They know about straight lines.

And what you would see is one of those neurons is tuned to respond to a straight line like this, and the next one over to align like this, align like this; different angles. Different ones tune to a straight line, moving in one direction, moving in the opposite direction, different speeds, different lengths. Every single one of the neurons in there knows one thing and one thing only—a fact about straight lines. What you see here is there is this hierarchy of extracting information. Layer one knows about dots, a whole bunch of them all together gives information about a line.

Okay, so that took Hubel and Wiesel a bunch of years, and then they move over to the next layer. And the same exact logic, this one extracts information from layer two, this one gets axonal projections from layer two and you can begin to imagine how the wiring works. What does this layer know about? It knows about moving straight lines, moving straight lines at different angles. What happens if you put a whole bunch of these together? You begin to get curves. This was amazing. People loved this stuff. Hubel and Wiesel were celebrated. They got their noble prize soon after this. And what everybody knew at that point is exactly what happens next, which is, you should be able to get to layer four and layer four would see a bunch of curves, and layer five would make them three dimensional, and you would go eleventy layers up until you got to this super duper layer, all the way up on top where you would get a neuron that knew one fact and one fact only; this is where you would find a neuron that knew how to recognize the head of your grandmother at this angle.

And next to it was another neuron that recognized her head at this angle; and next to that, and to the right of that would be a column that recognized your grandfather. And this is what everybody expected. You go all the way up and you would find these super specialized neurons that knew one thing and that responded to one thing and one thing only.

Literally what these neurons were called were *grandmother neurons*. The notion that these would be neurons so many layers up in this abstraction of information that you would get single neurons that were highly, highly specialized for recognizing things.

Now fortunately for Hubel and Wiesel, they didn't go and look for these super duper grandmother neurons, they moved onto another area of research that was at least as interesting. But everybody went looking for them, and to this day, basically they haven't found them. And if you think about it, this actually makes sense.

Do some math here. What you wind up seeing is a certain numerical constraint. How many photoreceptors do you have in your retina? You got some large number of them. How many neurons do you need in layer one? You need one neuron there for every photoreceptor in the eye—one-for-one correspondence. How many neurons do you need in layer two? Well, you need one neuron that specializes in this line and one in this line and one in this line, and one in the same line but a little bit shorter, and one a little bit longer, and one a little bit—you need like ten times, a hundred times as many neurons in layer two as you do in layer one.

Now we move up to layer three. How many neurons do you need there? For this line, for this line, for this line, for this combination, for that combination—you need like a hundred times more there. No wonder there's no layer four. You run out of neurons. And the whole field ran into a wall at this point, because what became clear is, if you think about single neurons knowing one fact and one fact only, all the way up in the cortex, it can't work that way because you don't have enough neurons. The whole field fell apart at this point. People were highly despairing. This notion of single neuron specializing went down the drain.

And what became clear in retrospect is the first two or three layers of the visual cortex worked like this. The first two or three layers of the auditory cortex: layer one would recognize a signal note, layer two would recognize an interval of two notes, layer three would recognize a chord, that sort of thing. And then it got into the great unwashed, undifferentiated cortex where it worked differently.

What you have now entered was 90% of the cortex, which is called *associational cortex*, which is a fancy way of saying we have no idea what it does. But what you've got there is this whole point-for-point, one neuron knows one thing and one thing only; went down the drain at that point. And what this has ushered in instead is an entirely new field of neuroscience for looking at how this stuff works, what are now called *neural networks*.

A lot of this comes from the realm of computational neuroscience, computer models, mathematics. Essentially, the way that this all works—or the basic notion—is information is not contained in a single neuron. Information is not contained in a single synapse, potentiated or otherwise. Information is contained in patterns of excitation, in networks of excitation, where the same neurons can overlap in different networks and be used in different settings. And it turns out this explains an enormous amount about how the nervous system works, and it has proved an enormously difficult thing to get after because it is very, very complicated.

Let me give you an example of a wildly, impossibly simplified neural network. And here we have one—and you can trust me that none actually exists like this, but this will give the idea. We've got a neural network consisting of two layers. The first layer has three neurons. Second layer has five neurons, neurons A through E. And what we've got is overlapping projections. The first neuron down here, in the lower layer, sends its projections to A, B, and C in the second layer. The second neuron in that first layer sends its projections to the B, C, and D; the third neuron to C, D, and E. What you can see here is there's partial overlap in each of these cases.

Okay, so what are these neurons about? Layer one is an imaginary network layer and this one has neurons that are Hubel-and-Wieselesque. These are neurons that know one fact and one fact only; they don't really work this way. But suppose the first one is a neuron that responds to Gauguin paintings, the second is a neuron that responds to Van Gogh, and the third one is the one that responds to Monet. So what's going on in the second layer?

What does neuron A know about? In the second layer, who does it get information from? Only the Gauguin neuron; it knows how to recognize Gauguin paintings. Meanwhile, neuron E only gets its inputs from Monet and knows how to recognize Monet paintings. They are highly specialized. What about neuron C? Neuron C is sitting there at the intersection of projections from all three of those neurons. What does neuron C know about? Neuron C is the one that knows how to recognize an impressionist painting. Neuron C is the one sitting there saying, "Don't ask me the name of the painter, certainly don't ask me the name of the painting, but its one of those impressionists. It's not a Cubist, it's not a Dutch master." Neuron C knows information that it could only extract out of the individual cases. Neuron C is at the center of the network where it gets that convergence.

And you look at neurons B and D, and they're both recognizing impressionist painting neurons as well. They're simply not as good as neuron C. They don't have as many examples to draw upon. And in a very artificial way, that's how these networks work.

Let's give an example showing how we exploit these networks, showing that we're perfectly conscious of this. Now this diagram shows an even more schematic version of a network, and it's the network which houses at its center, a neuron that responds to the name of what's-his-name. What was that guy? You're trying to remember that guy's name; he was a painter. He was a painter; he was one of those impressionist painters; he was always painting those Parisian women in the bars. He wasn't Degas He was that short guy with the beard, what was his name? Oh, I had this junior high school art appreciation teacher who is always going on about him. If I could remember her name, I'd remember his name. Oh, there's that time I was in museum and there was this really cute person and they liked this guy's paintings. I had to pretend I did too and never got the person's phone number. Oh yeah, there's this stupid pun about the tracks being too loose. Toulouse Lautrec! And suddenly it comes popping out there and this Toulouse Lautrec neuron again, which is hypothetical, this Toulouse Lautrec neuron is sitting there at the intersection of your network of short guys, or your network of guys with beards, your network of stupid puns or your network, and sitting there at the intersection of them is that output.

What are you doing there when you're sitting there saying, wait, wait, it was a lot of syllables, it started with a "t" sound, there was this pun, he was the short guy? You're tapping into all these different networks. What are you taking advantage of there? Back to Lecture Two, no single input is enough to pull out the guy's name. You're trying to get summation, integration of all those inputs, and sitting there at the intersection of those is the information popping out.

And what we've got here is a network in this dimension on this chart, and these same neurons are part of another network that goes perpendicular to that and another. At the intersection of all these, this is how we pull memories out there. We don't have a fact, we have a fact imbedded in context, and we are often trying to tap into enough pathways to get that to pop out.

We all use that in everyday sense; that's the tip of the tongue phenomenon. What was that called? You sense the number of syllables; you sense where you were when.... You're trying to tap into these networks. And one of the greatest ways of proving this is how this works is to look at people with early stage Alzheimer's disease.

Now what's one of the clichés of Alzheimer's? You lose some neuron. Last night was the night that some neuron died that remembers the name of your first grade teacher; never again will you find that name available. That's not how it works. What you see instead, early on, is the memory is still there, it just takes more work to pull it out. And thus you are trying to get the person, oriented in space and time, you're giving them... do you know what year it is, do you know where you are, what continent you are on, why you are here? And then you ask them a question: Who's the President right now? And, we have a current President and the person can't remember the guy's name.

So you start tapping into some of their networks. You say, let me give you a clue, let me give you a clue: it's a one syllable name. Still flailing, they can't get it. So you tap into another network: it's a word for something you might encounter in a park. Still not there, so you give even more strong priming cues there, you give them a forced verse. You say okay, is it President Tree, President Shrub, President Bench, President Rock, President Bush, President ...? Bush, Bush, yeah, he's the kid of the other President there. It's still in there, it just takes more work to pull it out.

And that's what dementia looks like in its early stages. That's proof that you don't have one neuron that knows one fact only. Instead you have these networks where you have to tap into them. And what's been happening in early stage Alzheimer's is one of these neurons dies, and one of these and one of these—this network that I'm showing here in the diagram—you lose a neuron here and there. Do you lose the capacity to pull out that name? No, it just takes more work. The remaining pieces of the network have to be stimulated more strongly.

Now I saw a wonderful example of what proves there are neural nets. A couple of years back with my daughter, who was about 3 years old at the time, and we met some guy who we interacted with for the afternoon, and his name happened to be Barney. Clearly showing what sort of network she had formed in her brain, she spent the entire afternoon, instead, calling him Elmo. We could not get that out of her head. Clearly she's got some sort of network of childhood cartoon characters or purple dinosaur puppets or whatever, and just calling this guy Barney, Elmo all afternoon. That's where we begin to have the intersection of facts. These are networks. And this seems to be much how the brain works once you get into the complex areas.

Let me show you another bit of circuitry. And this is one—back down to that boring part of the nervous system, down to your spinal cord—but an aspect of it that is far from boring: how do we feel pain? Now what we've got here are two types of inputs in pain pathways in the spine. Sitting here in this diagram is a neuron, which when stimulated, shoots a message up your spine and tells you that something is painful. But it turns out pain comes in a number of different varieties.

You can have a certain type of sharp pain. What may be obvious here is that we're just on a set and this is artificial, and I in fact am just a hologram, but were this a real window and I put my hand through it instead of it being fake here, I would be feeling very sharp pain as it goes through the glass—technical term, *epocritic* pain. What's a characteristic of that sharp pain? It is suddenly very, very intense and then goes away somewhat. We have here a pathway that explains it.

Here we have an input, a pathway from a pain receptor, which carries rapid sharp information, sends its axon to stimulate this neuron that we discussed before; excites it. This neuron has its action potential and you feel pain. The information shoots up your spine. Notice, however, this same pain-receptive neuron sends a collateral off to the second neuron. The second neuron inhibits the pain messenger neuron. This collateral stimulates that neuron. What is that about? This is a case of a feedback signal.

This neuron stimulates this one in order to feel pain. This incoming fast projection stimulates this pain neuron, and then a second later, by stimulating this feedback loop, it turns it off. A brief burst of excitation in that pain neuron, and then it's turned off. What is that? That's the pin prick. The very painful instant, and then it disappears.

Meanwhile, something very different on this side, we've got pain coming in, and here it stimulates that neuron to fire; to tell your spine that something is painful. And it sends its collateral off to that local inhibitory neuron; but in this case, it inhibits the inhibitory neuron. It blocks the ability of that inhibitory neuron to turn off that pain neuron.

What's that about? You stimulate this pathway and it keeps going and it keeps going. That's throbbing pain. That's a pulled muscle, that's a burn, that's a very different version of pain. Here we've got these two inputs, one of which gets a sharp pain pathway, the other which gets a slow, throbbing, chronic one. And this turns out to explain all sorts of aspects of pain perception.

For example, you've got a disease that damages these fast fibers, the ones that produce the sharp pain, and these fall of out action. What happens is you get stimulation of this pathway, and it just keeps going on and on and on. That's a certain type of pain perception people get with diabetes, something called a *diabetic neuropathy*. Things just keeping throbbing; for complex reasons you have killed these neurons and these guys just stimulate this pain neuron, and it just keeps going and going.

This also explains a very important thing that most of us master early on in life: when we get our first horrible, itchy, painful mosquito bite, and our mothers yell at us and say don't scratch it, it will get infected. What do we figure out to do instead? We scratch on either side of it. What's that about? We've got this throbbing pain here going through the slow chronic pathway, and by scratching on either side, we're stimulating this fast pathway; it adds a burst of pain, and then a second later, it turns off the pathway.

A sudden sharp pain inhibits throbbing pain. And that's why, if something really hurts, you squeeze. That's why we pay to have our fast pain pathways pummeled by somebody; that's why a massage feels good. You've got some sore muscles that are throbbing and a chronic unabated pain, and somebody comes in and mauls you and pushes the muscles around. By stimulating these fast pathways, you get a burst of pain, and then it turns off the system for a while afterward.

And here we see the interactions of the two. What is very striking— back to our final two themes, first off, at looking at plasticity—all of these networks change their function over time. Obviously, your Toulouse Lautrec network gets potentiated by learning about it. Obviously, all of these pathways can change their functioning. In this pain pathway for example, prior experience, projections starting up in your brain, can come down and change the excitability of this key neuron here.

What's that about? That's neurons and plasticity that, for example, put you in a complete panic when you get into the dentist's chair, if that happens to be your makeup. And you sit there, and the second the music comes on, your teeth already hurt. You've sensitized that pathway thanks to experience; that's all sorts of settings where if you were sufficiently excited and distracted, you twist your ankle in the middle of battle and you don't even notice it. Experience can very dramatically change how this pathway works. So this issue, always of plasticity.

Then back to individual differences. How do networks differ in one of us versus the other? In lots of ways; one of the most intriguing is to ask, what's creativity? What we see here are networks by which a neuron that has something to do with short guys, or guys with beards or whatever, can eventually overlap, and out comes the knowledge of the name of this painter. On a certain, very crude, simplistic level, what creativity is about is having broader networks than most people, making connections that most individuals don't.

And whereas most of us out there have networks of what encompasses a face—it involves two eyes on either side of your nose and some ears sticking out and all of that—every now and then you get someone with networks that are broader than everybody else's as to what constitutes a face, and you've just invented Picasso. On a certain crude level, what individual differences are about in creativity are making associations that never occur to anybody else. Put a whole bunch of chords together that would have been thought discordant, and you've just invented the "Rite of Spring." And in all these cases, what creativity is about is, no doubt, networks in places that most brains don't have.

So this now has given us a sense of how we have moved from the level of two neurons, to how to extract information to compute things, to process things in a much larger level. What this sets us up for now is to look at whole areas of your nervous system, by way of networks; now hundred thousands of neurons and they effect events throughout your entire body.

Lecture Six
The Limbic System

Scope:

Increasing the scale beyond that of single neural networks, this lecture examines the *limbic system*—the part of the brain most centrally involved in emotion and in generation of emotionally related behavior. We will begin with a brief overview of how the limbic system is organized anatomically, followed by an introduction to its roles in aggression, fear, anxiety, sexual behavior, and depression.

Outline

I. The brain is not one homogenous mass of undifferentiated neurons. Instead, there is structure and organization to it.

    A. Clusters of neuronal cell bodies, called *gray matter*, are the nuclei of cell bodies.

    B. Cables of axons are projections from those cell bodies. They are called *white matter* because they are wrapped in white myelin sheaths.

II. Now, we expand one step further to the neuroanatomy of the brain.

    A. First, we see the broad features of the mammalian brain. (Figure 6a)

        1. Heading down from the brain are the spinal cord, sensory afferents, and motor efferents, all of which carry sensory information and messages to all parts of the body.

        2. At the back of the brain are the hindbrain and brainstem, which control such activities as breathing and the beating of the heart.

        3. Sitting on top of the hindbrain and brainstem is the limbic system, which deals with regulation of emotions.

    4. Higher up is the cortex, involved in memory, learning, judgment, decision making, conscious commands to muscles, and complex processing of sensory information.

B. Species differences in neuroanatomical organization must be noted.

    1. The limbic system is a mammalian specialty; only mammals have complex emotions.

    2. The cortex, which is involved in social intelligence, is a primate specialty.

III. What is the limbic system? (Figure 6b)

A. Historically, people used to think that the limbic system was the *rhinencephalon*, or "nose-brain," because it was studied first in laboratory rats, for which olfaction and emotion are utterly intertwined.

B. The limbic system comprises many different subareas.

    1. These subareas send projections to one another and to other parts of the brain, particularly to the hypothalamus.

    2. All of the brain nuclei in the limbic system want to influence the hypothalamus.

    3. Conversely, these nuclei want to inhibit other limbic sites from influencing the hypothalamus.

    4. The hypothalamus controls all manner of autonomic (automatic) functions in your body. Future lectures will address the hypothalamus in more detail.

C. The best way to determine which limbic structure influences the hypothalamus most readily is to count synapse numbers. The fewer synapses it takes to get from one limbic structure to the hypothalamus, the more influential that structure is over the hypothalamus.

IV. Components of the limbic system include major structures, as well as major connections within the system. (Figures 6c and 6d)

A. Major structures within the limbic system include the amygdala, the hippocampus, the septum, the cingulate cortex and gyrus, the hypothalamus, the mammillary bodies, the thalamic nuclei, and the frontal cortex.

B. Major connections within the limbic system include the amygdalofugal pathway (amygdala to hippocampus); the fimbria/fornix (hippocampus to septum); the striae terminalis (amygdala to hypothalamus); the medial forebrain bundle (the highway between the mammillary bodies and the septum, passing through the hypothalamus); and the mammillothalamic tract (mammillaries to thalamus).

V. How do we know what the limbic system does?

A. Scientists come to understand what the limbic system does in the same ways that they discover how any brain region works.

  1. One way is to experimentally damage the part of the brain to be studied in research animals. Accidental wounds to the human brain can provide similar information.

  2. Other strategies are to stimulate certain parts of the brain or to record the electrical activity of certain clusters of neurons.

  3. A relatively new method is brain imaging.

  4. A more classical approach is neuroanatomy: determining which region talks to which.

  5. Some pitfalls of these approaches include redundancy, compensation, and mistaking the function of a nucleus for the function of the fibers passing through it.

B. Studying limbic function poses special challenges because this area of the brain deals with complex, subtle, interactive emotions; therefore, many factors must be kept in mind.

  1. What sort of sensory information is relevant in a particular species? For example, sexual arousal in one species can be about smell and in another, about sight.

  2. What does a behavior look like in a particular species? For example, maternal behavior in a rat is very different from that in a monkey.

  3. Who is the individual under study? Do dominant and subordinate animals express emotions in the same way?

VI. Simplified explanations of some functions for limbic structures are helpful to further understand the brain and behavior.

    A. The amygdala and septum have roles in aggression.

    B. The hippocampus is important in certain types of learning, memory, and stress-responsiveness.

    C. Mammillary bodies are associated with maternal behavior.

    D. The frontal cortex controls inhibition of socially inappropriate behaviors and inhibition of perseverative cognitions.

    E. The medial preoptic region of the hypothalamus is associated with sexual behavior.

    F. The lateral and ventromedial hypothalamus affect hunger and satiation.

    G. The suprachiasmatic nucleus of the hypothalamus is involved in circadian rhythmicity.

Further Reading:

For a particularly strong book on this topic:

M. Konner, *The Tangled Wing: Biological Constraints on the Human Spirit.*

For additional information on this subject:

J. LeDoux, *The Emotional Brain: The Mysterious Underpinnings of Emotional Life.*

J. LeDoux, *Synaptic Self: How Our Brains Become Who We Are.*

For a classic on the subject by one of the key people in the field:

P. MacLean, *The Triune Brain in Evolution: Role in Paleocerebral Functions.*

Questions to Consider:

1. What will the structure and function of the limbic system in a particular species tell you about the social behavior of that species?

2. How are interactions between the limbic system and the cortex particularly interesting in humans?

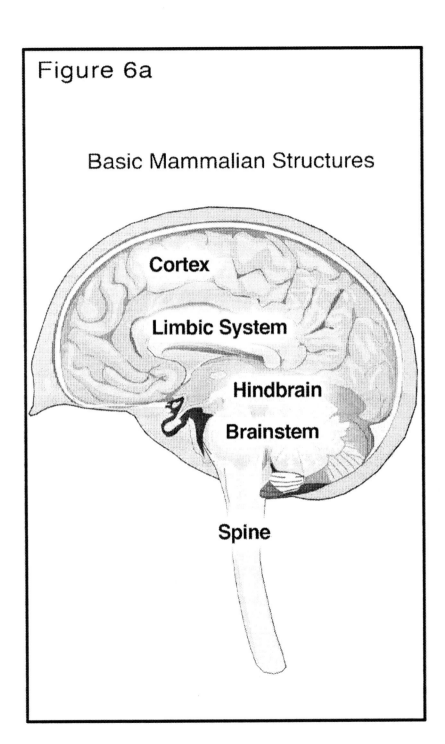

Figure 6a

Basic Mammalian Structures

Cortex

Limbic System

Hindbrain

Brainstem

Spine

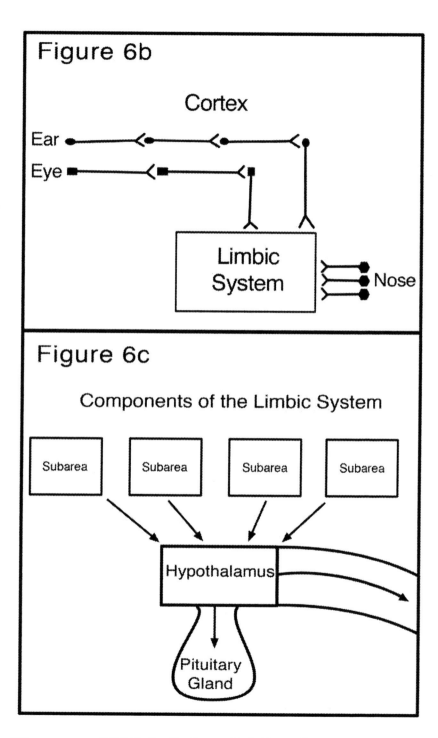

©2005 The Teaching Company Limited Partnership

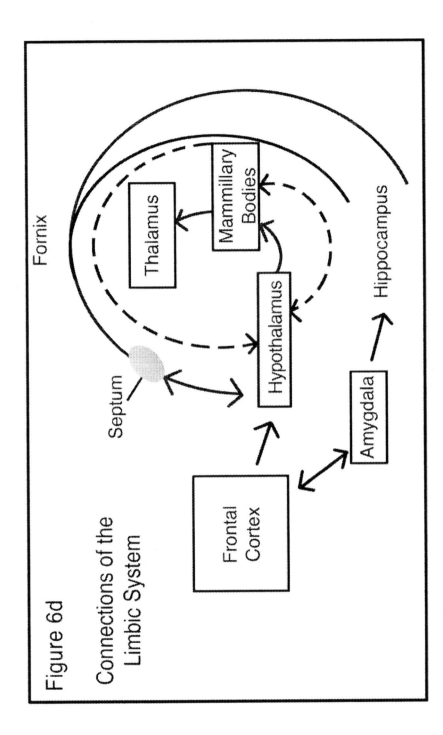

Figure 6d

Connections of the
Limbic System

Lecture Six—Transcript
The Limbic System

Back again. Let's see, since our last lecture, I've spent two months vacationing in the Mediterranean, so I am really charged and ready to go after the next subject, which is a good thing, because we are throwing all caution to the wind right now and are going to deal with hundreds of thousands of neurons now.

We have now graduated from one neuron to two to networks, all of that. We are now going to look at large areas of the brain in our ever expanding goal to understand where our behavior comes from. We're going to be looking at a very special area of the brain; not the part of the brain that makes your heart beat now and then, not the part of your brain that controls your spleen, but the parts of your brain that are involved in emotion. A part of the brain called the *limbic system*. The limbic system, not surprisingly, is going to be central to the rest of this course.

Now to begin to appreciate this limbic system, we have to return to a point from an earlier lecture. Your brain is not one homogeneous mass of undifferentiated neurons; instead, there's a structure to it, an organization, an anatomy, a neural anatomy. And one important structural feature of the brain is shown here in this first diagram. What we have are clusters, areas where there's whole bunches of cell bodies grouped together. And what they all do is send their axons projecting to another area with a cluster of cell bodies, which in turn, send their axons elsewhere. What we have here is a dichotomy between what are called nuclei, within the brain, the clusters of the cell bodies, and then cables, projections, areas where you send your axons on to the next bunch of cell bodies.

Another term for this, having to do with the color of this, all of the cell bodies grouped together are termed *grey matter*, and all of those cables, *white matter*. Why white? It turns out there's myelin sheets wrapped around the axons; they're a little bit fatty, they're white, which gives this characteristic white color. So, we've got grey matter and white matter. We have centers, clusters, nuclei of cell bodies sending projections, sending white matter, sending cables made up of axons, talking to the next part of the brain.

And given this organization, what we could now do in the next diagram is take a look at the broad features of the brain; not a bunch of neurons forming a network, but the neurons that make up entire regions, and we are talking about millions, tens of millions of neurons. And in a very, very simplistic way, as we approach here what the mammalian brain is about, we see some basic building blocks that are in every mammal's brain and spinal cord.

What do we have? We have the brain sitting there on top of it. Heading down the spine is the spinal cord, starting at that end. What you have is an organization built around projections, axons going to the spinal cord. What do they carry? Sensory information: information about touch, about pain, about temperature. And coming from the spinal cord are projections, axons heading out to the body, telling your muscles to contract, telling your body to have all sorts of things. So, projections to and from the spine.

Then, moving upward, you've got the back part of the brain, the brainstem—the hindbrain, for our purposes—not a very exciting part of the brain that makes you remember to breathe now and then. It makes your heart beat on its own, that sort of stuff; not very central to understanding emotion, until we get back to this later, but brainstem, hindbrain.

Then sitting on top of that is the limbic system. And for our purposes right now, the limbic system equals emotional regulation. And what we will see is how laughably simplistic that is. Nonetheless, that works for the moment, and then sitting on top of the limbic system, we've got the cortex. The cortex does all of the abstract, cognitive sort of stuff, and for our purposes right now, just as a limbic system is this fraw, the emotional part of the brain just marinating excess and impulsivity, the cortex is this gleaming, stainless steel computer up there. We will see how incorrect that is, as well.

Okay, so we've got this drawered organization going on here, and we're going to have a lot of focus here on the limbic system. Now interestingly, right off the bat, the limbic system and the cortex sitting on top of it are very different depending on what species you are looking at. You look at a human, you look at a lab rat, you look at a lizard, and the hindbrain and the brainstem and the spinal cords are surprisingly similar. You look at a limbic system and suddenly you are in the realm of a mammalian specialty. Lizards are not famous for their emotional lies. It's not until you get into mammals that you're getting complex emotions, and emotions that have a complex physiology underlying it.

By the time you get to the cortex, you are dealing with a part of the brain that is very much a primate specialization. It's not until us and our primate cousins that you have this much of the brain devoted to cortex. That's why primates are doing fancy stuff that all sorts of other species can't. Just as one measure of it, there's more than 150 different species of primates out there, and you look at how big the cortex is in any given species, how big it is relative to the rest of the brain, and what you see is the best predictor. The more individuals in the social group of that species, the bigger the cortex.

What is the cortex about in primates? It's about social intelligence. It's about keeping track of who's doing what to whom and small town gossip and all those things. That's a first hint that there is no way the cortex and its abstract function is going to be separate from the limbic system and emotion. We will see this in much more detail.

Okay, so the limbic system. The limbic system started off life early in the last century with a very different name. It was originally called the *rhinencephalon*. Rhine = nose, rhinencephalon, the nose-brain. What's that about? Why was it the nose-brain? Because the first species it was studied in was the laboratory rat; and what you see immediately is a very distinctive feature of wiring of the sensory systems.

What we see here is a limbic system in this diagram, carefully drawn to be just a black box, and what we see on top are the projections, how you get from the ear, from hearing, to the limbic system; how you get from the eyes, how you get from any sensory system; and we already know something about it. We do our whole Hubel and Wiesel number, a projection into the first layer of the cortex and the second and the third, and a whole bunch of synapses later you get some neuron that remembers to send its axons down to the limbic system and tell you something about what you're seeing, what you're hearing, all of that. That's a general property of the sensory systems, until you get to *olfaction*.

And the thing about olfaction is, you start with neurons that are the olfactory receptors, and you are one synapse away from the limbic system. Before your cortex knows anything about what you smell, the emotional part of your brain does. And suddenly we've got this whole world of smell and strong emotions that are not even conscious yet of smell and memory. Memory. Hippocampus. As we will see, the hippocampus is in the limbic system. Suddenly you've got that phenomenon where some smell wafts in the room, and suddenly you're back in kindergarten and you remember those little pastel colored chairs and the taste of a little page glue, and suddenly all of that is evoked. Smell is highly evocative of emotion of memory. We got the rhinencephalon; we've got the nose-brain.

It was only as scientists became more sophisticated and understood the behavior of rodents that they realized you can't talk about a rat's emotions without talking about what it's smelling in the world; a transition in the 1930s, recognizing this rhinencephalon of the rat is the emotional center for all sorts of species about there, and thus the term, the limbic system.

Now what we'll see is the limbic system is made up of a whole bunch of different sub areas, and you've already known one of them. One is the hippocampus. But we will see a lot more of these in detail. And in this diagram, we're not yet naming these structures, but all we see is there's a bunch of different parts of the limbic system, and they all have a very similar wiring scheme. They send projections to each other, they talk to the cortex, and they talk to various parts of the brain. But the main thing they all do is send projections down to this critical funnel in the brain, an area that we're going to hear about over and over and over, the *hypothalamus*.

Everybody in the limbic system wants to influence what the hypothalamus does. Now why is that? Why is that, is going to be the next two or three lectures because the hypothalamus plays this pivotal role in how your brain winds up influencing behavior. Just to give some dramatic foreshadowing here, your hypothalamus runs all sorts of autonomic, automatic things in your body. You get gooseflesh in the right setting and it's because your hypothalamus has sent some message down the spine.

As we'll see in two entire lectures, the hypothalamus controls all sorts of hormones you release. The hypothalamus plays this central role, so the selfish, narcissistic thing that every part of the limbic system wants to do is disproportionately influence the hypothalamus. And naturally the other thing they want to do is to keep the other limbic areas from influencing the hypothalamus. All of them jockeying, and you know the wiring already, which is going be a whole bunch of excitatory projections into the hypothalamus and a whole bunch of lateral inhibitory ones trying to turn each other off.

So a sense now of what all of these guys want to do in the limbic system. So how do you figure out who's doing what? No surprise, most of these limbic structures have a whole bunch of different ways of sending their projections into the hypothalamus, of inhibiting each other. And the way to begin to make sense of it is to use a trick we've already done in here—okay, how many synapses away from the limbic system is your nose, how many synapses away is your ear or your eyes—counting synapses. As a general rule, the fewer synapses it takes to get from structure A to structure B, the more powerfully influential A and going to be over B. And what you see are all sorts of different routes to get one part from one part of the limbic system to another. How many synapses away, in a very rough approximation. That gives you a good sense of who's influencing who.

Okay, all of this sets us up now for actually seeing the components of the limbic system. I'm going to put up a diagram right now, and before I do so, every single person watching this has to promise to shut their eyes and not look at it. This is an appalling diagram; do not memorize a single thing on this chart. What this shows are some of the mains structures of the limbic system. And do not panic, do not pay any attention. All of these areas will make a great deal of sense if you were schooled in Latin. We've already heard about the hippocampus, looking like a seahorse. Another area, the amygdala, looks like a walnut or almond or something or other I should have learned if I had gotten a decent classical education. All of these horrible multi-syllabic names, and even worse—so horrible I haven't even dared to write them down—all of these multi-syllabic names for the connections between them. You already know the logic of this, which is lots of these areas have some role in regulating emotion, in regulating how your body responds to emotion, all of that, all of them sending projections to each other, all of them sending projections down into the hypothalamus.

So areas of the limbic system, I will recite them now, and do not pay attention to these names, because the ones that are important we're going to hear about over and over again throughout the rest of this course. You've got areas like the amygdala, the hippocampus, the septum, the cingulate, hypothalamus, mammilary bodies, thalamic parts of the nuclei, nuclei found in the thalamus. Very interestingly, by definition, the limbic system used to be a sub-cortical part of the brain; the part of the brain that is below the surface, below the cortex, this is all this old, primitive, mammalian emotion—hate and lust and petulance and all that stuff. This is obviously going to be a part of the brain that's completely separate from the cortex sitting up there doing calculus for you. What people have come to realize is there's one part of the cortex, which by all logic anatomically should be considered part of the limbic system.

We've already heard about this area, this is the frontal cortex. And the frontal cortex is intimately involved in the limbic system in terms of impulsivity, gratification, postponement. We will hear lots about the frontal cortex, and there was this wondrous accomplished neuroanatomist, a man name Walle Nauta, a Dutch neuroanatomist, who's pretty much the best neuroanatomist over the last century, and in the 50s he convinced everybody he had just shot his career down the tubes by insisting the frontal cortex is part of the limbic system. This is a world where neuroanatomists could destroy their careers by saying this part of the brain is part of the limbic system. They have these concerns. He said, when you look at its wiring—and this was even before people knew a lot about its function—when you look at its wiring, this is part of the limbic system.

Since then it has become clear that the cortex is not separate from emotion, and instead it is vastly intertwined. There's a wonderful book from a wondrous neurologist named Antonio Damasio, a book called *Descartes Error*, a very, very influential book in the field. Descartes' view that there's this dramatic dichotomy between emotion and cognition, they are utterly disconnected. And what we have learned ever since then with modern neuroscience is they are completely intertwined. We will see endless functional examples of this where pure abstract cognition is deeply influenced, often altered, distorted, often assisted by emotion, and we will see ways in which your emotion is highly influenced by abstract things like memory, like thought. And Descartes error being that there's not a clean dichotomy between the cortical world of cognition and the limbic world of emotion, the frontal cortex is right where that's happening, very dramatic number of projections between the frontal cortex and the rest of the limbic system.

Now going back to this diagram that you're not supposed to be paying any attention to, what we have here in straight lines and dotted lines are just the connections amongst these areas. Amygdala, hippocampus, hypothalamus, mammilary bodies, thalamus, septum, frontal cortex; all of these areas you reel you off, and all of them are connected to each other. And when you look closely, you will see, as promised, some of the connections are very straightforward, and some of them are indirect and loop all over the place and have places where they bypass and other places where they stop along the way; this is part of this extremely complex circuitry. Once again, all built around this broad strategy of bossing around the hypothalamus and trying to keep other limbic areas from doing so.

So that sets us up now for beginning to look at what do these different sub areas of the limbic system do. We already have a sense of the hippocampus. Hippocampus, learning and memory, we heard that sentence before, a couple of lectures back about the amygdala, something with fear. What do these different areas do?

Imbedded in that is the question, how do you figure out what these areas do? How do you figure out what any part of the nervous system does, even a simple area like one little bit of cortex that controls the movement of this finger, and the area of cortex next to it that controls the movement of this finger? How do you figure out the function of a part of the brain that instead does nostalgia for you, or poignancy, or love or any such thing? How do you figure out the function and parts of the nervous system? And here's where we get into the realm of different experimental approaches.

How do figure out, you've got area X in the brain and you're trying to figure out what it does. What are some of the strategies? One version is experimentally to go in and damage that part of the brain. Do that in a laboratory animal; go in, cut a certain pathway, cut a whole bunch of axons connecting A to B, or go in—and the term given is *lesion*—damage a cluster of nucleus, an area of cell bodies, and then basically ask, what works differently now? What doesn't work anymore? You've just gotten some insight into what A does. Or by cutting the connection between A and B, what this communication is about between them; that's a classic approach. And that classic experimental approach has been vastly depressingly aided over the years by our endless capacity as humans to generate great study subjects for this sort of thing, soldiers coming back from wars with what are projectile wounds, some part of the brain has been blown away, and starting in the 19th century, neurobiologists got enormous amounts of information by studying people who have had parts of their brain lesioned by our political processes and wars on this planet. And what you get there is a whole lot of insight coming from that realm, as well. So you destroy a part of the brain; what doesn't work right anymore?

Another strategy is you can go in with an electrode and you stimulate a certain part of the brain. You artificially, electrically excite that part of the brain. You make those neurons have action potentials and you see what happens next. And it was indeed these sorts of classical studies where you would stimulate a part of the brain and, as mentioned before, an area of the cortex in an animal, primate, and suddenly it uncontrollably moves this finger. And move the stimulated electrode over a little bit and you move the next finger. You're mapping out function that way.

Other versions. Now you stick in a different type of an electrode, this is not one which stimulates the neuron, it instead records it; it tells you when that neuron is getting excited. That was the Hubel and Wiesel approach, sticking recording electrodes into the neurons in the first layer of the visual cortex. Ah ha, this one gets excited if, and only if, this one single photoreceptor in the eye is being stimulated. You are getting, in a sense, a read out, what things in the outside world excite this neuron.

Those used to be the classical approaches: lesioning, damaging nervous system, stimulate it, record from it. In recent years, a whole new area has become possible. And this is taking advantage of this whole revolution in neuroradiology, using these imaging machines; CT scanners, PT scans, MRIs, functional MRIs, where basically you can look at activity in the part of the brain while you're doing something. And you can show things like play a certain sound to somebody in a functional scanner and up lights up the auditory cortex, things like that. Give somebody a problem to think about and you can see what pathways in the brain light up. So that's another approach that has been extremely powerful.

Finally, the classical approach, the most straightforward one is to do boring old neuroanatomy. If A sends a projection to B, and A sends a projection to all of these places, and in turn, A gets inputs from these places. If you know what a whole bunch of them do, you can begin to figure out what the function is of A. These are some of the classic approaches to figure out what does this part of the brain does. And with these classical approaches come a whole bunch of pitfalls.

The first one being, you can go damage a certain part of the brain and nothing changes at all. Does that mean that this part of the brain has no function? Obviously not, it means some other area may have taken over this function. There's the capacity for compensation. That's been immensely sort of challenging, and the capacity for that compensation is so strong in the cortex that there was this famous neurobiologist, Carl Ashley, who, about a half century ago, was looking for where our individual memory is stored in the cortex. As we know already, they're not stored in individual places, they're stored in networks; and networks that can compensate for damage. He came up with this famously depressed paper towards the end of his career where you basically concluded in the end that there's no place in the brain where memories are stored, because he was dealing with the old notion that this particular part of the cortex would have a certain type of memory, and would see in an animal trained with certain memory tasks, it would have no effect at all. You lesion an area and some other place could take over. So that makes things extremely difficult.

Another major problem is you damage a certain part of the brain and a function is stopped as a result and now you figured out what that part of the brain does. Some of the time, you have not gotten useful information, because what you have damaged is not a nucleus, an area of a whole bunch of neuronal cell bodies, but you've instead damaged a cable, a passage way. And that's like saying you're trying to understand how much of some bread is being delivered to some city, and you go and you lesion the main highway into that city and no bread comes in anymore. And what you conclude about that spot on the highway that you lesioned, you say, aw, that's obviously where bread is made, because when we destroy that part of the highway, no more bread gets delivered. No, you have not destroyed the bread making center, you've destroyed what is termed a *fiber of passage*. So another way in which you get into trouble is by not recognizing when you are dealing with a nucleus, an area of neuronal cell bodies, and when you are dealing with a cable, just some highway running through there.

Okay, so these are the sorts of things that make any neurobiologist crazy. All of these issues are that much more awful. When now, instead of trying to figure out what part of the brain makes your finger do this, you are now trying to figure out, complex, subtle interactive emotions. And when you get to the limbic system, these challenges become far more challenging.

For example, you are trying to figure out what part of the limbic system is involved in sexual behavior. What's the sort of clues you have to get? You better know a lot about the species that you're studying, because different species have different sensory systems that are relevant to sexual behavior. We've already heard about rodents paying a whole lot of attention to olfaction; our rhinencephalon, our Wellesley effect from oh so many lectures ago. Meanwhile, if you're studying an electric fish, electric fish get sexually excited by electricity, by the electrical call from a number of other individuals in their species. They communicate electrically. Some other species communicate with visual cues. What that's going to tell you is you better know what species and what behavior you're dealing with, because in one species, you would expect to see olfactory projections coming in, and in another, you should expect to see heavy auditory ones. Things like that, figuring out something, you better know what sort of species you're dealing with in terms of behavior.

Another example of that: you've got some part of the limbic system and you are studying a lab rat, and you stimulate that part of the limbic system and this rat quickly runs over to the corner where there's a pile of papers, newspapers or whatever, and she shreds up the newspapers and stuffs them all in the corner. Phew, what's that about? Some sort of behavior. Then you study the same part of the brain in a rhesus monkey, and you stimulate that area and what does this rhesus monkey do? She runs over to the other side of the cage and takes a water bottle and holds it like this and rocks it back and forth. What are you looking at? You are looking at a part of the brain relevant to maternal behavior. You better know that rats go about being maternal by building nests out of shredded up things and primates go about maternal behavior by cuddling their child in a position where it could nurse; and you need to know what species you're looking at.

Next version of needing to know what you're dealing with. Now we've got a part of the brain, a part of the limbic system, which for our purposes right here, simplistically has something to do with aggression. So you take some male baboon and you stimulate that part of the brain and he suddenly displays his canines and he gets this whole aggressive position and he looks like it's about to be bad news. Okay, you've just learned this part of the brain has something to do with aggressive displays. Being a good scientist, you want to replicate this. So you check this out in the next baboon and you stimulate that part of the brain and nothing happens. The guy just sits there. Uh oh, there goes your doctoral thesis. What's happening here? One guy you get this floor dominance display, in the next guy nothing happens. What's going on? Eventually you figure it out; the second guy is socially subordinate. The second guy is sure feeling those aggressive emotions, but he has been trained by experience, you don't go making those threatening gestures, because you're going to get your head handed back to you. Suddenly do you not only need to know about the species, you need to know about the individual member of that species. So trying to figure out what the limbic system does is very, very challenging.

Now, given all of those endless caveats, here we will have a very superficial, mindlessly so, four minute overview of what some of these limbic areas do. And we will be returning to a whole bunch of them in far more detail.

Amygdala. Amygdala we already know about. Amygdala is fear; amygdala is trauma. Of tremendously insightful importance, the amygdala also plays a key role in aggression, and that will dominate some of our final lectures—just one thought there to file away in preparation for it—a part of the brain that is central to aggression is a part of the brain that responds to fear, and lots of ways you cannot make sense of aggressive behavior outside of that aggressive organism, feeling fearful.

Another part of the limbic system, the septum, has a very opposite role. It tends to inhibit aggressive behavior. Ah ha, back to that theme, different limbic structures inhibiting each other. Metaphorically, one is putting your foot on the gas, the other on the brake; areas working in opposition.

Hippocampus. We know the hippocampus ad nauseam already. The hippocampus, learning and memory, but only certain types of learning and memory, ones that are called *explicit* conscious facts that you are aware of:—I am a mammal; I have a dentist appointment next Tuesday—things that you know and that you know that you know. When things are automatic—how to do a backhand in tennis, doing the trill on a piano piece, things like that that—you don't have to think about that in a sense your hands, your body knows before you do, that's a different part of the nervous system. The hippocampus, learning and memory, but this is a conscious, explicit sort of memory.

Moving on in this simplistic overview to mammilary bodies; mammilary bodies have something to do with maternal behavior. We've heard about that before and what we're going to see are different areas in the limbic system, very different in their responsiveness to different hormones.

Moving on to the frontal cortex, we already know it's going to do interesting stuff. The frontal cortex keeps you from doing socially inappropriate things. And in a very, very mindless way, what you can think of is the front cortex trying to wrestle the limbic system into submission and good manners, and often not very successfully. We will return to that in vast detail when considering the neurobiology of aggression.

Finally, the hypothalamus, rare at the center of all these influences, the hypothalamus is made up of a dozen different substructures with all sorts of different roles. There's one area, the medial pre-optic area—do not remember that term—the medial pre-optic area has something to do with sexual behavior. There's two hypothalamic nuclei, the lateral hypothalamus, the ventral medial hypothalamus that has something to do with appetite. One mediates hunger, the other mediates satiation. A part of a hypothalamus called the superchiasmatic nucleus; and that's involved in daily rhythm, circadian rhythms, and things of that sort. What we have is this very crude first pass.

You already know, number one, it's not going to be one function to one structure. You already know, ad nauseam by now, number two, the strengths of these connections can change over time. And now when you think about LTP happening in limbic areas, you are not getting pathways of emotion that are more readily occurring than others. You learn to love something, you learn to fear something, you learn to respond emotionally—tremendous plasticity in here. Just as your brain can learn a new fact, your brain can learn a new reality about emotions.

And finally, it should be no problem at all to begin to recognize—insofar as we all have different neurons and different synaptic patterns of communication and different networks, etc—by the time we get into the limbic system and those individual differences, we are beginning to imagine a part of the brain relevant to why we differ and how we love and how we hate and how we feel despair and how we feel all of those things.

What this sets us up now for is the obvious next step, now we've gotten to how large chunks of the brain influence the hypothalamus. What is the hypothalamus now to do?

Lecture Seven
The Autonomic Nervous System (ANS)

Scope:

This lecture examines the workings of the *autonomic nervous system* and its subparts, the *sympathetic nervous system* and the *parasympathetic nervous system*. The lecture also investigates how the autonomic nervous system regulates the organs of the body, how different levels of the brain activate the system, and how the system is strengthened. The lecture ends with a glimpse into ways that the autonomic nervous system influences individual differences.

Outline

I. We start with the basics of the ANS.

    A. The voluntary nervous system controls the rapid regulation of skeletal muscles.

    B. In contrast, the ANS regulates involuntary function throughout the body.

    C. The ANS has two components.

        1. The *sympathetic nervous system* (SNS), which releases epinephrine and norepinephrine (adrenalin and noradrenalin), is used for emergencies.

        2. The *parasympathetic nervous system* (PNS) releases acetylcholine, which triggers a calm, vegetative state.

II. The SNS and PNS work in choreographed opposition in all parts of the body. (Figure 7a)

    A. Although the heart is able to beat on its own, the brain tells it whether to speed up or slow down.

        1. The SNS causes the heart to beat faster and blood pressure to increase, all as a strategy to deliver energy to exercising muscle.

        2. The PNS does the opposite, slowing down the heart.

    B. SNS and PNS also interact during digestion.

        1. Under normal circumstances, the PNS stimulates the digestive tract.

2. During an emergency, the SNS has the opposite effects. It shuts down digestion and blood flow to the gastrointestinal tract to ensure that energy is not wasted there.

C. The SNS and PNS work in a more coordinated fashion when a male becomes aroused.

1. In order for the penis of a male to become erect, the PNS must be activated and, thus, requires that he be in a calm state.

2. The SNS, however, slowly takes over, and when the PNS is turned off, ejaculation occurs.

3. Syndromes of erectile dysfunction include stress-induced erectile dysfunction, during which stress prevents a man from attaining a state of calm and, thus, an erection, and premature ejaculation, during which the transition from PNS to SNS occurs more quickly than desired. Both are disorders of the choreography between the PNS and SNS.

III. The ANS is activated and regulated differently in three layers of the brain. (Figure 7b)

A. The first regulation of the ANS is directly influenced by the hypothalamus. For example, if a person is injured and his or her blood pressure is dropping, a blood pressure sensor sends a message up the spinal cord to the hypothalamus, which stimulates the SNS, increasing blood pressure and heart rate.

B. In the second layer, the ANS is regulated by the limbic system. For example, the scent or the sight of a threatening rival is detected, causing an emotional response and sending a message to the hypothalamus, which in turn, activates the ANS.

C. In the third layer, we have cortical regulation of the ANS in a way that is fairly unique to primates.

1. Cortical projections are sent to the limbic system, including the hypothalamus, to activate the ANS.

2. Thought and memory serve as stimulants of the ANS.

3. This method of activation gives us insight into the cause of clinical depression.

    a. On a certain level, depression can be thought of as the cortex sending abstractly depressive thoughts into limbic and hypothalamic regions, resulting in the affect of depression (as well as overactivity of the stress response).

    b. A clinically depressed person feels grief, exhaustion, and an absence of pleasure, called *anhedonia*.

IV. Plasticity in ANS function over time manifests itself in three ways.

    A. *Habituation* is the process whereby the same stimulus will not have the same effect on the ANS.

    B. *Sensitization* is the process whereby a stimulus that once did not have an effect on the ANS now does.

    C. *Biofeedback* is a conscious tool for controlling the unconscious workings of the ANS; for example, thinking relaxing thoughts can reduce the SNS response.

V. Individual differences in ANS function explain why some of us are more vulnerable to depression or anxiety disorders than others.

Further Reading:

For a particularly nice, accessible treatment of the subject:

J. Kalat, *Biological Psychology*, 8th ed.

Questions to Consider:

1. How does the autonomic nervous system translate events in the mind into changes in the body?

2. What are the distinctive features of autonomic function in humans?

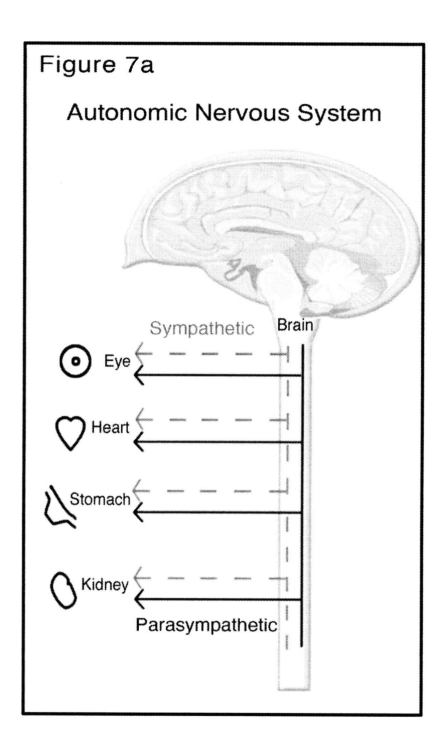

Figure 7a

Autonomic Nervous System

Sympathetic   Brain

Eye

Heart

Stomach

Kidney

Parasympathetic

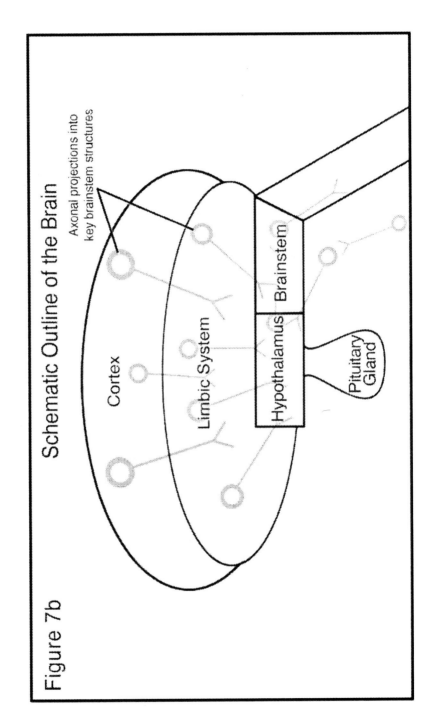

Figure 7b

Schematic Outline of the Brain

Axonal projections into key brainstem structures

Cortex

Limbic System

Hypothalamus

Brainstem

Pituitary Gland

Lecture Seven—Transcript
The Autonomic Nervous System (ANS)

"As she melted small and wonderful in his arms, she became infinitely desirable to him. All his blood vessels seem to scald with intense, yet tender, desire for her. For her softness, for the penetrating beauty of her in his arms, passing into his blood, and softly, with that marvelous swoon like caress of his hand, and pure soft desire, softly he stroked the silky slope of her loins. She yielded with a quiver that was like death. She went all open to him."

Why have you stopped eating your potato chips all of a sudden? Think about what I just read to you, or better yet, later at a quiet moment alone, think about what I just read to you, and if D.H. Lawrence happens to be your thing, something interesting might have happened to your body just now. You won't have just run up a flight of stairs, but your heart may be beating faster. You won't have done anything physically exhausting, yet your breathing rate may have changed. You may suddenly be aware of tingling in all sorts of unlikely outposts in your body. You would have just learned the main point of this lecture, which is sometimes all you need to do, is think a thought, have a memory, have an emotion, and every single organ in your body will work differently.

This is what we've gotten to so far: expanding from one neuron, to a pair of neurons, to networks, to networks changing over time to entire areas of the brain, the limbic system. And as we saw in the last lecture, the entire desire—the limbic system—is to influence the hypothalamus, and thus we get to this section. How does the hypothalamus go about its business? What's so important about the hypothalamus?

What we will see in the next lecture is its control of hormones. What we will see in this lecture is its control of all sorts of neural responses throughout the body, and all sorts of things you have no control over.

Okay, most of your spinal cord does boring stuff. It makes you shake hands and sign checks and shift the gears in the car; but then there's this whole part of your spinal cord and the brain that commands it that does the good stuff, that does things you normally don't have any control over—blushing and gooseflesh and orgasms and papillary contractions—all those things that could be evoked simply by a passage of a book, all these things that are automatic; things that you don't normally have a whole lot of control over.

And thus, this part of the nervous system is called the *autonomic* nervous system. The automatic nervous system, the part of your nervous system that does not have a whole lot of conscious control, and the center of it is, you guessed, it the hypothalamus. Have something emotionally arousing, emotionally stressful, emotionally anything and you get a bodily response two seconds later. That's your autonomic nervous system. So we have this contrast between the voluntary nervous system—ooh, I think I'm going to extend my arm and thus I do it, and is very conscious, voluntary way, controlling skeletal muscles—and then you've got this autonomic nervous system that's sending projections to your liver and your gonads and your diaphragm and you're sending projections to virtually every single spot along your skin, causing you to get gooseflesh. This autonomic nervous system under the control of the hypothalamus doesn't bother with these voluntary skeletal muscles; instead, it is changing functions all throughout the body.

This is the first way—and in lots of ways, the most dramatic way—by which your brain can sit there and reach out and take control of organs throughout your body—first by way of the autonomic nervous system, this lecture, and then by way of hormones, the next lecture.

Okay, so focusing in on what the autonomic nervous system does. For starters, we need to see how it's constructed. The autonomic nervous system comes in two halves, and there's this theme that will go throughout a lot of these sections, different parts of the body working in opposition, different parts of the brain. We've got two different components to the autonomic nervous system and for the most part, they work in opposition.

First part: the sympathetic nervous system—don't worry about the terminology, because this will become very comfortable and familiar by the end of this course—the sympathetic nervous system. All hell is breaking loose, emergency, arousal, fear, terror, excitement, stress, and adrenaline, everything kicking into gear. As it is stated, and this is an obligatory joke that all first year medical students have to hear, a sympathetic nervous system subsumes the four Fs of behavior: fear, flight, fright and sex. Okay. That's required; I loose my license if I don't give that joke. That's what the sympathetic nervous does; it does all of this emergency arousal stuff.

Meanwhile, next door to it, in your brain, in your hypothalamus, in your spinal cord, is the other half, termed the *parasympathetic* nervous system. Parasympathetic is just the opposite—calm, vegetative function. You take a nap; you turn on the parasympathetic nervous system. You eat a big heavy, starchy meal; you turn on the parasympathetic nervous system. You get disemboweled by a predator; you turn off the parasympathetic nervous system. You turn on the sympathetic. They work in opposition.

And you can bet already what the wiring is going to be like, straight out of the network lecture, the parasympathetic axons have a collateral that inhibit the sympathetic ones, the sympathetic axons have a collateral that inhibits the parasympathetic. A system that is brilliantly involved, to make sure you never put your feet on the gas and the brake at the same time, they work in opposition.

Alright, so what do these two halves of the autonomic nervous system do? Lots of different things throughout the body; and where we start off is with this diagram, getting a sense of the sheer range of autonomic function. Here we've got coming down the spine all the stuff not diagramed, there are projections, the axons for the voluntary nervous system going out to all of your skeletal muscles, but shown here instead are the descending projections of the autonomic nervous system. I haven't even labeled which is sympathetic and which is parasympathetic; it doesn't matter in this case. You see parallel projections, two separate cables descending the spine, and each one of them exiting at various points to send a projection to different organs.

The actual anatomy of this is somewhat different, but this is basically the notion there. What you've got is a parasympathetic projection to this organ, a sympathetic projection to the same organ. Parasympathetic here, sympathetic there, to all of the organs throughout the body, you've got the heart, you've got the kidney, you've got the stomach—I'm actually not sure if this is an eyeball or a breast, but it works the same in either case—you've got these projections going all over the place to these target organs, working in opposition.

What would be an example of how this works? Here we see what's happening in the heart—the heart, which in real life looks exactly like that. The heart is very interesting. You take somebody's heart out and put it on a table, it's going to go on beating all on its own. The heart has its own endogenous rhythm, what is called a *myogenic rhythm*, a rhythm generated by muscle myogenic. The heart beats on its own, all your brain does is tells it to slow down or speed up. All it does is send bidirectional messages by way of the autonomic nervous system. Thus, you have a sympathetic projection to the heart—fear, arousal, anxiety, all hell breaking loose, the four F's. It stimulates heart muscle to beat faster, indirectly to beat harder, increasing heart rate, increasing blood pressure. Meanwhile, you've got the parasympathetic doing exactly the opposite, slowing down the heart, that sort of thing, working opposition.

So that makes a great deal of sense. Meanwhile, you've got another autonomic outpost. You've got, for example, your gut, your stomach, and your small intestines. What's going on there? Something very different; something in the opposite direction. Now what did I describe before? The parasympathetic nervous system is about is calm, vegetative function. You take a nap. You eat a big meal. Calm, vegetative is a perfect time to be doing digestion. This is a wonderful time. What happens in your gut? The parasympathetic nervous system stimulates it, stimulates it to go about its business. You do digestion, your stomach churns and contracts and empties out various enzymes that degrade your food and your small intestines does this rhythmic sort of congo line thing called *peristalsis* where it moves food down the line there, and this is digestion. This is precisely what is stimulated by your parasympathetic nervous system. Eat that big starchy Thanksgiving meal, you turn on the parasympathetic in order to stimulate digestion.

Meanwhile, what is your sympathetic nervous system doing to your gut, your stomach and your intestines? Exactly the opposite. The lion is chasing you; you got much better things to do at that point than worry about digesting breakfast if you're trying to avoid being somebody's lunch. You don't mobilize energy to run for your life away from a lion with your thigh muscles. You don't mobilize that by increasing the rate at which your stomach is churning. That takes hours. For running for your life you borrow energy from your fat cells. Digestion takes hours, slow, expensive, and you're trying to avoid this, you've got better things to do right now with your energy. What do you do during a crisis, during a stressful event? What do you do with your sympathetic nervous system? You turn off action in your gut, you inhibit there.

So what you see now are two very different ways in which the autonomic nervous system works. And here we see on sort of a more diagramed level we've got the heart, and just for convenience, we have purely the sympathetic projection into there, your stomach, your gut, sympathetic there. Okay, in general, what the sympathetic nervous system is about is fear, emergency, arousal, everything turning on. What we see is, in some cases, in some parts of your body, it accomplishes it by stimulating an organ. At the heart, the sympathetic nervous system and the neurotransmitters it releases works in an excitatory way. And sometimes in order to accomplish that same emergency switch to a crisis budget, some of the time what the sympathetic nervous system does is turn off the activity in organ. In this case, going to the gut, the neurotransmitter it releases there having an inhibitory role.

So down on a local cellular level, it could be either excitatory or inhibitory. Same thing with the parasympathetic nervous system, inhibiting the heart, stimulating the gut, so now at cellular level, very local effects, but fitting within this large picture, sympathetic nervous system, emergency arousal, parasympathetic, calm, vegetative function.

So you wind up getting these two branches of the autonomic nervous system working in dramatic opposition to each other; except, there's a few outposts where, in fact, they work in a coordinated fashion. One of the best examples of this is, looking at how your autonomic nervous system regulates erections. Okay, we have finally come to this point in the course—seven lectures in there—where we need to deal with how does your brain regulate erections. Finally, something useful in this course here; get out those pens, write down this information. What you've got is, is this remarkably subtle choreography between the parasympathetic and the sympathetic.

Okay, we start off with our first rule. In order for a male of any mammalian species out there, in order for a male to get an erection, he has to turn on the parasympathetic nervous system, a calm, vegetative function. Okay, that's great. So he's got the erection, what happens next? Maybe it is something having to do obscurely with the social setting that brought about the erection in the first place. Maybe for some obscure reason the guy starts feeling a little bit less calm and vegetative. Maybe he starts breathing a little bit faster. Maybe his heart rate begins to increase; maybe he is slowly turning on the sympathetic nervous system.

More time goes by, breathing faster, heart racing, gasping, toes curled, sweating, all of that, eventually he reaches this point where his whole body is screamingly sympathetic except for this one lone outpost where he's desperately holding onto parasympathetic tone, as long as possible, finally can't take it anymore, you turn off the parasympathetic, turn on the sympathetic and you ejaculate.

Okay, so that's how erections work. How do erections work and how can this go wrong? What happens during stress for example? During stress you're not feeling very calm and vegetative. You have trouble getting that parasympathetic tone. What happens then? You can't get the erection—stress induced erectile dysfunction. Or, you can have a second problem. Suppose you've managed to get that erection and suddenly you're thinking, "Oh no the prime lending rate," whatever it is, you have something that stresses you, it accelerates the transition from parasympathetic to sympathetic, it accelerates that transition and everything occurs more quickly than you would like, premature ejaculation. Either of these things can happen and they stupendously common amongst stressed males of every species out there. Current estimates are something like 60% of the doctors visits in this country of men complaining about erectile dysfunction, it turns out there is no organic basis, there's not a spinal tumor, there's not something wrong with the hypothalamus, it is instead, stress related. And what that essentially is, is a disorder of getting the choreography between the parasympathetic and the sympathetic out of whack.

Okay, so we've got a sense now of how the two branches of the sympathetic nervous system and the parasympathetic, these two components forming the autonomic nervous system, we've got a sense by now how they regulate events throughout the body. What we need to look at now is what regulates the centers in your brain that direct the autonomic nervous system.

Now what we have in the next diagram is a very schematic outline of the brain as a whole, and we've seen some of these broad categories before. Midbrain, hindbrain, hypothalamus, limbic system, cortex, we'll be framing it a little bit differently here, and what we've got is the hypothalamus sitting there at the very center, and below it the pituitary—next lecture—hormonal regulation of the body by way of the hypothalamus and the pituitary. Then we've got, with the hypothalamus, a bunch of axonal projections into key brain stem structures, which then send their projections down the spine. We've got the autonomic nervous system.

And now the question becomes: What regulates the hypothalamus in telling the midbrain brain stem what to do with its autonomic projections? And what we have here in this schematic form is this grand formulation of brain function, something come up with in the 1950's by this eminent neuroscientist, Paul McLean, what is termed the *triune organization* of the brain. The three-layered organization of the brain, basically built around hypothalamus, brainstem, and midbrain as one area. The second layer, the rest of the limbic system layered on top, the third layer of the cortex. And this actually gives us a lot of insight into the regulation going on here.

Okay, first type of event that could turn on, cause changes in the autonomic nervous system. You're sitting there and you've hemorrhaged, you've just had some horrible injury, massive amounts of blood flowing out, your blood pressure is dropping and what you need to do now is constrict certain blood vessels to preserve your blood pressure. This is a classic job for the autonomic nervous system. How does the autonomic nervous system know how to do it? The blood pressure sensors throughout your body send signals up the spine, get to those hypothalamic neurons, stimulate them and then they send their message down the spinal cord to have an appropriate response.

This exactly how it works in us, in a rat, in a lizard, all you need are your basis ancient building blocks in the nervous system. In this case, when you are taking care of shifting the function of organs in response to some physical damage, in this case, all you need to run the autonomic nervous system are these very local circuits.

Now we move to the next layer. We move the limbic system. And as we know from the previous lecture, we are now in the realm no longer of lizards, but of those emotional labial mammals, suddenly you've got a huge chunk of the brain devoted to emotional regulation. Lizards have limbic systems; they're just not very big.

It's not until mammals that you have all that stuff going on there. And as we know from the last lecture, what's happening, all those complex projections down into the limbic system, all of those emotionally relevant brain structures wanting to regulate the ability of the hypothalamus to regulate the autonomic nervous system. And suddenly you have world in which you're some wildebeest, and the right menacing, threatening wildebeest has shown up in the edge of your territory and your heart is racing, merely by the emotional arousal in this case. That's your limbic system. You are not injured, you are not hemorrhaging, all you are is seeing this guy who you hate more than any other wildebeest on earth and your heart is speeding up.

Or in another circumstance, all you need to do is see the person who makes your blood run scalding like no one else on earth, and your heart has sped up. In all these cases, we are not dealing with some local little loop in the brainstem and the hypothalamus, instead we have limbic structures. Suddenly we are in a world in which olfaction, sensory input, smell, etc., can change functioning throughout your body. So that's our second layer.

Then we move up to our third layer, and by the time we get up to the cortex, we are dealing with stuff that is much more the realm of primates, including us. Suddenly we have a world where you are not changing autonomic function, you are not changing blood pressure, you are not changing heart rate because you're hemorrhaging, you're not changing it because you're smelling your rival, you're not changing it because of the sight right now of someone who is emotionally arousing to you, you're changing it thinking about the fact that, oh my gosh, someday I'm going to die. You're changing it thinking about refugees on the other side of the planet. You're changing it thinking about the late Beethoven. You're changing it thinking. And suddenly we're in this realm where thought and memory can change how our spleen functions, and how our gut digests and the rate of our heart beating, and we're in the realm of thought influencing the rest of the body.

And this is suddenly a very different realm and a very, very primate specialized one. And here we've got something that happens like no other species other than primates, massive projections from the cortex down into the limbic system, down into the hypothalamus. We've already heard how big the cortex is by the time you get to primates, and that's not just for them to sit around and do fancy math and baseball statistics. By the time you're getting a big cortex, some of what it's doing is having lots of neurons up there to send lots of projections down south into the limbic system and the hypothalamus, suddenly to have this abstract cognitive part of your brain mucking around with your emotions and mucking around with how your body responds to those emotions.

Suddenly we have this realm of an enormous capacity for the cortex, for thought, for memory, to regulate bodily functions. And once again, all you need to do is the experiment to prove that, just sit there and really, really think about the fact that your heart is going to stop beating someday. You're not hemorrhaging, you're not running for your life, and you're not smelling the pheromones of a rival, simply with thought, and you will be turning on aspects of your sympathetic nervous system.

Now the fact that the cortex as shown here has such strong projections down into the limbic system, down into the hypothalamus, this gives us insight into one of the most prevalent, one of the most disastrous, one of the most primate specific diseases out there, major clinical depression.

What is a depression about? Okay. Let's think about this: finish watching this lecture, step outside, and unexpectedly get gored by an elephant. What's going to happen at that point? You're going to turn on your sympathetic nervous system. You're going to be bleeding, in pain, all of that; you're going to be turning on all of those pain relevant pathways, hemorrhage relevant pathways, all that brain stem, midbrain stuff, you're going to feel unhappy, you're going to feel an absence of pleasure, a sense of grief, you're going to feel exhausted, a big buffet may not be the top thing on your list at that point, sex may not seem like the highest priority, this is what your body does during a physical crisis like that.

Go and have yourself a major clinical depression, and what you do, you turn on a lot of the same stress responsive pathways, you feel a similar sense of grief, of exhaustion, appetite is lost, interest in sex is lost, pleasure goes down the tubes, the defining symptom of depression is *hedonia*—hedonism, the pursuit of pleasure—and an hedonia is the inability to feel pleasure. In a very, very simplified level, what a depression is about is, your cortex comes up with these abstract, sad thoughts, and gets your hypothalamus to go along with it just as if you had been gored by an elephant. On that very simplistic level, it is a disease of having an overgrown cortex with a capacity to regulate limbic and hypothalamic areas.

Now given this idiotically simplistic notion, depression is a cortex that thinks too many sad thoughts and whispers it to the hypothalamus. What's a solution for depression? What's a treatment? I know, go in with a pair of scissors and cut along the dotted line, disconnect the cortex from the rest of the brain. Oh right, that is going to work. Remarkably enough, there is some evidence that a very extreme version of depression can be made better by a procedure kind of like that. This is not a frontal lobotomy where you are lopping out the front part of the brain, in this case it's called a singulotomy, a singulumbundal cut, it is disconnecting one part of the cortex from the underlying brain, and the notion is, you are making it impossible now for this cortex to come up with these abstractly sad thoughts and get the rest of the brain to go along with it.

Now naturally somewhere along there, amid these studies suggesting that this can help in some types of depression—and these are controversial findings—naturally what you also want to wonder is, what else is different in somebody where you've gone in and disconnected part of their cortex? Do they lose the capacity for abstract pleasure? Yes, indeed. And suddenly we have this great sort of philosophical debate over the dinner table and George Bernard Shaw play of, "are we more human for our pains in addition to our pleasures," and great philosophical arguments. Anybody who's a candidate for a songulumbundal cut is not feeling a whole lot of abstract pleasures; this is someone in the back ward of a state hospital. Every antidepressant, every combination, electric convulsive therapy even tried, and none of them make a dent and they're slashing their wrists every three months. This is the sort of person where remarkably enough, this may help. You take the most sophisticated clinician on earth and you run by them this idiotically simplistic notion, ooh, what this procedure's about is you disconnect that sad, overly influential cortex from the rest of the brain and it can't tell the sad thoughts to the limbic system, they can't come up with a more sophisticated explanation for what this is about.

So here we see layered is the most subtle way by which your brain, via your cortex, can regulate autonomic function throughout the body. So now of course, we switch to our two themes, plasticity and individual differences. Plasticity, how does the working of the autonomic nervous system change over time? In a whole bunch of ways, one is the same sort of stimulus that would trigger an autonomic response becomes less effective as you do it over and over, you habituate. And that's very often the case for certain stimuli that are frightening. The first time you're on the roller coaster your heart races, and the 47th time in a row that you're on it your heart is not as responsive, your autonomic nervous system is habituating. Some of the time it goes in the opposite direction. With each exposure, your autonomic response becomes more extreme, sensitization, and that appears to be relevant to some anxiety disorders built around trauma. You can change the functioning; you could change the sensitivity in one direction or other.

What is most remarkable is you can change function in the autonomic nervous system in a conscious, volitional way. Let me give you an example of this. Sit there and think very carefully for a moment, if you had to, could you urinate right now? I bet a fair percentage of people watching this could. I could, probably lots of you can. Now ask the question, how many of you are urinating right now? My bet is very few of you. How come? Because back when we were about three years old, we learned you gain control over your bladder, you get toilet trained. You get toilet trained and you remain that way for the rest of your life. What is that in a neurobiological level? Somewhere up in the cortex you LTP, you potentiated a pathway by which you could now consciously control autonomic regulation of your bladder, you have learned how to do that. That's a pathway that was not very strong before, but back to a bunch of lectures ago you have made those synaptic connections stronger, you have learned how to regulate that aspect of the autonomic nervous system.

Another example of this is one that is clinically very relevant, you get some guy with elevated blood pressure. What's one solution? Pour a whole bunch of drugs into him, many of which wind up not working very well or with side effects. An alternative is *biofeedback*. What is biofeedback about? You sit the person down and you hook them up to a blood pressure monitor, and if sitting they're going too high, you tell them, think about your favorite piece of music, think about your favorite food, think about a recent vacation, and suddenly you get some thought where down goes the blood pressure. Ah ha, what did you just think about? Oh, it was the vacation, the Hawaiian vacation. Think about that again, think about…oh, down goes the blood pressure again, and what the person is slowing learning to do is how to consciously, cortically pull forth certain memories, certain thoughts that are ones that strengthen the parasympathetic nervous system, ones that decrease blood pressure.

And what biofeedback is about then is LTPing, strengthening, potentiating those pathways so that you get better and better at evoking some cortical state that's real good at toning down the autonomic nervous system. So that tells us a whole lot there, just like any other part of the nervous system that could change over time.

Finally we come to our other finishing topic here, the whole notion of how the autonomic nervous system works differently between one person and the next. You know exactly the sort of ways in which that could play out. At this point there are lots of reasons to think that differences in autonomic function have something to do with why some of us are more vulnerable to clinical depression, why some of us are more vulnerable to anxiety disorders. It is clear this tremendous variability in this realm, once again, nothing here in set in stone; once again, no nervous system is exactly the same as the one in the neighboring person, tremendous individual variability, which can response the changes in experience.

So on that note I assume everybody needs to go to the bathroom at this point and they probably should, and we will call it the end of this lecture. What we will now do in the subsequent one is the other half of the role of the hypothalamus, the control of hormones.

Module III

The Neuroendocrinology of Behavior

Module Scope:

The lectures on the brain ended with an overview of how the brain (via the limbic system) regulates the body by way of the ANS. Starting with Lecture Eight, this module first examines how the limbic system also regulates the body through the release of hormones. Following that is a review of the different types of hormones and what sort of effects they have. Lecture Nine considers the converse of the brain's regulation of hormones, namely, the hormones' regulation of the brain. How can hormones change the function and even the very structure of the brain? The main point of these lectures is to refute the notion that hormones "cause" behaviors to occur (for example, the notion that testosterone "causes" aggression) and, instead, to explain how hormones interact with the nervous system to change the likelihood of behaviors occurring in certain environments.

Lecture Eight
The Regulation of Hormones by the Brain

Scope:

Lecture Seven introduced the ANS, a means by which the brain can regulate the function of organs throughout the body. This lecture introduces the other route by which the brain can accomplish this regulation, namely, by regulating the release of numerous types of hormones. The nature of this regulation is reviewed, as are the basic ways in which hormones work.

Outline

I. What is the difference between a neurotransmitter and a hormone?

    A. Neurotransmitters travel across synapses and influence the next neuron in line, while hormones travel in the bloodstream.

    B. There are three other major differences between neurons and hormones.

        1. Hormones work more slowly than neurotransmitters.

        2. Neurons communicate only with neurons; hormones influence every cell in the body and can be secreted from various parts of the body.

        3. Hormones have a broader effect on cells.

    C. The brain plays a critical role in regulating the endocrine systems.

II. The hypothalamus is the center of the endocrine world, and the limbic system tries to tell the hypothalamus what to do. (Figure 8a)

    A. The earlier view was that peripheral glands were autonomous and self-regulating.

    B. This notion then gave way to the equally incorrect idea that the pituitary was the "master gland."

C. It is understood now that the brain is an endocrine gland and that the hypothalamus secretes an array of hormones, which in turn, regulate the pituitary gland.

III. The anterior pituitary is a hormonal system that is entirely under the control of the brain.

   A. The hypothalamus releases hormones to stimulate or inhibit the pituitary gland cells.

   B. The anterior pituitary, in turn, regulates hormonal release from peripheral glands.

IV. The posterior pituitary is another hormonal system that is entirely under the control of the brain.

   A. The posterior pituitary can be considered an outpost of the brain.

   B. The posterior pituitary releases oxytocin and vasopressin, hormones that play roles in birth and lactation.

V. The body also has hormonal systems that are under partial control by the brain.

   A. One example is the pancreas, which produces a number of hormones, the most recognized of which is insulin.

   B. Insulin secretion is triggered by blood glucose, and it is also triggered through the PNS by the expectation of food.

VI. The body also has hormonal systems that are independent of the brain. In such cases, hormones are derived from all sorts of unlikely sources, such as the heart and the immune system. (Figure 8b)

   A. When the heart senses high blood pressure, it releases a hormone, ANF, to the kidneys to tell them to make more urine, thereby reducing the amount of fluid in circulation; as a result, blood volume is reduced and blood pressure is lowered.

B. The immune system also has messengers that act as hormones. One of them, Interleukin 1, triggers white blood cells to proliferate and mount an immune defense against a pathogen that the system has detected. Interleukin 1 can also affect brain function, bringing about fatigue or fever and making one's body ache by sensitizing pain pathways, and it can trigger a stress response. All these events are ways to make a person decrease activity during illness.

VII. There are two broad classes of hormones.

    A. Steroid hormones include estrogens, androgens, progestins, glucocorticoids, and mineralocorticoids.

    B. The other class of hormones is made from amino acids; that is, they are protein based. They include insulin, follicle-stimulating hormone (FSH), and growth hormone.

    C. For both classes, we see the themes of cheap and plentiful starting material, short synthetic pathways, and multiple messengers derived from the same precursors. But cheap messengers require very fancy and expensive receptors to tell apart these structurally similar hormones.

VIII. Hormone receptors are as critical to the endocrine system as the hormones they receive.

    A. Hormones bind to receptors and, thereby, activate events in cells.

    B. Amino acid-derived hormones tend to influence the activity of proteins that already exist in the cell (for example, epinephrine mobilizing energy from storage sites during an emergency).

    C. Steroid hormones tend to alter the synthesis of new proteins.

    D. The amount of a hormone in the bloodstream is important, but so are the amount and function and possible mutation of hormone receptors.

IX. A great deal of crosstalk exists between different endocrine systems. An example of such crosstalk is seen in the effects of stress on female reproduction. (Figure 8c)

    A. The ovarian axis illustrates the pathway.

1. The hypothalamus releases the luteinizing hormone releasing hormone (LHRH).
2. The LHRH causes the anterior pituitary to release the luteinizing hormone.
3. The ovaries are then triggered to release estrogen, causing the uterine wall to mature.

B. If you add any major form of stress, such as starvation or psychological trauma, stress hormones will influence every step in that pathway.

1. Stress and its effects on hormone release from fat cells show that starvation is an antireproductive form of stress. Likewise, excessive amounts of exercise can cause the release of beta-endorphins, which, along with other stress hormones, can also have antireproductive effects.
2. Stress-induced release of prolactin disrupts uterine maturation.

Further Reading:

For two excellent texts:

J. Becker, M. Breedlove, D. Crews, and M. McCarthy, *Behavioral Endocrinology*, 2nd ed.

R. Nelson, *An Introduction to Behavioral Endocrinology*, 2nd ed.

For the (very difficult) bible of the field:

P. Larsen et al., *Williams Textbook of Endocrinology*, 10th ed.

Questions to Consider:

1. What are ways in which the brain can regulate hormone release?
2. What are steps that could give rise to differences between two individuals in the functioning of a particular endocrine system?

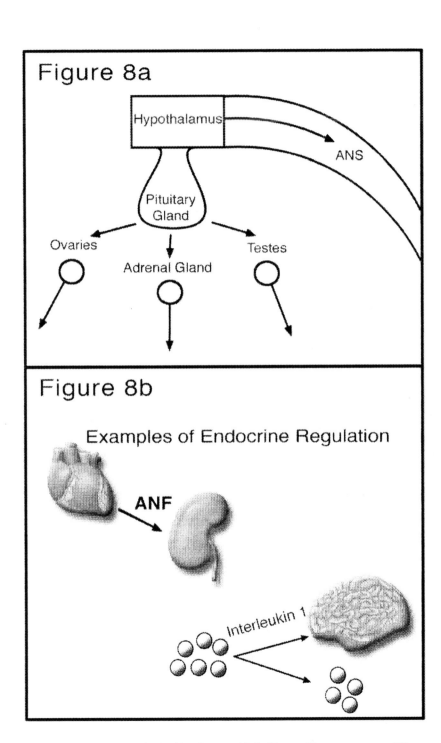

Figure 8a

Hypothalamus

ANS

Pituitary
Gland

Ovaries

Adrenal Gland

Testes

Figure 8b

Examples of Endocrine Regulation

ANF

Interleukin 1

Figure 8c

Why Female Mammals Are Less Likely to Ovulate under Stress

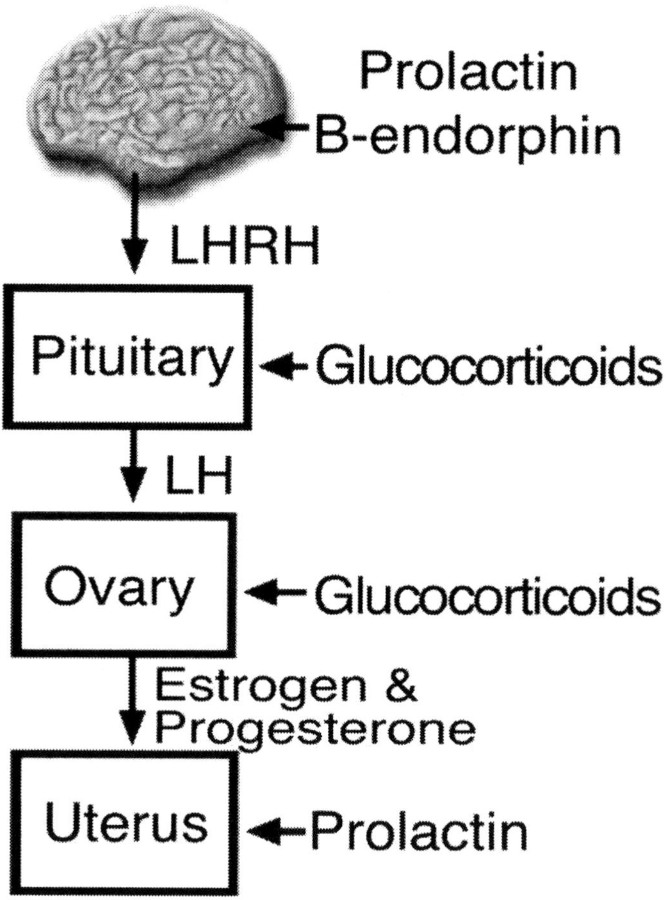

Prolactin
B-endorphin

LHRH

Pituitary ← Glucocorticoids

LH

Ovary ← Glucocorticoids

Estrogen & Progesterone

Uterus ← Prolactin

Lecture Eight—Transcript
The Regulation of Hormones by the Brain

We're back. I've changed my shirt since the last lecture and thus feel wildly invigorated, and that's a great thing because we are talking hormones today. Okay, where were we at in the last lecture? We have now taken this grand expanding view of how the nervous system works, starting with one neuron and then a pair of neurons and networks and whole areas of the brain, the limbic system and where we left off, finally seeing why it is everyone in the limbic system is so concerned about the hypothalamus' opinion. Why? Number one, the last lecture discussed the ability of the hypothalamus to regulate all sorts of aspects of the body by way of that autonomic nervous system. Number two, today's lecture discusses the ability of the hypothalamus to regulate hormones throughout your body.

Okay, so we've just introduced some new jargon, hormones, what's the deal? What is a hormone compared to what is a neurotransmitter? Neurotransmitters we're amply familiar with by now, and we have a really simply difference in explanations here and their definitions as shown on this diagram. By definition, you've got some axon terminal, it dribbles out a chemical messenger, that's to an action potential, and if the chemical messenger goes floating a thousand of an inch across the synapse and does something or other to the next neuron in line, you got a neurotransmitter. And just as clearly by definition, if the axon terminal releases the same messenger, any other messenger, whatever it is it releases, if it instead gets into the bloodstream, you now have a hormone.

Hormones are blood born, and what that winds up meaning is they circulate throughout the entire body, they could be coming out of neurons and we will see lots of cases for that, or as shown at the bottom of the diagram, you can have all sorts of endocrine glands throughout the body, ovaries, testes, adrenals, pancreas, whatever and once again, if the cells there secrete some sort of messenger that gets into the bloodstream, you've got a hormone on your hand. It can be the exact same chemical as the neurotransmitter, it could be epinephrine, it could be neuroepinephrine, it could be oregano, whatever it is; goes floating across the synapse, it's a neurotransmitter; gets into the bloodstream, it's a hormone.

Now what that sets us up for are some major differences in what neurotransmitters do, what hormones do. By definition, the neurotransmitter is affecting events a hundredth-of-an-inch away; hormones are affecting events in every cell in the body. By definition, neurotransmitters are doing their thing in incredibly short amounts of time. We saw in previous lectures you can have 50 action potentials a second; in contrast, hormones could take minutes to start working, they could take days. As we will see, some hormones have their effects decades later.

Finally, what the neurotransmitters do is change some excitable event in the next neuron in line. What the hormones do is virtually anything out there. They change the function of cells. They can cause cells to divide. They can cause cells to die and everything in between, extremely versatile.

Now as we already know, a whole lot of the business of hormone regulation is centered around the brain, centered around the hypothalamus, and we have by now, our flow chart describing the last lecture in this. You've got your hypothalamus there and we know all of those influences up north, the limbic system, the cortex heading down into the hypothalamus. We saw from the last lecture the hypothalamus regulating the autonomic nervous system heading down your spinal cord, and what we will see today is how for a large percentage of hormonal systems, the key is the hypothalamus tells the pituitary what to do. The pituitary, this is gland sitting right under the base of the hypothalamus, the hypothalamus tells the pituitary what to do. The pituitary in turn dumps all sorts of different types of hormones into the bloodstream where they have peripheral actions; they cause some peripheral gland to secrete something or other—pancreas, adrenals, thyroid gland, ovaries, testes. What you have here is termed a *neuroendocrine cascade*. The brain commands the pituitary, which commands all sorts of peripheral glands.

Now the whole notion of the brain commanding hormonal outflow throughout the body has had a pretty exciting controversial history, if you have no more exciting things in your life than the exciting endocrinologist does. But what you have is a very unlikely pathway by which this occurs. You've got the pituitary basically broken into two different parts, the anterior and the posterior pituitary. It's in the anterior pituitary where all of this controversy occurred, and it was built around the notion of how does the brain regulate the pituitary.

Now back around 1900 or so, nobody knew that the pituitary secreted hormones, people basically did not have a hormone concept then. They sort of knew these peripheral glands secreted something or other that altered physiology, altered behavior. Actually, the discovery that peripheral glands secrete hormones is the oldest fact in physiology, it's probably about ten thousand years old, when some farmer discovered the bull that chasing him around the backyard too much, if you wrestle that bull down and removed his testes, he was suddenly a much more attractable guy and suddenly you realize, something or other comes out the testes that has something or other to do with what a pain in the neck males can be very frequently. Ah ha, these peripheral glands release these factors—soon named hormones—that could change events throughout the body.

The original view was these hormones knew exactly what they were doing by way of these peripheral glands, which knew exactly what they were doing. These peripheral glands had all the information needed. It wasn't until some decades later people began to figure out, no, actually these peripheral glands have no idea what they're doing, left to their own devices. They can't figure out when they should be secreting insulin or estrogen or things like that, they are actually under the command of the pituitary. And that gave rise to the most persistent, celebrated, and incorrect saying in all of endocrinology that the pituitary is the "master gland" and that was in scribes and endless Reader Digest articles by the time I was a kid. The pituitary is a master gland. The pituitary is making all the decisions as to when those peripheral glands do their things, and when they release their hormones.

It wasn't until around the 1950s that people began to figure out the pituitary was not a master gland. Somehow or another it was getting its directions from the brain, from the hypothalamus. And somebody at that time came up with the notion—a British scientist, an endocrinologist pioneer, named Geoffrey Harris—and this guy came up with the notion that what you have is the brain working as a endocrine gland. When you look at the anterior pituitary, it is not exactly connected with the base of the hypothalamus as shown here in this diagram. What you have instead is a tiny, tiny circulating system connecting the hypothalamus with the anterior pituitary. The notion then was that the hypothalamus secreted hormones, which then went down to the anterior pituitary and told those cells which hormones to secrete into the main circulation.

Neurobiologists hated this concept simply because something seemed kind of demeaning and disgusting and yucky about the brain being an endocrine gland. The brain does this sort of gleaming calculation stuff for you, and here it is drooling out hormones instead. There is tremendous resistance to the idea of the brain as an endocrine gland. It took a number of scientists, a pair of them in fact, decades to prove this was in fact the case, and they got their noble prizes out of this showing the brain is an endocrine organ.

What you wind up seeing in the anterior pituitary world is all of the hormone release coming out of there is directly under endocrine control of the hypothalamus. You've got the hypothalamus with its hypothalamic hormone secreting neurons there, dumping their hormones into that local circulation where they go down and their job is to stimulate, to inhibit, to regulate what these pituitary gland cells are doing. We have a first pass here of the brain as the central regulator of endocrine systems.

Okay, the second way in which the brain is completely in charge is at the much more conventional reassuring posterior pituitary, which people had known how that had worked for decades and none of this sort to heretical revisionism about the brain is an endocrine gland. This one was much simpler to make sense of. It turns out the posterior pituitary, as shown in this next diagram, is really just an outpost of the brain. The brain in this case just has this little bit of hypothalamic tissue dribbling down there and happened to merge with the anterior pituitary; and in this case, you didn't have to come up with this weird scenario of hormones circulating in this tiny little local system. Here instead you simply have the cell bodies of those neurons sending their projections down to the posterior pituitary, and it's those exact same axon terminals that are releasing the hormones in those cases.

There are two principle hormones at the posterior pituitary, oxytocin, vasopressin, and these have a whole lot to do with giving birth, with milk let down with contraction of the uterus. In this case we have complete control of these hormones by way of the brain, once again, in this case by way of these axons coursing down into the posterior pituitary.

Now this is great. We've got these scenarios here, where forget these peripheral glands knowing what they're doing. Forget the pituitary is the master gland. The brain is entirely in charge of when these hormones are released. And we will see about some of these hormones in far more detail. For example, the anterior pituitary hormones, which trigger ovulation, which trigger sperm production, releasing hormones like luteinizing hormone, follicle stimulating hormone—do not panic if these are all new terms, the important ones we will come back to again and again—a whole branch of other hormones relating to the anterior pituitary system regulating growth, growth hormone, hormones having to do with thyroid function, regulating them, a class of hormones in this hypothalamic anterior pituitary system, having to do with stress. And what you wind up seeing is, depending on the stressful event, which hormones come out of the hypothalamus to kick the anterior pituitary into gear. So, you have a different hormonal profile if you were stressed, for example, because you just had your leg broken versus if you were stressed because you were stuck in traffic; in those cases, very different stressors, physical, psychological, wind up being coded for with different hypothalamic hormones. We have a system here of great complexity, but entirely built around the brain runs the system.

Now what we have in some cases though are endocrine systems where the brain has something to say about it, but it's not the only thing it has something to say. Where there's partial regulation about by brain. And this is shown in the next diagram. What we have is one of everybody's favorite endocrine organs in the body, the pancreas. What does the pancreas do? It secretes insulin, people have known this forever; and when it fails to secrete insulin, you've got juvenile onset diabetes. What you also have, as it turns out, is a whole bunch of other hormones coming out of the pancreas, but it is most famous, most celebrated for its release of insulin, and people used to think they understood everything about insulin secretion.

Okay, what does insulin do? Insulin tells your body to store energy, to take circulating glucose and stick it away in various storage sites in your body. Insulin is this wildly optimistic, forward-looking hormone. It says we've got enough energy onboard, we've got enough stuff in our bloodstream to keep us perfectly happy and energized right now, take the extra stuff and store it away for some building project next spring.

So you ask the question, how does the pancreas know when to secrete insulin? It turns out it has this wonderfully logical little regulatory loop from the bloodstream. By definition, how does the pancreas know when you've got tons of glucose in the bloodstream, good idea to store it. It measures the amount of your circulating glucose. There are receptors on pancreatic cells as shown in the diagram here that are glucose receptors, they measure glucose. Circulating glucose is sensed there and there's a local little regulatory loop which, when glucose levels get high in the blood stream, that tells you to secrete insulin. Wonderful! That explains everything, except, there's an additional step in there, where the nervous system comes in. And if you are a well conditioned westernized human, what happens? You have dinner every night at say 6:00 o'clock or so and what happens in addition is, right around a quarter of 6:00 you start secreting insulin. Is that because your blood glucose levels have gone up? Absolutely not. You're not eating yet. Blood glucose isn't going to go up for at least 15 minutes, you start secreting insulin in anticipation. How do you pull that off when circulating glucose levels have not changed yet? In this case it's your brain doing that.

And back to the last lecture, which branch of the autonomic nervous system is all about calm, vegetative planning for the future; it's the parasympathetic nervous system. As shown here on the diagram there's a big old axonal projection from the parasympathetic nervous system going into the pancreas, and forget circulating glucose levels, when you are sophisticated enough of a primate to know, ooh, 15 minutes until dinner, your PNS is already working to cause anticipatory insulin secretion. So in those cases we have an endocrine system only partially under control of the brain, but no surprise, the way in which it's controlling there is the most cerebral events; we're one of the only species out there that can sit there and anticipate a Thanksgiving dinner.

Okay, in some cases though, you've got endocrine systems that are completely independent on the brain. This is one that—once people got on board with the notion that the brain is the master gland, and even does unseemly things like secrete hormones itself—people were really quite surprised to discover that organs in the body, in cases, could get along just fine without the brain putting in its two cents of endocrine regulation. We've got all sorts of versions of this.

One of them is shown on the top of this diagram. What we've got in this case is a hormone called ANF, which has so many syllables in its actual name I'm not going to actually say it, but it comes out of, of all places, what turned out to be one of the most unlikely endocrine glands anybody could imagine, your heart. Your heart turns out to be yet another endocrine organ. What do we mean by that? It secretes something or other which gets into the bloodstream and effects events someplace else in the body. It secretes this hormone ANF, and it secretes it at a wonderfully logical time.

So you've got high blood pressure. By definition the problem with high blood pressure is your heart is pumping too hard, resistance in your blood vessels is incorrect. Whatever it is, there's too much blood pressure; so what's a way to solve it. One way, which your heart thinks of, is let's get rid of some blood volume. How can you do that? You can get rid of red blood cells, and that's another clever thing for your body to do, or you can decrease the amount of fluid, the amount of water in your circulation. How are you going to do that? I know, those kidneys down there, they're all adept to this sort of thing. What ANF does is, it is sent down into the circulation and it has effects at the kidney, it is a diuretic, it makes your kidneys make more urine and your blood volume goes down.

When does the heart secrete ANF? By definition, if your heart muscles are getting extended, that means you're slamming blood with too much pressure into it, stretching of heart muscle triggers ANF release, which goes and talks to the pituitary, you go and pee, blood pressure goes down, everybody's happy. And here we've got this wonderfully logical endocrine loop that's got nothing to do with the brain.

This diagram on the bottom shows another example of this, and this one completely caught people by surprise, because it turns out another branch of your body contains endocrine glands. In these cases these are individual cells of your immune system, white blood cells. And you talk to immunologists, and they do not, in their classical form, think a whole lot about hormones, and suddenly it turns out, your immune cells secrete hormones as well.

Now one of the things your immune system has as a major challenge is, it's not a single organ. You've got your thymus gland and your bone marrow and your spleen and all sorts of immune cells in this circulation. By definition then, that's going to be a system that has to involve secreting a whole lot of messengers that go all over the place; there's a whole family of these immune messengers that send information from one type of blood cell to another, that sort of thing. And it turns out a whole lot of these immune messengers have effects elsewhere in the body work as hormones.

In some ways, the most shocking example was the discovery that there's a whole class of immune messengers that work as hormones affecting brain function, and this is an immune messenger called interleukin one. Interleukin one does all sorts of nice logical things to other white blood cells; it triggers them to divide and proliferate and mounts some whole immune defense against some sort of pathogen that's gotten into you. Meanwhile, interleukin one gets into your brain, where it does all sorts of interesting stuff. It makes you sleepy. It's called a *somnogen*. It makes sleep onset more readily occur. It changes your threshold of temperature regulation. It is a *pyrogen*.

Those of you who are pyromaniacs or Pyrex fans will know that pyro—temperature, fire—makes your body run a temperature. It changes pain threshold so that your body aches, your tooth roots and your eyeballs throb. It triggers a stress response. What is interleukin one doing? It's making you feel terrible. Interleukin one is the messenger that makes you feel crummy when you're sick. It makes you sleepy, lethargic, it makes you run a temperature, it makes you feverish, and it makes everything ache. It turns out it decreases appetite, it decreases sex drive, all sorts of things built around this logic. You feel awful, you have some pathogen, hunger down there, forget going out hunting; just lie still. The pain is probably a way to make you decrease your activity as well. You've got this whole branch of the immune system which turns out to be able to direct events all over your brain.

A couple of interesting additional implications of that; it turns out with interleukin one can affect aspects of learning and memory. Basically along the lines of disrupting LTP, you remember from umpteen lectures ago, LTP synaptic plasticity. Interleukin one tends to inhibit LTP. Ah ha, you're running a high fever, that's not a great day for being at your cognitive best. In addition, it's looking as if a whole lot of interleukin one can increase your risk of a depression. And that has something to do with all sorts of chronic immune activational diseases, increasing the risk of depression there as well.

Okay, so we've got this enormously varied array of endocrine systems entirely under the control of the brain via the anterior pituitary, the posterior partially under the control of the brain, entirely independent of the nervous system, independent, and of all outlandish things, actually then regulating the brain by way of peripheral hormones, the subject of our next lecture. What we see here is an enormous range of ways in which hormones can operate.

So what we now need to shift to is, what are the actual hormones involved? And there are two broad classes, and you are going to recognize some of the exact same themes as from the neurotransmitter lecture. First off you've got a class of hormones called steroid hormones. Steroids, everybody's heard of steroids. Steroids get you thrown out of the Olympics, steroids get you in trouble with Congress if you're a baseball player; steroids is just a way of describing the chemical structure of a class of hormones. There are five different families of steroid hormones, once again, do not panic. If these are important names we will come back to them. Estrogen-related steroid hormones, progesterone related-ones, testosterone-related ones and regenic—anabolic hormones are the other terms for those—ones that are related to stress, and we will hear about those plenty, and a class of them that are related to kidney function—five different classes of steroid hormones.

That should already give you a hint of where we are heading, the same exact themes of cheapness that ran all through our neurotransmitter lecture, the same rules. In the case of steroid hormones you start with a cheap, plentiful precursor—in this case, cholesterol. And you should not panic and suddenly say, oh my gosh, if I cut down cholesterol in my diet I'm going to run out of estrogen and androgens and all that. It is such a tiny percentage of the cholesterol that is used to make these hormone messengers that you don't need to worry about it. No dietary change in cholesterol intake is going to have an effect on steroid production. But you've got a plentiful, cheap precursor, cholesterol. So we fulfill our first requirement, the same one as with the neurotransmitters—cheap precursor. Just a couple of biosynthetic steps and you've made your steroid hormones, and we already see our next principle straight out of the neurotransmitter lecture generate multiple messengers out of the same precursor.

What you have in that case is from that same cholesterol beginning, a couple of steps here, a couple of construction steps in an opposite direction and you've produced estrogens or androgens or progesterones or different classes. The remarkable thing is that there are hundreds of different types of minor steroid hormones in the body, all of which fit in those five classes. Look at that efficiency, that cheapness you've got going on there. One simple precursor and you can generate a gazillion different messengers. That's great.

However, it comes with a downside. If you are going to be very cheap in producing your hormone messengers so that you produce testosterone that structurally looks almost like estrogen, it's just a couple of steps different and great, you've generated two messengers from different sort of pathways. Suddenly you've got a problem, which is you never, ever, ever want to have your testosterone receptor, for example, mistake estrogen for testosterone. You don't have your receptors get fooled and suddenly you've got a no-free-lunch scenario. If you're going to have very structurally similar hormones, you've got to have very fancy, expensive receptors that can tell them apart. You don't want your receptors to confuse androgens and estrogens.

So, we see at one end generating the messengers, this very simple rule once again of economy generating lots of different messengers out of the same precursor; and, then we see steroid hormone receptors are some of the fanciest ones around.

Then we have our other class of hormones, and these are ones that are protein based and a couple of lectures from now we are going to see in great detail, what does it mean to have a protein and how do you construct it, and what part of your body gives the instructions. But what we have here are hormones made out of protein precursors and the exact same logic again, plentiful precursors here, amino acids, just string a bunch of them together and you've made this type of peptide protein-based hormone, growth hormone. String another version of them together and you've made insulin, another version and you've made follicle-stimulating hormone. Same principle again, plentiful precursors, relatively few steps and you can generate a whole bunch of hormones that are structurally quite similar to each other based on just a few synthetic steps.

Once again you've got the same downside; you definitely want receptors that can tell the difference between a hormone that tends to stimulate ovulation versus a hormone that tends to inhibit it. If you are cheap in generating your messengers, you are going to have to be very expensive in designing receptors that can tell the difference.

Okay, so that brings us to the point of receptors. And a big theme throughout endocrinology used to be, just tell me how much of a hormone is in the bloodstream and that tells me what's going to be happening in the body. What people have since realized is how much hormone in the bloodstream is half the story. The other half is, how many receptors, where they're working and how well they're working; that's the other half of the deal.

That became clearer when people began to identify some wild endocrine disorders where there was nothing wrong with the levels of the hormones in the bloodstream. What there were instead were mutations and receptors and one wild example, you have a syndrome of someone who appears to be a girl and who appears to be having a problem because she's not hitting puberty yet and she's really quite delayed and the physician checks her out and discovers the great shock that this girl is a boy. This individual is a boy genetically—X Y chromosomes. This individual is a boy in terms of having testes. This individual is a boy having those testes way up, undescended, those testes secreting boatloads of testosterone. What's the problem in this case, they can have testosterone being poured out 'til the cows come home, but there's a mutation in the testosterone receptor. That testosterone's doing nothing and in this case, the hormone signal is just fine, the response to the signal is impaired. We're really wild endocrine disorder.

So what we've got there are two halves of a story. How much of an endocrine signal, and how much tissue sensitivity there is to it are critical. Now this gives us a broad picture of endocrine systems, but it's a very, very artificial one. It's basically saying, okay in the brain you've got your neuroendocrine pathway having to do with ovulation, these hormones getting into the ovaries. Meanwhile you've got your neuroendocrine cascade having to do with stress, and then here's the one with temperature regulation, and here's the one with growth. It's this very artificial picture of separate branches, and what you have instead is enormous amounts of cross talk between these endocrine branches.

Let me give you one really interesting example of this, and this is, as shown on this diagram, asking the question why is it that if you are a female mammal, and you are under stress, you tend to be less likely to ovulate. You tend to have more fertility problems?

What we have here, as starters in the diagram, is the boring straightforward neuroendocrine cascade, the brain secretes its hypothalamic hormone, LHRH, luteinizing hormone, releasing hormone, which then triggers the pituitary to release luteinizing hormone, which gets the ovaries to make estrogen and progesterone, and progesterone causes the uterine wall to mature. Great, we've got one of our classic neuroendocrine cascades. But then you throw in some major stress, physical stress, starvation, psychological stress and what you see is there's a whole family of stress hormones that work to disrupt this pathway at different levels. One stress hormone is a hormone secreted in response to stress, *prolactin*. Prolactin works up at the level of the brain to make you less likely to secrete this LHRH.

Another hormone that's responsive to this stress, beta endorphin works up at the hypothalamus to do the same thing. Ah ha, some of you may be saying beta endorphin and endorphin, runners high, your endorphin high, it is secreted by the physical stress of large amounts of exercise. This is a hint as to why individuals who do massive amounts of exercise, and this is not the government recommended go out and do 30 minutes of aerobics, something or other, every day; this is the ultra marathoners, what you wind up seeing, this can occasionally have anti-reproductive effects.

Meanwhile, down south at the pituitary, another class of stress hormones called *glucocorticoid* make the pituitary less sensitive to whatever LHRH is coming out of the brain. Down at the ovaries glucocoricoids work there to make the ovaries less sensitive to LHRH. Meanwhile, down at the uterus, prolactin works to make it less likely that the uterine walls are going to thicken and you've got just effects all over the place here. Less hypothalamic hormone, less pituitary sensitivity to it, less pituitary hormone secreted, less ovarian sensitivity to it, and then a hormone working down at the uterus to block the effects of progesterone. What you have here, from the reproductive standpoint, is a whole bunch of ways that stress can effect the system from the learning about endocrinology standpoint, obvious punch line, it is far more complicated than one hormonal pathway, tremendous amounts of cross talk.

Now what this sets us up for is our next lecture, looking at in some ways the most interesting outpost of endocrinology, neuroendocrinology. Not how the brain regulates hormone release, but how hormones regulate the brain in return. So that will be our next step in the next lecture.

Lecture Nine
The Regulation of the Brain by Hormones

Scope:

This lecture examines the other half of the endocrine cycle: how hormones regulate the brain. This lecture will focus on both the *organizational* effects of hormones (which is how exposure to hormones early in life, beginning with fetal life, can alter the structure and function of the brain forever after) and the *activational* effects of hormones (which is how hormones can alter brain function on a much shorter timespan).

Outline

I. Hormones have effects on cells, including cells in the brain.

    A. Both neurons and glial cells have hormone receptors.

    B. Hormones can alter protein function and synthesis in the brain, just as they do throughout the rest of the body.

    C. Hormones can alter neurotransmitter actions in the brain. (Figure 9a)

        1. Dopamine is a neurotransmitter of pleasure in the brain.

        2. Steroid hormones called glucocorticoids are released during stress, and these hormones have an effect on dopamine release.

            a. During short-term stress (stimulation), a transient rise in glucocorticoid levels occurs, resulting in increased synaptic release of dopamine. This can produce pleasurable effects. LTP is enhanced as well.

            b. During long-term stress, however, a chronic rise in glucocorticoid levels occurs; thus, the dopamine neurons are depleted, leading to anhedonia, or the inability to feel pleasure.

    D. Hormones can also alter the plasticity of synapses.

        1. Glucocorticoid levels affect the hippocampus and the amygdala differently.

> a. A transient rise in glucocorticoid levels in the hippocampus brought on by short-term stress enhances LTP, while sustained glucocorticoid exposure in the hippocampus can disrupt LTP.
>
> b. On the other hand, chronic stress enhances LTP in the amygdala, thereby enhancing the ability of the amygdala to "file away" memories of trauma.
>
> c. This factor might explain free-floating anxiety, in which the hippocampus does not recall an explicit traumatic memory, but the amygdala recognizes the source of the trauma and activates the sympathetic nervous system.

2. Estrogen is another hormone that enhances LTP in the hippocampus.

E. Hormones can change the structure of neural networks, causing neurons to grow more elaborate dendritic branches or to shrivel up.

1. Chronic stress and the resulting chronic glucocorticoid exposure cause atrophy of hippocampal neurons, thus inhibiting learning.

2. Chronic stress and the resulting chronic glucocorticoid exposure cause expansion of dendritic branches in the amygdala, thus increasing anxiety.

3. Higher estrogen levels cause the growth of new dendritic branches in hippocampal neurons, thus enhancing learning and memory.

F. Hormones can affect the birth and death of neurons. The discovery of adult *neurogenesis* is an exciting new finding in neurobiology.

1. Estrogen enhances the birth of new neurons in the adult brain, while glucocorticoids inhibit such neurogenesis.

2. Estrogen makes neurons more likely to survive a neurological insult, while glucocorticoids do the opposite in response to such an insult.

G. Hormones can influence how the brain regulates the body and behavior.

1. For example, it used to be thought that glucose levels in the bloodstream alone controlled our appetites.

2. Now it is known that an array of hormones released by the gastrointestinal tract, fat cells, liver, and pancreas regulate appetite.

II. A theme that runs through behavioral neuroendocrinology is that hormones may "cause" some behaviors, such as aggression, to occur. Instead, however, hormones alter a preexisting tendency for the behavior to occur in the context of interaction with the environment. This notion will be studied more in depth in the lectures on aggression.

Further Reading:

For two excellent texts:

J. Becker, M. Breedlove, D. Crews, and M. McCarthy, *Behavioral Endocrinology*, 2nd ed.

R. Nelson, *An Introduction to Behavioral Endocrinology*, 2nd ed.

For the (very difficult) bible of the field:

P. Larsen et al., *Williams Textbook of Endocrinology*, 10th ed.

Questions to Consider:

1. What would brain function be like if hormones could not get access to the brain?

2. Could one claim (in a courtroom, for example) that a behavior was caused by hormones?

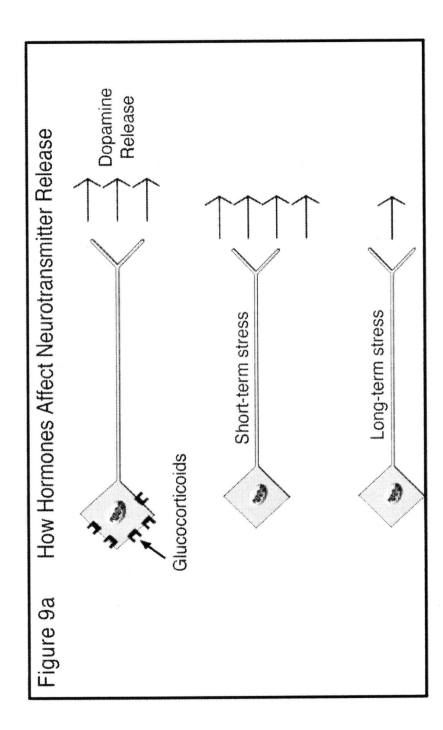

Figure 9a   How Hormones Affect Neurotransmitter Release

Dopamine Release

Glucocorticoids

Short-term stress

Long-term stress

Lecture Nine—Transcript
The Regulation of the Brain by Hormones

You are back just in time for neuroendocrinology. Neuroendocrinology, where have we gotten to so far? We started with our neuron and expanded ever outward. We've looked at which, by which, large parts of the brain can regulate the body: number one, by way of the autonomic nervous system, number two, as seen in the last lecture, by way of hormones. The brain as a neuroendocrine gland, the brain as controlling hormones released throughout the body.

What we do in this lecture is one of the things that science often does, which is to complete a loop, show a big, old regulatory loop. Now looking at not how the brain regulates hormones, but how hormones in the circulation get back into the brain and regulate brain function.

Now pristine, card-carrying neurobiologists have often been very resistant to the ideas that hormones can muck around with brain function, but it should be obvious for two reasons. The first one, as we heard in the last lecture is, the oldest experiment in endocrinology going back millennia and showed that hormones coming out of the testes could affect the brain, could affect behavior produced by the brain. Testosterone has some effect on aggression. The other reason this should not be surprising is built around the simple definition of what hormones do. Hormones affect cells—neurons are cells; glial cells are cells. All the cells in the brain are as much subject to hormonal effects as anywhere else in the body. So what you can immediately predict is hormone receptors occur throughout the brain—neurons, glial receptors for virtually every hormone out there, and in all the logical interesting places.

So what we'll be doing in this lecture is looking at some of the ways that hormones can affect brain function, and what we will see is, they can do some really dramatic things, ranging from changing the amount of neurotransmitter coming out of a neuron to changing whether neurons live or whether neurons die. Remarkably powerful effects, and as we'll see, some of these have tremendous implications for some psychiatric diseases. Some of this will have tremendous implications as well. For the lectures to come, looking at the biology and thus as part of it, the neuroendocrinology of aggression.

Now starting off with the first case: how do hormones affect neurotransmitter release, neurotransmitter synthesis, neurotransmitter breakdown? They affect it in exactly the ways you can imagine, by the way of a hormone binding to receptors and some neurons. It could change the synthesis of a neurotransmitter, it could change the amount of some enzyme that degrades it in the synapse, and it could affect the amount of receptors for a neurotransmitter, all the usual suspects in terms of effects.

Let's look at an example of this, and a very interesting one. As shown in the first diagram here, we have a neuron up on top that releases a neurotransmitter that we talked about a bit in different context, but now having a very interesting function, the neurotransmitter dopamine. You remember back we heard about dopamine in one part of the brain having to do with sequential, logical thoughts, schizophrenia. Dopamine in another part of the brain has to do with fine-motor control, Parkinson's disease. Here we've got dopamine in another place in the brain having everything to do with pleasure and the anticipation of pleasure; this is the system worked on by cocaine and other euphorians. Dopamine in this part of the brain is about pleasure and about the anticipation of it, and, it turns out, all sorts of hormones affect this dopamine system.

One really interesting example, you remember from the last lecture I made reference to some steroid hormones released during stress. We come back to them now in more detail. These are called *glucocorticoids*. The human version known as cortisol, hydrocortisone, there's a rodent version related to it, structurally similar; these are hormones released during stress, and they get into the brain, where there are plenty of glucocorticoid receptors on these dopamine neurons, and glucocorticoids do two really interesting things there.

Short-term stress, talking about a couple of minutes maybe an hour or so, short-term stress, that is not too extreme, causes a transient rise in glucocorticoid levels, only for a certain amount of time and not too high; and under those circumstances, what those glucocorticoids do is really interesting, they increase the amount of dopamine coming out of those neurons. Hum. What is that about? What do we call short-term transient stress? We've seen this principle earlier in the LTP lecture. It's stimulation, and stimulation feels good. The right amount of stimulation and you secrete these stress hormones and among other things, they make you think more clearly, they enhance LTP; we know that already, and they increase the amount of dopamine coming out of these neurons. Hum. What's that about? We know what that's about. Stimulation feels stimulatory. It feels great, it feels wonderful. We pay to be stressed in the right way. We pay to see a good scary movie; we pay for a really great roller coaster, and what we see in those cases is a transient moderate rise in glucocorticoid levels it feels wonderful, addictively so in some cases, and this is the reason for it, it increases dopamine release. This is such a clear mechanism that a laboratory rat will actually work at pressing a lever over and over and over to get infused with just the right amount of glucocorticoids that maximizes dopamine release, so short-term stress feels wonderful by way of dopamine release.

Now the key thing here is short-term, moderate stress. Massive stress, no matter how short term it is, having your limbs twisted painfully are not going to lead to wondrous dopamine release, and I feel wonderful and alive and all of that. Likewise, no matter how moderate of a stressor, if it's really chronic, that's not going to feel great either. It's not by chance that roller coaster rides are not three weeks long. The transients, once you have glucocorticoids now being secreted long term, what we see in the bottom of this diagram, they do just the opposite, they deplete dopamine neurons of dopamine.

And what's that about? You begin to feel awful. Technical term we heard a few lectures back, an hedonia—hedonism, the pursuit of pleasure—an hedonia, the inability to feel pleasure, sustained stress triggers an hedonia, and this is the mechanism for it, depletion of dopamine. And there're lot and lots of reasons to think this is one mechanism linking chronic stress with the onset of clinical depression.

Okay, so we see here a way in which hormones in circulation can get into your brain and alter aspects of neurotransmitter trafficking. Now we look at another aspect. We've already seen an example of this, but let's look at this in more detail, back from that LTP lecture. LTP, you remember LTP, synaptic plasticity thanks to repeated experience, those glutamate systems passing a threshold and suddenly triggering a synapse to now be more excitatory for the rest of time. At the end of that lecture, we looked at some factors that

©2005 The Teaching Company Limited Partnership

modulate LTP. Lots of energy facilitates it, energy shortage disrupts it, alcohol disrupts it. And we saw that same dichotomy in there before as we just looked at. Short-term stress and glucocorticoids enhance LTP, and as we saw also, long-term glucocorticoids disrupt it. It's shown here in the diagram. On top we have our classical pattern of LTP, stimulate a neuron you get a little bit of your dendritic activation. Now stimulate it like crazy, over and over and over, and you get your LTP, your potentiated response.

What we see in the second case is prolonged glucocorticoid exposure, and you block that induction of LTP; and that is not a good thing. Now that's what's going on in the hippocampus. Meanwhile, next door in the amygdala, something very different is happening with glucocorticoids. You remember the amygdala—amygdala and fear, amygdala and anxiety, amygdala and aggression—as we will hear about. What glucocorticoids do there is just the opposite. Glucocorticoids and stress enhance LTP. Chronic stress makes the amygdala more excitable, and when do you see that? You see that with individuals with trauma disorders—post traumatic stress disorder. You do brain imaging on these folks and you flash up a scary image to anybody and you could show the amygdala lights up. In these individuals the amygdala lights up and stays on much longer. What traumatic experience does is often make the amygdala hyper excitable and literally what happens there is, the synapses undergo LTP, and glucocorticoids drive that affect.

So we see this interesting contrast in the hippocampus, short term, glucocorticoids enhance LTP; long term they disrupt it very dramatically. Meanwhile in the amygdala, chronic stress enhances LTP. Now put those pieces together and you get something very interesting going on there. Okay, massive sustained stressor comes along, and what is it doing? By way of glucocorticoids it's facilitating synaptic activity in the amygdale; it's disrupting synaptic activity in the hippocampus. What happens when you put those two pieces together? Hippocampus filing away conscious explicit memories, with enough of a stressor, your hippocampus is pretty much going offline. Meanwhile the amygdala sure is filing away the autonomic, the arousal aspects of the emergency of the trauma and what happens next time something like that comes along, the amygdala kicks into gear like crazy, and you find yourself by way of the hypothalamus and the autonomic nervous system, you find yourself with your heart racing and getting sweaty and all of that, and you haven't a clue why, because your hippocampus never filed away. Your amygdala surely remembers; your hippocampus doesn't. What have we got here?

A neuroscientist at New York University, Joel LeDoux, has put forth this model where this is somewhat of an explanation for free-floating anxiety, this sense of panic and you have no idea why. Now a question becomes, how can glucocorticoids, say in the hippocampus, do this business? Short term, they enhance LTP, short term they enhance dopamine release. Long term they do just the opposite. How does that work mechanistically? The trick was sorted out about a decade ago. There are two different classes of glucocorticoid receptors in those parts of the brain, one of which works really fast, one of which works slower. So we see there, this very interesting contrast between short-term stress and long-term stress and between what happens in one part of the brain and another.

Meanwhile, at the bottom of this diagram is another very interesting neuroendocrine interaction with LTP; estrogen turns out to enhance LTP in the hippocampus, and as shown here, we get our usual response; stimulate the neuron like crazy, and when there's estrogen onboard, you get a vast potentiation of the potentiation. Estrogen makes LTP occur more readily.

Now these same themes continue with the next level. We already know a whole big aspect of the story of neurons as these ten thousand dendritic spines and the axon terminals and, it turns out, this is a very dynamic, plastic process, to use the jargon for earlier lectures. And what you wind up seeing is different types of event experiences can cause neurons to grow more elaborate, dendritic branches, can cause them to shrivel up, and we see the exact same theme here. Chronic stress, chronic glucocorticoids and those dendritic branches in the hippocampus shrivel up. What's the consequence of that? That's straight out of the network lecture. What you're doing is you're disconnecting networks, and that's sure going to disrupt things. It's bad enough if you've got a synapse, which thanks to chronic stress, is not doing LTP very well anymore; it's even worse if you're ripping that synapse apart because your dendritic spines are shriveling up.

Chronic stress, chronic glucocorticoid exposure causes atrophy of these dendritic arbors, these dendritic branches throughout the hippocampus. And you guessed it, meanwhile next door in the amygdala, not only do glucocorticoids enhance LTP, glucocorticoids stimulate amygdala neurons to grow new branches. That's part of that story again about how this amygdala is this hyper excitable part of the brain with anxiety disorders, with post traumatic stress disorder.

Next, just like with the LTP story, along comes estrogen, and what estrogen does is stimulate hippocampal neurons to grow new processes. Ah ha, so you were sitting there and saying this generates all sorts of predictions. When estrogen levels are high, hormones, working in the hippocampus, estrogenic hormones cause hippocampal neurons to grow new processes. For synapses to work better does that mean that learning and memory gets better when estrogen levels are high? Absolutely, that is shown in humans and all sorts of circumstances naturally over the course of the ovulatory cycle. It is shown in humans where hormone levels are manipulated for any of a number of reasons. It's shown in laboratory rats.

Here's how amazing the effect is. In a laboratory rat, just as we heard in the very first lecture as with hamsters, various rodents, there's a four-day ovulatory cycle. Every four days estrogen goes up, goes down, ovulate, that sort of thing. It's a four-day cycle as opposed to the 28-day one in primates, humans, and what you've got there is this amazing phenomenon over the course of this very short cycle. The hippocampus in a female rat gets bigger for two days and then gets smaller and gets bigger; it's like this accordion getting bigger and stronger. As you grow new processes and retract them, memory, cognition, hippocampal dependent, learning and memory peak when estrogen levels are highest. It oscillates back and forth—absolutely remarkable.

Now what's even more remarkable is the next step. We've now gone through these hormones effecting neurotransmitter release, which is a very transient effect, affecting LTP, a much longer-lasting effect, affecting the actual structure of neurons. The next remarkable thing is some of these hormones can affect the life and death of these neurons in there, and this brings up some really interesting issues.

The first question being, what are you talking about—the birth of new neurons in the brain? Everybody who has taken introductory neuroscience anytime in the last thousand years, somewhere in the first week learns the exact same cliché, which is the brain is a non-dividing organ. Neurons do not divide. Once you're about year old, you've got the most neurons you are ever going to have for the rest of your life, all you can do is squander them with abuse of alcohol and staying up too late and who knows what else. You don't get any more neurons, so you better be careful with your brain.

Naturally this turns out to be totally wrong, and this is the biggest revolution in neuroscience in a long time. This is the hottest subject there is—the discovery of adult neurogenesis, that the adult brain can indeed make new neurons—and this is a recent finding that has swept through the field, except as one of those classic, great history-of-science stories, it's not such a recent finding. There were a couple of pioneers back in the 60s who saw the first evidence of this and were roundly ignored and often viewed as having their careers greatly impaired by them for coming up with this observation that everybody knew that was not true—the adult brain does not make new neurons; go back and check your experiment, this can't be true. And by the recent decade, it has become clear the adult brain makes new neurons. It makes it in two interesting places.

One is the olfactory system. That's not so interesting. You smell some really strong order, some toxic sort of smell, some very abrasive order, you kill a bunch of cells there, and it takes a couple of weeks to grow new neurons. That's not very exciting, except for the suggestion that hormones released during pregnancy, probably prolactin, causes you to grow a gazillion new neurons there in your olfactory system. What's that about? It's right in time to give birth. You've got this spanking new, renovated olfactory system perfect for imprinting on the smell of your child—very cool.

What that also probably explains is, if you spend all of pregnancy ripping out the scaffolding in your nose there and changing all the olfactory neurons and putting in new ones that are not quite working yet, no wonder stuff smells weird and your taste is all out of whack during pregnancy; that's one area where this occurs, and as we see there, a very powerful hormone effect on this.

Meanwhile, the one other place in the brain where there clearly is a lot of this adult neurogenesis is so interesting, it's just perfect. Where is it? You guessed it, in the hippocampus. And when does it occur? For exactly the logical reasons, the same exact circumstances you would pick, stimulating environment, learn something new, enriched setting, all sorts of aspects of voluntary exercise; and you stimulate neurogenesis there, and there're increasing reasons to believe that these new neurons actually get integrated into networks, function. That's very controversial at this point, but it's beginning to look as if that's the case.

So along come our hormones, and two effects that are right up there that are very clear at this point. What's the single biggest inhibitor of adult neurogenesis? You guess it, glucocorticoids. Have something stressful come along, and your hippocampus is not going to be making a whole lot of new neurons. Conversely, along comes estrogen, and not only are you enhancing LTP and growing new processes in the neurons already there, but that stimulates neurogenesis. Everyone is very interested these days to see how much that winds up explaining changes in cognition when your hormones are changing.

Now that glucocorticoid angle is very interesting because there's one additional step in that story. It looks as if under circumstances of truly massive amounts of stress, glucocorticoids can actually kill neurons in the hippocampus. Even better documented, lots of stress, lots of glucocorticoids can endanger hippocampal neurons, making it harder for those neurons to survive all sorts of insults. So what you wind up getting in the realm of glucocorticoids is, that these stress hormones can disrupt aspects of synaptic plasticity, can cause the neurons to retract their processes, can cause the neurons to fail to be born, inhibit adult neurogenesis and make the neurons more fragile in the face of all sorts of traumas, and maybe even as an extreme, might kill the neurons.

So you sit there and you say, uh oh, this is not a good thing. Does this mean prolonged stress? There's bad stuff in your hippocampus. There's beginning to be reasons to think that this story, mostly a laboratory rat story, begins to apply to the human brain. There are three circumstances in which this is relevant, and they're of increasingly bad news.

The first one is a fairly rare endocrine disorder called Cushing's disease. You get a tumor in some weird, unexpected place in the body and even more bizarrely, this tumor often in the lungs, of all places, secretes some hormones that stimulate glucocorticoid release. You get elevated glucocorticoid levels, all sorts of things go wrong.

In Cushing's disease, one of the things that happens though is you begin to get severe memory problems. It's in fact called Cushingoid dementia, and the first few brain imaging studies are now being done showing that people with Cushing's disease begin to get atrophy of their hippocampus. Their hippocampus shrinks, it seems to be only the hippocampus. The higher the glucocorticoid levels, the more shrinkage and the more memory problems.

Now how fast does this affect? The best guesses are it emerges over the course of a couple of years. Is this due to killing the neurons? Almost certainly not, because what the most recent studies are showing is, you go in and you correct the tumor and over the next year or so, the hippocampus comes back to normal size. What's that about? That's the flipside of what we've heard already. Lots of stress and glucocorticoids and those hippocampal neurons have their dendritic processes shrivel up. End of stress, end of glucocorticoid exposure, and very slowly they can regenerate.

The next model is worse news, simply for the number of people involved—people with a history of severe stress. People with PTSD, post traumatic stress disorder—combat vets, childhood abuse, it is known that they get memory problems. There is, by now, very clear literature showing a smaller hippocampal volume; the more severe the history of trauma, in some of the studies, the more shrinkage, the more memory problems. Is this reversible? Seemingly not, because these are people decades after Vietnam, decades after the child abuse, and the atrophy is still there.

Now, in that particular literature there is a wildly incendiary controversy right now built around the trauma, which caused the hippocampus to shrink, or are they coming into the trauma with the small hippocampus, setting them up for being more vulnerable to the PTSD; there's evidence for both at this point. The jury is still out.

The third syndrome is the most worrisome one, because it applies to merely 10%, 15%, 20% of us or so and it's one that's been floating around in a bunch of these lectures—major clinical depression, elevated glucocorticoids; you find that in about half of depressives. It is a classical psychiatric disease of sustained stress. We've already seen how sustained glucocorticoid exposure could give rise to the an hedonia, the dopamine depletion. It also could give rise to hippocampal damage. Does that occur? A handful of studies now showing big-time, long-term depresses, atrophy of the hippocampus, pretty much *only* in the hippocampus—the more severe the depression history, the more hippocampal atrophy, the more memory problems. This also appears to be a syndrome that does not reverse with time because you look at some of these folks years, decades after the depressions have gotten under control with medication, and the volume loss is still there. These are very disturbing studies.

There's also additional literature to worry about—people who take synthetic glucocorticoids, prednisone, dexamethasone. There's a suggestion that those taking very high doses long term get problems there as well. This is a very, very fertile area of research these days. The one thing that should be emphasized at this point is, if you are stressed like you're stuck in traffic jams every day or you're in a lousy relationship or you've got an abusive boss, there is zero evidence at this point to think that's rotting out your hippocampus. Do not panic, these are major league stressors, major league examples of glucocorticoid exposures. So don't panic too much there.

A final example here is of how hormones can affect the brain, and this is an enormously complex area built around the fact that a whole bunch of different hormones from very unlikely places can affect appetite. Now no surprise, this is a massively studied subject. Since our lack of control over appetite has something to do what is fast becoming the number-one killer in this country, metabolic syndrome related to adult-onset diabetes. How does your brain figure out when enough is enough? How does it figure out when it should make you feel hungry and go out foraging out in the grasslands or the supermarket? What it's doing is getting an enormous amount of endocrine information from the body. People used to think the easiest thing was it just measured, as shown in this diagram, how much glucose do you have in your bloodstream. Glucose levels go up, you stop feeling as hungry, glucose levels go down you start feeling real hungry. It makes perfect sense.

It turns out there's a whole orchestrated set of hormones that come from all sorts of unlikely places. Your pancreas, okay, that's not so unlikely; insulin, that makes sense, but hormones coming out of your gut, intestinal hormones? No one ever considered that getting into your circulation. Hormones come out of your liver, out of your muscles. Recognized in the last couple of years, muscles are endocrine glands; fat cells are endocrine glands. All sorts of hormones are secreted under those circumstances, which collectively, get into the bloodstream, and the part of your brain figuring out, are we still hungry, is still there and getting endocrine input from all these different hormonal systems that reflect something about your energy state—your metabolic state—ranging from, do you have a whole big lump of food distending the walls of your intestines, to how much fat you have stored away, and that regulates which hormones your fat cells make. And no surprise, this is a frantic area of research because if people can understand how some of these things can work, and can make some artificial version, some pharmacological imitators of these hormones, these may be important regulators of appetite, things of that sort.

Okay, so this has been a very quick tour of some different ways that hormones can affect the brain. The main point of that is, not only to teach these specific examples, but to get a very important point across, and this is one that's going to come back to haunt us in the aggressional lectures. Okay, aggression, we're going to think a lot about testosterone and why males, on the average, are more aggressive than females, on the average. And what's testosterone doing in the brain? It's going to be all over the places you would guess, the limbic system, the amygdale, like crazy, and then you get this temptation to start getting this very deterministic model of the world. Ah ha, hormones control aspects of the brain! Ah ha, hormones determine certain behaviors! Ah ha, as we will see down the line, the temptation to say, testosterone causes aggression. We will see that's not how testosterone works, and that's not how hormones work in the brain. They do not cause behaviors; they make pre-existing tendencies more or less capable of eliciting those behaviors.

This is a first example of us looking at function of the brain and the brain is not sitting there in vacuo, instead, hormones modulating how sensitive the brain is to the outside world. Thus, for example, if there is some environmental trigger that tends to cause aggression, pain, frustration—things of that sort. What you wind up seeing is testosterone lowers the threshold for pain to elicit aggression. Does testosterone cause aggression in and of itself? Not at all; this is a theme that runs through the endocrine literature. Hormones are no more master messengers than the brain is at controlling everything. The interaction between the two, as we will see over and over, is the interaction between the two in the context of the environment.

Now this brings us to a perfect point here to summarize because we've now pretty much completed our overview of the nervous system, complete with how the nervous system does not control the entire world all on its own, but is instead subject to hormonal control. Now that sets up perfectly for the coming dozen lectures or so, to see that we understand a bit about how the brain works and how it might produce behavior, what we now shift to, how things regulate the brain.

Today, this lecture, how hormones regulate the brain, and now beginning to look at how early experience does—how ecological factors regulate brain development, how the brain evolved, the evolutionary pressures that brought about this sort of brains that we have and of course, the intervening step in there, the evolutionary pressures which gave rise to certain patterns of genes which, note here, do not cause behaviors, but have an influence on what sort of behaviors occur. This is our segue now to begin to consider all of these factors that regulate brain development, brain evolution, brain function.

What we will switch to next on our time chart, is here comes the behavior out the very right end of it, under the control of the brain. Switching back to the very beginning, how do we think about the evolution of behavior? What we're saying there is how do we think about the evolution of the brain? How our brains have evolved with the structure, the functions that we've seen? How our brains have evolved to regulate behavior. So that's our next subject.

Lecture Ten
The Evolution of Behavior

Scope:

We all understand the evolutionary biology of how, for example, the giraffe evolved its long neck as an adaptive trait. This lecture introduces the idea that behavior and the brain that produces behavior have also evolved, sculpted toward adaptive features by natural selection. Then, the lecture provides an overview of the various ways in which species can maximize the number of copies of their genes passed on to the next generation through behavioral means.

Outline

I. The evolutionary biology taught in high school was built around certain key points that help to explain such phenomena as how giraffes evolved long necks.

   A. The first key point is the inheritance of traits across generations; that is, traits can be passed on from one generation to the next.

   B. The second key point is the variability in those heritable traits among individuals. In modern genetic molecular terms, mutations in genes can be passed from one generation to the next.

   C. The third key point is known as *differential fitness*; that is, some versions of those genetic variants are more adaptive, more fit, than others. (Figure 10a)

      1. Organisms with maladaptive mutations do not reproduce; they do not survive, and therefore, they do not pass on copies of their genes.

      2. Organisms having beneficial mutations, however, do reproduce; thus, the new version of a trait becomes more plentiful.

      3. Intrinsic to this key point is the debunking of a great urban legend of evolution, which is *survival* of the fittest. Instead, the key is *reproduction* of the fittest.

II. How did behavior evolve?

   A. The notion exists that behavior is sculpted by evolution, by the same forces of nature that influenced the length of our necks and the functioning of our hearts and kidneys.

   B. That notion leads, however, to the inflammatory issue of heritability of behavior: the issue of whether a certain behavior has a genetic component.

III. Building block #1 in considering the evolution of behavior is *individual selection*.

   A. The old notion of group selection, that is, the idea that animals behave "for the good of the species" and that behaviors are driven by ways to increase the likelihood of the species surviving and multiplying, has been proven wildly incorrect.

   B. Instead, by the early 1960s, the concept of individual selection was accepted.

   1. This idea proposed that evolution is not about animals behaving for the good of the species but, rather, behaving to optimize the number of copies of their own genes to pass on to the next generation.

   2. This idea brought about the oversimplified and somewhat erroneous notion of the *selfish gene*: the idea that a gene's purpose is to maximize one's own ability to reproduce and to pass on copies of one's own genes.

   3. Another way to illustrate this idea is a quote from an early evolutionist, Samuel Butler: "A chicken is just an egg's way of making another egg."

   C. A rather grim example of the logic of individual selection is competitive infanticide, as seen in a number of species, even those as endangered as the gorilla.

IV. Building block #2 in considering the evolution of behavior is *kin selection* (*inclusive fitness*).

   A. What does it mean to be related to someone? It means you share genes with that individual.

B. Kin selection is a way to help your relatives reproduce as much as they can—passing on copies of your genes by helping relatives.

C. Degrees of relatedness on a genetic level come into play here because we are "more related" to some individuals than others. For example, full siblings are closer genetically than half siblings; a parent is closer genetically to a child than is a grandparent. In short, the more steps away relatives are from one another, the fewer genes they share in common.

D. One of the implications of kin selection is an obsession with kinship. For the most part, data support the logic that we are cooperative with relatives as a function of how related they are to us; hence the quote of evolutionary geneticist J. B. S. Haldane: "I will lay down my life for two brothers or eight cousins."

E. Some examples of kin selection in the animal world include adelphic polyandry, food sharing in inbred species, and parent-offspring conflict.

    1. *Polyandry*, in which a single female mates with more than one male, occurs fairly rarely in the animal kingdom and among humans. However, when it does occur, it is often *adelphic polyandry*, in which the males are brothers.

    2. Many studies show that the degree of relatedness is an accurate predictor of how much one animal shares food with another.

    3. Parent-offspring conflict stems from the idea that whereas a parent wants to balance the survival of current offspring with that of future offspring, those current offspring want more care than the parent cares to offer. For example, conflict may occur between a mother baboon who wishes to wean her year-old offspring so that she can ovulate and possibly produce another, while that young baboon wants to continue nursing.

V. Building block #3 in considering the evolution of behavior is *reciprocal altruism.*

    A. This notion is based on the concept that many hands make the task light. Such cooperation ensures the distribution of risk- and food-sharing among hunters.

    B. Reciprocity is very common in all sorts of social species, even among nonrelatives.

    C. However, species that exhibit such patterns of cooperation must possess certain characteristics.

        1. Reciprocity will work only in a species with stable social groups.

        2. The species involved must live long enough to benefit from the cooperation.

        3. The members of the species must have enough social intelligence to recognize other members of their species.

    D. In games of reciprocal altruism, which we will discuss in Lecture Twelve, individuals will try to cheat whenever they can; thus, another requirement is vigilance against cheaters.

    E. Potential examples of reciprocal altruism include blood-sharing among vampire bats and coalitions among male baboons.

Further Reading:

For good introductions to evolution and the neurobiology of behavior:

D. Barash, *The Survival Game: How Game Theory Explains the Biology of Cooperation and Competition.*

A. Brown, *The Darwin Wars: The Scientific Battle for the Soul of Man.*

M. Ridley, *The Origins of Virtue: Human Instincts and the Evolution of Cooperation.*

For the most magisterial book on the subject:

E. O. Wilson, *Sociobiology: The New Synthesis, Twenty-fifth Anniversary Edition.*

Questions to Consider:

1. How has evolutionary thought shifted from an emphasis on groups to an emphasis on individuals?

2. What are the ways in which modern evolutionary thought is not merely about selection at the individual level?

Figure 10a

Differential Fitness

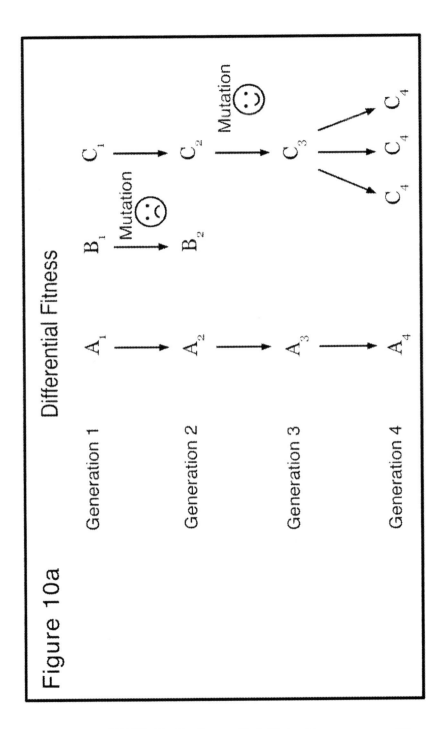

Lecture Ten—Transcript
The Evolution of Behavior

Hi there. I've just had my batteries changed, I feel wonderful and energized, and it is just in time because we're having a major shift now in this lecture. Okay, lets go back to that chart we began this whole course with, our big grand scheme for thinking about the biology behavior, and what we had was on the far right, the behavior is produced. And what we've just spent umpteen lectures on is looking at what's gone on a second before that, how did that brain, how did that nervous system produce that behavior? We've got a pretty good sense of it by now. We've got a feel for the basics of neurobiology from the level of a single neuron up to the level of whole parts of the nervous system. How the nervous system regulates the body and how the body in turn, by way of hormones can regulate the nervous system. We've got this bucket now well in place. And as you remember from the song and dance in the first lecture, another major goal of this course is to avoid thinking in terms of buckets, categories, to think that, okay, we've got neurons and neurobiology under our belt; that's all you need to do to explain the whole world. What we now devote much of the rest of the course to is seeing all of the other factors that give rise to how the brain functions.

As shown here, again on this diagram, what in the environment a second before made that brain have its responses that trigger that behavior to occur. As we had a first pass in the last lecture, what sort of hormone levels that hour, that day, maybe individual, more or less sensitive, to that environmental trigger which caused the brain to produce the behavior and so on. This is our strategy, working back over time.

What we are going to do in this lecture is transition to a detailed look at the first of those things that came beforehand that regulate how the brain regulates behavior, starting at the basic, starting at what, in lots of ways is, the central concept of all of biology. You cannot think of biology without thinking about the role of evolution. How has evolution, how has natural selection, given rise to the sort of fetal life, the sort of hormones, the sort of brain that has something to do with understanding our behaviors?

What we'll focus on in the next couple of lectures is basically the evolution of behavior. Now what is imbedded in that concept is that anytime you talk about evolution, evolution of behavior, evolution of kidney function, evolution of anything, what you're talking about is the evolution of genes that have something to do with those behaviors, that kidney function and so on. Following these lectures we will look at a very different aspect of the story, very molecular—how do genes get affected by evolution, on one hand, how do genes have something to do with the sort of brains we have?

So beginning all the way on the left side of this chart, how have the events of evolution and natural selective pressures over millennia, over millions of years, sculpted the sort of brains and behaviors that we have? Now, in introducing the subject of evolution, that's straightforward, we all know how evolution works; we all learned about it in ninth grade biology when we learned now come giraffes have long necks, and we all know the basic rules of evolution built around a couple of key points.

The first one is certain traits are heritable. Certain traits are passed on from one generation to the next; for example, the length of your neck. The second key point is that there is variation that can occur in how those traits are passed on, variation we now understand in modern genetic molecular terms; there could be mutations in genes passed on from one generation to the next. The third critical point is that there is then selection. Some of those genetic variants are more fit, are more adaptive than others, and those individuals leave more copies of their genes.

As shown in this chart, this is the basic sort of logic of evolution. You've got multiple generations of one pedigree here, passing on whatever trait is heritable, whatever trait has a genetic component. We see in pedigree B there is a mutation, a source of variability, and this happens to be a wildly maladaptive one and, as a result, by the second generation, B pedigree goes extinct; they don't reproduce, they don't survive, they don't pass on copies of their genes. Meanwhile, you can have a beneficial mutation, a beneficial source of variability, selection does its thing then, and as a result, this pedigree, this version of this trait becomes more plentiful. That's the basic building blocks of evolution. We understand all of that, and all you do now in the next couple of lectures is substitute how the giraffe evolved the long neck, and all of its adaptive features, to that. How we evolve certain behaviors. That's all there is to it.

The whole notion that the way behaviors occur is as much sculpted by evolution, by the forces of natural selection, as how our heart has evolved to pump blood and how necks or whatever are shaped and how our kidneys do whatever they do to retain water; ah, the same rules for behavior. Except there is one hell of an inflammatory concept tucked away in there—the notion of genes, of heritability, having anything to do with behavior. That is immensely controversial in certain quarters, and in other quarters that's taken as well, say, of course. It's perfectly obvious what we will be doing a lot in the coming lectures is wrestling with the issue of how do you tell if a certain behavior has a genetic component; how do you figure out, if ever, how much of a genetic component, and does that tell you anything about inevitability, genetic destiny—very, very rarely.

So we begin to think here about the evolution of behavior, and we all learned about how evolution applies to behavior. We all learned this thoroughly, back when we were kids or, only if you were the right generation, we all got taught our evolution biology by Marlin Perkins. Okay, remember Marlin Perkins; maybe you're not of the right age group, but Marlin Perkins was the host of this wildly successful show that I watched all throughout my childhood called "Wild Kingdom". They would cruise around and film animals in different interesting places, and he had this poor toddy of a guy named Jim, who always had the job of having to wrestle the giant boa constrictor and Marlin Perkins would sit off on the side there and tell us what was going on. Marlin Perkins taught all of us about evolutionary biology.

And here's the sort of scene where we all learn the subject. Okay, it's dawn in the savannah, and you're sitting there in East Africa, and there's some herd of a gazillion wildebeests; wildebeests travel around in these huge herds of million animals following the rains. The rains move across the plains of the Serengeti, and the wildebeests follow it around after that. What you wind up seeing is, the wildebeests are always trying to find the grass that's greener on the next field, and they head over there and mow it down and move on; and, you've got a problem here today, which is, you've got this huge herd of a gazillion wildebeests and there's this wonderful field over there just full of grass, and they can taste it already, and the one problem is, right in front of them there's a river. A river teaming with crocodiles that are just ready to shred one of these wildebeests as soon as it gets in the water, and they're all there and hemming and hawing in a panic and what are they going to do? Suddenly a Marlin Perkinesque solution emerges from the back of the crowd of the wildebeests. This elderly wildebeest fights its way up to the front, and he says I sacrifice myself for you *mein kinder* and throws itself into the river, and he's instantly ripped apart by the crocs; and while they're busy with him, everybody else tip toes around the other way, and why did he do that?

Why did he get killed and why did he fling himself in voluntarily; Marlin Perkins taught us the answer. Because animals behave for the good of the species, and this was the central concept that we all got hammered into our head. This was wildly incorrect. This got discredited in the early 60s, in scientific circles, and stuck around with Marin Perkins, and sticks around to this day in the general notion: behavior has evolved for the good of the species; but it has not at all. This old notion of what is termed a group selection argument—behaviors driven by ways to increase the likelihood of the species surviving and multiplying—makes no sense at all.

All you have to do to appreciate it is if you watch those wildebeests a little bit longer than Marlin and his film crew did, because something else was going on. You look at all these wildebeests, and they're all in a panic, and how are we going to get across the river and they're all milling there and suddenly up comes this elderly wildebeest to the front. Why is he up there? He did not push his way to the front, he got pushed up there. They said, "Yeah, get the old guy up to the front." He's the only one who couldn't, sort of, withstand it; he gets pushed to the front, and he gets pushed into the river. Volunteering? No way, he gets pushed in by everybody else and he gets done in at that point. There is no sacrificing himself for the good of the species. Evolution is not about evolving behaviors that optimize the survival of your species.

By the early 60s what got ushered in instead, was what is now, the central concept of the field, what is termed individual selection. Animals behave not for the good of the species; animals behave to optimize the number of copies of their own genes they pass on to the next generation. Evolution is not about survival of the fittest, evolution is not about optimizing the survival of your species, the good of your species; what evolution is about is passing on as many copies of your genes as possible into the next generation, and we will see some very important implications of this individual selection.

Now, in lots of ways, probably the best way to think about it, or the one that's most caught the public's imagination and one that is somewhat erroneous, is the notion of the selfish gene. The notion that your DNA—and we will see shortly what DNA is all about—but your DNA that makes up genes, what your genes are about is not helping the species to survive, but the purpose of your genes are to maximize your own ability to reproduce, to pass on copies of your genes.

A far better way of summarizing this was this wonderful quote by an early evolutionist late in the 19th century. A man named Samuel Butler, who came up with this great aphorism. He said sometimes a chicken is just an egg's way of making another egg, and that's a wonderful way of viewing it. A chicken is just an egg's way of making all of this behavior stuff, and all of this social interaction stuff, is just this epiphenomenon to get some mating, and to get a copy of the genes into the next generation. Sometimes an egg, in order to make another egg, produces this chicken with its behavior stuff. Sometimes behavior can be thought of as merely a way to optimize, to maximize the numbers of copies of genes that are passed on to a next generation, and this really has become the central concept in the field, in lots of ways. This notion of individual selection, animals do not behave to enhance the survival of their own species, they behave to maximize the number of copies of their own genes.

As we will see, this is not so straightforward, and it is not so selfish on either the gene level or the individual level. It has a whole lot of interesting elaborations, but this is the building block of the whole system, and what this winds up producing is an explanation for an awful lot of animal behavior. There are a lot of versions of behaviors that don't make any sense until you frame it as individual selection rather than group selection.

Let me give you one very grim example of this from the world of animal behavior as shown in this diagram. This is one that makes no sense at all, as wildly pathologic if you were schooled in Marlin Perkins, and makes wonderful, horrible, tragic sense if instead you think in terms of contemporary evolutionary biology. Okay, you have a species, gorillas for example, or lions or langer monkeys, a whole bunch of species that show this pattern. What you have is a stable, social group made up of a whole bunch of females and their kids and, typically, just one male in there. What is typically called a harem structure, but is just as readily called a gigolo structure. You've got a single male doing all the mating with the females. Where are all the other males? They are off in the periphery, bachelors herds is what it's called in some species, a bunch of these males off by themselves or individual isolate males, and what do they want out of life? Of course, to take over this harem, to boot out the guy who's resident! And every now and them one of them manages to do that at some big, aggressive interaction, and boots out the previous guy.

Okay, what happens at that point? What happens was first discovered in the 1970s, and people still imbued with sort of a group selection notion, simply did not have any idea how to make sense of this. This new male comes in, becomes the resident male in this all-female group and what does he proceed to do? He goes about systematically killing all of the infants he can in the group. This floored people. Number one, because there was a dominant notion at the time that, Oh my gosh, you're not aggressive to infants; infants have all sorts of features that inhibit aggression, and here you are having infanticide going on. This was totally bizarre until you begin to see a pattern. This was at first identified by a primatologist named Sarah Hrdy, studying this first in langer monkeys—a type of monkey found in India—seeing there's a pattern to it. A whole bunch of species now where you see this infanticide, and they all have the same populational structure. It's shown here on this chart.

Okay, suppose the female gives birth to an infant? What does she proceed to do as a good monkey mother. She nurses the kid, often for a year or for two years, a long nursing period. As is a feature of nursing, thanks to stuff we learned in the endocrine lecture, you boost up levels of prolactin; prolactinal, a hormone having to do with nursing, and prolactin inhibits ovulation. While the female is nursing for that period, she doesn't ovulate.

Shortly after giving birth, the resident male, the male who fathered that infant gets dumped by a new male who comes in and takes over, and the key point is, on the average, the length of time this new male is going to be in this group before he himself gets dumped, the average length of time is shorter than the amount of time that female is going to be nursing. What does this wind up meaning? This means is this guy spent the last six years going down to the gym and working out and he's finally all buffed up and tosses out this guy and he's going to be long gone and forgotten by the time this female is ovulating again. And what is the horrible, selfish, evolutionary logic for this guy to do at this point, as shown on the bottom, come in, and after he becomes the new resident male, kill the infant. The female stops nursing, ovulates a short time afterward and he fathers the next kid, and this grim piece of evolutionary logic, that makes no sense if you're Marlin Perkins, makes perfect sense from the standpoint of this male's trying to maximize the number of copies of his genes in the next generation. There're a dozen species now that have this social structure, as shown on top, where you wind up seeing this infanticide.

Now naturally the female is sitting there, and she's just as interested in evolutionary biology. She's not thrilled about losing her copy of genes into the next generation. What you wind up seeing is females resist like crazy trying to protect their kids. This all makes perfect sense from the individual selection level, and the greatest way of seeing just how much this is the case, how much animals do not behave for the good of the species, is that you see exactly this pattern of competitive infanticide in one of the most endangered species on this planet, a species that's probably going to be extinct within our lifetime, the gorilla.

The gorilla has this social structure, and they are close to extinction for a bunch of reasons—habitat degradation, warfare around there, hunting of them, killing of them for trophies—all sorts of tragic things, and on top of that, every now and then a male gorilla kills the infants there. Animals do not behave for the good of the species. So we have this first building block of modern evolutionary biology: sometime a chicken is an egg's way of making another egg.

Now we shift to the second building block, and it has to do with a very important notion, which is you are related to relatives. What does that mean in biological terms? You share genes with that individual. The whole notion of this second level, kin selection, inclusive fitness, is the simple idea that sometimes the best way to pass on copies of your genes, as many as possible to the next generation, is to reproduce as much as you can. Sometimes, the best way is to help your relatives reproduce as much as they can, and this notion of kin selection begins to describe a central feature of every social species out there, including us, which is an obsession with kinship. Who do you cooperate with, who do you fight with? Who's "them", who's "us"—built around lines of relativeness?

Now the important thing to appreciate here, and shown in this diagram that is so complex that you have to pay no attention to it, is some relatives you're more related to than others. A full sibling you're more related to than a half sibling, a parent more than a grandparent, and that could be stated mathematically—what percentage of your genes you share in common—and ignoring the details to the numbers, the simple fact is the more steps away a relative is, the fewer genes you share in common.

The logic and, for most part, the data support this logic. What you wind up seeing in this kin selection notion is that you will be more cooperative with relatives as a function of how related they are to you, the more genes you have in common. And what kin selection, inclusive fitness, is about is sometimes the best way to pass on a copy of your genes is to reproduce once. Sometimes, if you have a full sibling who shares half of your genes with you, if you help that sibling in a way that allows them to reproduce twice, to hand on two sets of copies of their genes, mathematically, one set of yours or two copies of someone sharing half of your genes with you, it's identical from a genetic standpoint. Either of those behaviors have the exact same impact on evolution.

And this was wonderfully summarized in a quote of this geneticist, [John Burdon Sanderson] Haldane, early in the last century, who apparently was sitting in a bar once, trying to describe this concept to the other guys there and did some calculations and said, I would gladly lay down my life for two brothers or eight cousins. Mathematically that's exactly how it works. What this begins to explain is this wild obsession with relatedness, with kinship, with relatives throughout the animal world. You get some social anthropologist, and he spends his entire career trying to understand the kinship terms of this one tribe in the Upper Volta River of West Africa. This is nothing compared to animal obsession. With patterns of relatedness, ·because it completely determines who you cooperate with and who you don't.

A couple of examples: there're lots and lots of species out there, and there're lots of human cultures that have polygamy—where one male will mate with multiple females, where one male will pass on copies of his genes with multiple females. Far rarer in the animal world, and in the human world of human cultures, is polyandry—a single female with more than one male. Among animals it's found occasionally in lions; it's found in marmoset monkeys in the new world, and there're a bunch of bird species. Among humans there are a number of cultures in Asia, particularly in Tibet and Nepal where you see this pattern, and in every single one of these cases, it's a very special type of polyandry. It's something called *adelphic polyandry*. Who are the two males? Who are the resident males in this lion pride? Who are the two males who are the husbands of this woman in Nepal? They're brothers. They're brothers! That's the pattern you always see. This adelphic polyandry makes perfect sense. Why should these two perfect stranger males cooperate in a marriage? They're not perfect stranger males, they're sharing 50% of their genes. This is exactly the sort of thing that's predicted by kin selection.

Some more examples of how to think about kin selection, and this one is so obvious it doesn't even count as an interesting observation until you think about it. You've got some food, you're some baboon, you're some whatever, and you share it with someone. Who do you share it with? Food sharing, in all sorts of species, goes along lines of relatedness. Well yes, obviously mothers feed their kids in all sorts of species; but even things like, you've got a kill, who do you allow to feed off of it as well? In lots of studies you see the degree of relatedness is a wonderful predictor of how much you share food with another individual.

More examples of this: this is one that you wind up seeing, which will seem terribly familiar to anyone who's a parent; this goes by the official jargon in the evolutionary biology world, of parent-offspring conflict—basically built around the following math, which seems bizarre to apply in almost economic terms to thinking about stuff, but you are this mother, you are this primate mother, you are this bird mother, you are this any mother, and you've got this offspring. You're doing your evolutionary calculations, and this brings up an important point, no animal is sitting there consciously aware of any of these principles; these have evolved and been sculpted by evolution. When I see what this bird wants to do, what this brine shrimp maximizes at that point, there's no conscious volition there, this has simply been sculpted by evolution.

So you're that parent sitting there and what you want is, of course, your offspring to survive. Are you willing to give up ever bit of your future reproduction potential to help this offspring survive as well as possible? Absolutely not, you are balancing the survival of this offspring with that of future individuals. In contrast, what does the kid want? They want all of the investment, and that's actually the economic term that's used by these folks; they want all of the investment possible. What you wind up getting is conflict between the kid wanting more care from the parent than the parent offers. Where is this seen in animals—when mothers try to wean their kids; you get parent-offspring conflict. You look at some baboons, and there will be a mother walking along, and there's the year-old kid she's trying to wean who's literally throwing a tantrum, and she's pushing the kid off—stop nursing, stop nursing, because once I stop nursing, I'm going to ovulate. Again, not a conscious strategy, this is what you wind up seeing. However, suppose it's an older female who's not likely to have more kids, you don't see the weaning battles then. You see this selection between generations, in a sense, in a battle for energetic investment. This makes no sense until you think about it in evolutionary terms.

Okay, so that gives us the second building block. First one, forget Marlin Perkins' group selection, individual selection; sometimes a chicken is an egg's way of making another egg. Second level, kin selection; sometimes the best way to pass on copies of your genes are to help relatives to do—I'll lay down my life for two brothers or eight cousins. The third final building block is what's termed reciprocal altruism.

Even amongst non-relatives, sometimes it makes sense to cooperate, and we've got all these great proverbs for it—many hands make the task light; or who knows what amongst hunters, for example; if you all share the kill, that distributes the risk each time when it's something that has a low success rate. Reciprocity is a very, very common thing in all sorts of social species, even among non-relatives. What you then have are all sorts of rules for when does reciprocity evolve. This is subject we will return to in some subsequent lectures, in tremendous detail, because this turns out to be a whole field that mathematicians work on—all sorts of mathematics of games; and this is a formal term in economics and math, of game theory, when do you cooperate, when do you fail to?—very complex mathematical models. So when do you wind up seeing this? We will look at this again in far more detail, but as a first pass, what sort of species do you see reciprocal altruism, patterns of cooperation among non-relatives?

Well it makes sense. First off, you have to have a social species. You're not going to see it in orangutans for example, where these are very solitary animals, nomadic in many cases; you've got to have a social species. Next thing you have to have is not only social groups, but stable social groups. It makes no sense at all to lend you the money to buy a hamburger today, and you'll pay me back next Tuesday; if our social group is fluid enough, then I'm going to be long gone in the next valley by then.

What else do you need? You need to have species that are long lived enough that you're actually going to be alive next Tuesday. Then you need to have a certain amount of social intelligence so you could recognize who the individual is. You remember who it is, you have to see this in more socially complex, more cognitively complex species. And remember that finding we had in the earlier lecture, across a hundred-fifty different primate species, the bigger the social group, the bigger the relative size of your cortex; and the argument has been, that has evolution sculpting our brains to keep track of social economics, social commerce, social interactions with reciprocity being a big piece of it.

The final thing that you see, and this is the basis of all of the mathematics, all of the game theory, the final thing that goes on in these games of reciprocal altruism is, you want to cheat whenever you can, and you want to be incredibly vigilant against other individuals who might cheat against you. We will see all sorts of mechanisms, ways in which this is involved in animal species.

What we see here though, are just a very few quick examples of how this reciprocity works. One example is with vampire bats, which despite their horrible reputation are actually warm, affectionate mothers who go out each night to get blood from cows typically, who fill up a throat sack full of blood and come back to their nest where they discord the blood, discord it to feed babies—discord it to feed babies, not just their babies, all the females feed each other's babies, even among non-relatives. This is a system of reciprocity.

How can you prove it? You engineer experimentally a way in which one of the females fails to do that, and her kids are not fed the next time—reciprocal altruism in this sense.

Other versions of this: you find amongst baboons, males will occasionally form coalitions, partnerships, backing them up in fights, and you look across years in a social group, and the coalitions are not random who forms the coalitions with each other, partners who have reciprocated in previous settings, it's a structure like that as well.

Another example, this is a great one that you see with stickleback fish, of all things, a species you can study this complex mathematics of behavior and cooperation in, turns out sticklebacks have been evolved to do this as well. Okay, you make a stickleback fish believe it is being threatened by another stickleback fish—these are not some of the smarter animals around—so it's done quite easily. You stick a mirror up on the side of the fish tank, and before you know it the fish is bashing its lips against the glass there to keep this other guy away and doing this whole defensive thing.

Now make it think that it has a partner. Take a second mirror and put it perpendicular to this fish so it's glancing over there; it sees its reflection, it sees its reflection of its reflection, it's sitting there saying, okay, I don't know who this guy is, but he's really backing me up here, because there's a second fish attacking and every time I attack this guy, he's there, I can really trust this guy, great I got a partner here.

Now make the fish he's being cheated against. Take the mirror and angle it a little bit so that the reflection is set back a few inches and he's sitting there saying, that son of a bitch, I can't believe that guy, here I am blistering my lips protecting our territory and sure he's pretending to go forward, but I see him hanging back a few inches there. He believes he's being cheated against, and the next time, he fails to attack his image. He is reciprocating against the cheating there. Cheat against me, and the next time I will cheat back. We will see complex mathematical models, which have often been exactly the ones that animals have evolved.

So with this first pass at thinking about the evolution of biology, we have moved past the notion that animals behave for the good of the species—survival of the fittest instead, individual selection, maximizing the numbers of copies of your genes. Kin selection, sometimes the best way to do that is to help relatives pass on copies of theirs. Reciprocal altruism, sometimes one of the best ways to do it is to set up systems of cooperation, even with non-relatives, but with very strict rules of vigilance against cheating.

This whole structure, and this is essentially the structure of modern evolutionary biology, thinking about behavior is highly explanatory. What we will now do, in subsequent lectures, is look at more detailed examples of this, beginning to frame it, how does all of this sculpt the bio-evolution to maximize this or that passing on your genes. How does this translate into the sort of brains we have evolved?

Lecture Eleven
The Evolution of Behavior—Some Examples

Scope:

Lecture Ten introduced the principles of the evolution of behavior. This lecture will explore how that conceptual framework helps explain, and even predict, social behavior in numerous species that vary in how aggressive they are, whether they are monogamous or polygamous, whether males participate in childcare, and so on. Throughout this lecture, links will be made to previous lectures to establish how the evolution of these behaviors translates into the neurobiology of these behaviors.

Outline

I. How can we successfully predict the social structure of an entire species (tournament versus pair-bonding) based on just one fact? Figure 11a lists the cluster of traits common to each type of species.

II. Imprinted genes and intersexual competition also play roles in evolutionary biology. (Figure 11b)

    A. Mendel theorized that a gene is a gene, regardless of which parent you inherited it from.

    B. Imprinted genes—genes that produce different outcomes in offspring depending on which parent they come from—have been discovered to be an exception to the laws of Mendelian heredity. For example, during fetal life, some male-derived genes push for more fetal growth, while female-derived genes favor the opposite.

    C. The logic of imprinted genesis is that in polygamous species, males and females have different investments in any given pregnancy. The male would like the female to expend all her energy raising his offspring, even at the expense of her ability to reproduce again. The female, however, wishes to balance her investment in her current offspring with her investment in her future reproductive potential.

D. The effects of imprinted genes in the brain on behavior after birth provide a marked contrast, with male-derived genes favoring more feeding and growth and female-derived genes the opposite, trying to slow the growth down.

E. Generally, polygamous species have large numbers of imprinted genes, whereas monogamous species have virtually none.

F. Humans are neither a classic pair-bonding species nor a classic tournament species; we are somewhere in between. Therefore, we have some imprinted genes.

III. Fruit flies and sperm competition also illustrate this intersexual competition.

A. Numerous male fruit flies mate with the female; thus, sperm from many different males is inside the female fruit fly's body.

B. The male sperm release toxins in an effort to kill its competitors' sperm. These toxins are damaging to the female fruit fly.

C. However, female fruit flies' bodies have evolved so that they now produce detoxifying defenses.

IV. Kin-based defense systems also illustrate the notion of kin selection.

A. When female vervet monkey A attacks female vervet monkey B for "no reason," the underlying cause for the attack can actually be that the child of monkey B had attacked the child of monkey A.

B. Patterns of aggression that closely follow the lines of kin selection are another way to ensure that the maximum number of copies of one's genes is passed on to the next generation.

Further Reading:

For good introductions to evolution and the neurobiology of behavior:

D. Barash, *The Survival Game: How Game Theory Explains the Biology of Cooperation and Competition.*

A. Brown, *The Darwin Wars: The Scientific Battle for the Soul of Man*.

M. Ridley, *The Origins of Virtue: Human Instincts and the Evolution of Cooperation*.

For the most magisterial book on the subject:

E. O. Wilson, *Sociobiology: The New Synthesis, Twenty-fifth Anniversary Edition*.

Questions to Consider:

1. How can an infant be viewed as the outcome of intersexual evolutionary competition?

2. What is the role of kinship in making sense of the evolution of behavior?

Figure 11a

Tournament	Pair Bond
Polygamous	Monogamous
No Paternalism	High Paternalism
Low ♂ Pickiness	High ♂ Pickiness
High ♂♂ Aggressor, Variance	Low ♂♂ Aggressor, Variance
High Sexual Dimorphism	Low Sexual Dimorphism
♀ Seek Good Sperm	♀ Seek Good Fathers
No Cuckoldry	Cuckoldry

Figure 11b

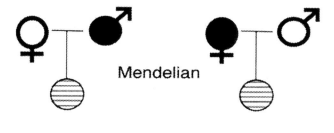

Mendelian

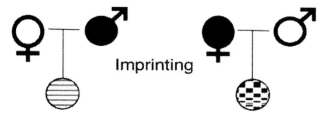

Imprinting

Lecture Eleven—Transcript
The Evolution of Behavior—Some Examples

We are back again and now beginning to look at more detailed versions of the evolution of behavior. Now, what have we accomplished so far? We have spent a huge number of lectures looking at how the nervous system works, starting at the level of a single neuron and our usual story of expansion there, up to the level now of vast parts of your nervous system regulating behavior, how your body changes during behavior, and what we shifted to in the last lecture was the start of a next long stretch of these, namely looking at the things that modify how your nervous system works.

What we started off with in the last lecture, the long view, if you're talking about nervous systems, genes for behavior, genes for how the nervous system works, what you are implicitly talking about thus is where do those gene come from, how do they evolve? Looking at the evolution of behavior, what we saw in the last lecture was the same sort of Darwinian logic that tells you where the giraffe got its long neck from, tells you how we've evolved, the optimal, the evolutionarily optimal set of behaviors.

What we first did was trash the Marlin Perkins world of animal behavior for the good of the species, and instead, shifted to the three building blocks of contemporary evolutionary biology. Number one, not for the good of the species, individual selection passing on as many copies of your genes as possible, a chicken is an egg's way of making another egg. Then the next layer, sometimes the way you maximize those copies of genes, helping relatives, kin selection, I'll gladly lay down my life for two brothers or eight cousins. Then the third layer is that world of reciprocal altruism with very strict rules with which that happens.

Now what we're going to do in this lecture is focus in more detail on a couple of ways in which these principles apply, in this lecture, focusing mostly on those first two levels, individual selection and kin selection. Now the first example is a fabulous one, simply because of how explanatory it is, how predictive it is.

Okay, you are off on an expedition in your local neighborhood park and unexpectedly you discover a new species of primates in there. You know next to nothing about it except as follows. You observe the animal whose skull I'm holding here and what you see, the only single fact you get about this animal before it tragically falls out of tree and you wind up with its skull is this was a female. She was nursing a baby.

Meanwhile, equally tragically, over in the next tree you have another individual—here the skull I am holding—and what you have in this case is, you know this guy was a male. You saw he had a penis, so you got the sexes sorted out and what you'll see is in this individual, who you know is a male, versus this individual, adult female, what you see is a vast difference in what the skulls look like. The male skull is far bigger than the female, amid the brain case, the area that the brain fits into, being exactly the same size, but the rest of the skull much bigger, long muzzle and most strikingly, this huge whopping great pair of sharp canines in the male, and meanwhile in the female, these very tiny canines. You know nothing more than these two facts that I've just outlined, what the gender is of each of these animals, and the fact that the male has these huge conspicuous canines and the female doesn't.

Now using the principles we went over in the last lecture, you could now generate an astonishing number of absolutely correct predictions about the social structure of this species, how these animals go about their mating, all sorts of other personal facts about them—aspects of their diseases that they get, all of this is predictable, simply from those two facts. What we look at here is a classic sort of way of dichotomizing different species, summarized in this diagram, that are broadly called tournament species versus pair bonding species. What we'll see shortly is this is a classic tournament species, these skulls that I was just holding up.

Okay, so we start off working here working through the logic derived from the rules we had in the last lecture, individual selection, kin selection, etc., and we go and we look at typical features of tournament versus pair-bonded species. What you see first off is a pair-bonded species which by definition is pair bonded, they pair for life, are monogamous; they're monogamous. Male and female mate with each other, and they stay together for the rest of their lives. In contrast, what you see in the tournament species is marked dramatic polygamy, males mating with a lot of different females, females often mating with many different males during one cycle.

Okay, so what's the next trait that goes in that? How about paternalization? How much care, how much energy does the male expend raising the offspring? In this case, what you see is a dramatic difference. Over in those pair-bonded, monogamous beasts you see very high levels of male paternalism. In fact in a lot of the species the males invest as many calories, as much energy, in taking care of kids as the female does. Meanwhile, across the great divide into these tournament species, you've got a male who has just mated with 47 different females; 23 of them give birth, and he is not doing any male paternalism stuff. He's got too many kids in that case, very low levels or non-existent levels of paternalism.

Next, this allows us through perfect logic to predict the next set of traits about this species. How picky are these males as to who they mate with? Over at the tournament end, this guy, if he mates with a female and she gives birth, what are his obligations after? They're zero, this guy is gone; he could be a nomadic male and never see that female again. He will, to be a little bit crude, he will mate with anybody who's willing to mate with him. You see here, very low male pickiness. Meanwhile, in that pair bonded, that monogamous species, if their rule is you get her pregnant and she gives birth, you take care of the kids for the rest of time. Males are suddenly far more picky whom they mate with. Is she healthy, does she appear to be a competent parent and things of that sort. What you get there is very high levels in male pickiness.

Next we move on to two traits, which wind up being really interesting, how much aggression is there in each of these species? What you can frame that as, given the individual selection stuff on the part of the male, is how much is he willing to aggress with another male in order to get a chance to mate with a female? What you see in the tournament species is tremendous amounts of male-male aggression. Because of another trait, tremendous variance, and the reproductive success of males, you get some tournament species where 95% of the reproducing is accounted for 4%/5% of the males and in those species, enormous amounts of male-male aggression. Meanwhile, over in the monogamous species, what you see is very low levels of male aggression, and pretty much each male fathers a couple of kids, but not huge numbers, none of this variance of 95% accounted for—low levels of aggression.

Then you shift to another trait. Okay, monogamous species, what you've got there is a male who what he mostly wants to be in this world from an evolutionary standpoint is almost as competent a parent as the female is. That's what he's being selected for, parental competence, and what you wind up seeing there is, he winds up having a body that's as close to the female as you can get, not a dramatic difference in appearance. Meanwhile over in those tournament species, what are males being selected for physically? Not to have the same physical attributes of a female where if only he could also lactate, what he's being selected for instead is male-male combat, and suddenly you have this world of these huge neon antlers and these huge canines and things of that sort and very conspicuous displays. You have big physical differences between males and females. Jargon in the field, *dimorphism*—morphism, morphology, the shape of the body—high degrees of sexual dimorphism. Males and females look real different and males selected for their combat ability, as opposed to those monogamous species with virtually non-existent sexual dimorphism; males and females are being selected for having very similar bodies.

Okay, meanwhile, what do the females want out of their evolutionary perspective on the whole field? What you're looking for if you're a female is what do you want out of the guy you're going to mate with? In the case of tournament species, what are you going to get from this guy? You are going to get competent parental care, is he going to be the greatest granddad somewhere down ... no, you're never going to see this guy again after you mate with him. What's being selected for there is the only thing you're getting out of this guy, which is good sperm containing good genes. All you look for there are markers of good genetic attributes, big, healthy, muscular, etc. Meanwhile over in those monogamous species, what do females select for—guys who are competent parents, and suddenly you have these species where how does a male court a female? He goes and gets her a worm and delivers it to her if you're a monogamous bird species trying to show, look, I'm capable of doing this sort of stuff.

Finally, a very insidious bit of behavior that only makes sense from this world of sort of evolution of behavior; you're in one of those monogamous species and you're a female, the rule is, if the guy has gotten you pregnant and you've given birth, he is going to take care of that kid for the rest of time until the child is independent. What would be a viciously, genetically logical thing for you to do? To abandon your nest, and as you'll see, it's mostly birds that show this trait. Abandon your nest and go get pregnant again with somebody else, because this guy is going to stay back at home and raise your kids. That's the, in effect, wiring of the system, and you are not increasing the number of copies of your genes in future generations, blah, blah. Cuckoldry, I believe is the formal term for it, you see cuckoldry in monogamous species; you never see it in polygamists, in tournament species because if you abandon your kids, nobody else is going to raise them—dramatic differences.

And what we see with the skulls I was displaying before, a classic tournament species, you get these huge whopping canines in the males and you don't get them in the females. That's telling you, you are not selecting males in this species for being able to be competent mothers, just like the females do, classic tournament species. In this case, a case, a savannah baboon, and you see lots of other species showing those traits. This is the world of peacocks, male peacocks with their peacockery or whatever the term is with huge caloric investment on these secondary sexual displays, where they look utterly different from the females, in mandrel baboons where the males have this dramatic facial coloration which you don't see in the females. The males have twice the body size.

Meanwhile, over at the monogamous end, you've got about 600 species of birds and your wondrous poetic swans pining away for each other when their mate dies, or in the primate world, a whole bunch of South American monkeys like Marmoset monkeys, where you look at a picture of them, and it's a pair but you can't even tell which is which sex, and you look at them, and you look at who's taking care of the kids, and you can't tell which sex. What we see here is not just a whole bunch of explanations, but enormous predictive power. Again, go out there and know only one of those facts from this chart about some new species and you've got a pretty good chance of predicting lots of the rest of the world.

Okay, so that's one example. Another example now, and this one is a world of really bizarre genetics that was only recently recognized. To appreciate it, we need to spend 30 seconds on Mendel, one of those people we heard about in high school biology and probably have not thought about since, from whom we learned our Mendelian rules, and one of the rules that was critical to it is as follows.

Okay, here we have on this chart one of those classic pedigree diagrams you've got your female and your male, by the classic symbols they have mated and produced this individual. One of the rules of Mendelian genetics, Mendelian heredity, is it doesn't matter which parent you get which genes from. As shown here, the open circle represents one genetic trait, the closed one a different version, and it happens in this case, when the two of them mate, it combines this trait. Here we see switched around, now it's the female who has the closed circle trait, the male who has the open one and it produces the same exact outcome; it doesn't matter which parent you get which version of a gene from. That is classic Mendelian science.

What people have discovered in the last couple of decades are a whole bunch of genes that violate that rule. Where, in this case, we start off with the open circle-closed circle trait, producing this outcome in the offspring, and in this diagram, now we flip the traits—which parent applies which—and, depending on which parent it comes from, you get a completely different profile on the offspring. Mendel rolls over in his grave, this is not common in genetics. Best estimates are less than 1% of genes show this trait, but these are genes that are now called imprinted genes.

People were highly puzzled what these were about, what they were good for, until it finally became clear. Actually a geneticist at Harvard named David Haig has been the person really giving the clarifying insights, and it comes straight out of our kin selection, inclusive selection, individual selection, our evolutionary principles.

Okay, where do you see imprinted genes? First bit of a clue, you see it in polygamous species, tournament species. Back to the logic of that, the male mates with a female and he is out of there, he is gone, no tuition payments, nothing on his part, he is out there, once again, he mates with a female once and he never sees her again, and she raises the kids.

This thus brings up a term, which originally is a term that economists would use, and is something used all the time by evolutionary biologists—a very hard-nosed term, but a very appropriate one— here is dramatically different energetic investment in the kids on the part of this male and female. What is the male investing in this case? All the energy it took to produce a couple of sperm and deliver them. And what's the female investing? She's raising the kids all on her own. Now to take that very hard nosed, unsentimental evolutionary view, the male has a choice, and again, back to the last lecture, the male is not sitting there reading a textbook of evolutionary biology; the male wants, the male chooses, is just a shorthand for saying, over the course of a gazillion years, males who have this trait have been selected for, passed on more copies of their genes, blah, blah, we know that's just a convenient shorthand.

Okay, what does this male want out of this female? What does this male want out of the reproductive biology of this female? He's got a choice, once again, not the real term, but it is evolved that what is to his advantage that the female invest a gazillion tons of calories on raising his off spring, so that the kid is that much more likely to grow up and survive and pass on copies of some of his genes, etc. What if in the female, expending that much energy, completely wipes out her ability to mate again, to reproduce again in the future? He could care less. Not only could he care less, he thinks that's a great thing, because she's going to be mating with some other guy in the future.

Meanwhile, what is her evolutionary logic? Yes, she wants this kid to survive, but if she is a female who's not old enough to having this as probably her last kid, she wants to balance the number of calories she invests in this offspring with her "future" reproductive potential. Suddenly you have a conflict, an inter sexual conflict between the number of kids that the male wants with this female, he's never going to see her again, so he would love for her to invest a ton in his offspring, even at the cost of her future reproductive success, whereas she wants to do a much more balanced strategy, and it turns out that explains the imprinted genes. Because every single imprinted gene where it differs which parent it's coming from, shows the same trait. Every version of the gene derived from the male pushes for more fetal growth, and every version of the gene from the female does exactly the opposite, tries to slow it down, and this turns out to be a pattern in every single one of these genes.

Let me give you one example. In this case, the gene derived from the male is for a growth factor. A protein, which among other things, stimulates the fetus to grow faster—to pull more energy out of the mother for growth—and what you see from the female, the equivalently matched, imprinted gene is a receptor for that growth factor. Back to our obligatory cliché, our key going into the lock, and it's evolved in this evolutionary arms race that the more potent of a growth factor males have been selected for, the more dosey and lousy of a receptor the females have been selected for to try to offset this, and this keeps up on being this trade off you see there, and this is an arms race. This is an arms race that makes no sense at all with swans that have the exact same interest in each mating being for a certain degree of success with balancing it against the future. This is what you see in these polygamous species instead, where all the male wants out of this female is for her to invest a ton of calories in this offspring, and all the female wants is instead, a much more balance strategy. These are all these imprinted genes.

So that very example, if you see a mutant version of one of these, where it winds up producing a disease, a mutant, an overactive version for example, of a gene derived from a female and a fertilized egg doesn't implant in the uterus. This gene is so anti-fetal growth, that in an extreme version, it slows it down to that extent. Meanwhile, a mutated version in a male that drives her over activity, what this produces is this wild placental cancer of overgrowth and you see here, this totally bizarre world of non-Mendelian genes which only make sense in the context that males and females, even when they're mating, do not have identical genetic interests in the off spring, and let alone, in each other—very interesting.

So okay, what about us humans? Us humans going about our mating business and trying to make sense of us in the world of evolutionary biology, do we have any of these imprinted genes? Yes indeed. We have a whole bunch of them. Not as many as in some other species, and there's a whole bunch of rodent species where they're very, very similar except for the sort of features we heard about before. Some species, they're polygamous; some they're monogamous, and all the pair bonded versus tournament species with traits going along with them and what you find is, the polygamous version has huge numbers of imprinted genes, and the monogamous version has like no imprinted genes, and then you look at us and we've got some imprinted genes.

Thus you have that disturbing issue, wait a second—we're the species that came up with Paul Newman and Joanne Woodward; we're the species unto death and 'til whatever does us apart and 50-year wedding anniversaries—what are we doing with imprinted genes? What you've got there is this answer; we are not a classic pair-bonded species. We're not a classic polygamous tournament species either. In terms of human measures of sexual dimorphism, males are somewhat bigger than females, on the average, even males have somewhat bigger canines than human females do, but not in the typical tournament range. What we are officially, by sort of the jargon of the field of evolutionary biology, what we are is a tragically confused species. We're not quite monogamous, we're not quite polygamous, and this is great because this accounts for about 90% of our great literature; but nonetheless, evolutionarily we're somewhere in between and we've got some of these imprinted genes.

Now more examples of this inter-sexual, genetic competition comes through in other realms. You see one of these in drosophila, fruit flies, and people who study these guys, again have all of these things to make sense of, which make no sense except in the realm of evolutionary biology, our principles of passing on as many copies of your genes. Once again, polygamous species where a whole bunch of males will mate with the same female and what you've got then is this bizarre world where inside the female's body now are sperm from different males. This is going to sound grotesquely science fiction, but there has been tremendous evolutionary selection for sperm competition, for the sperm from these different males to compete with each other and leaving on as many copies of their genes as they want. If we've gone through this sort of formal exercise in saying a baboon is not sitting there, what he wants his genes to do, that certainly applies to the sperm sitting there; they are not wanting their genes to do something.

But what has evolved instead is competition between sperm of different males. It turns out in drosophila, these male sperm, release toxins that kill the other guys' sperm. There's inter-male competition releasing these toxins, and you sit there and you say this is totally bizarre, and you see an even more bizarre trait which is, okay, you're the female and you've got all these toxic sperm drooling stuff all over inside you, punching it out with each other, are these toxins good for you? Absolutely not, and what you see is, over the course of a lifetime being exposed to these toxins, if the female had not evolved something, these toxins would be wiping out her health after a while. Isn't the male concerned about her? No, absolutely not, that same tournament species logic again. He's never going to see this female again and if in the process he secretes enough toxins that she's never going to be able to reproduce again, but in the process this time, he wipes out the other guys' sperm, this is great, exactly what he wants to do. Males have evolved increasingly toxic sperm over time and some really interesting experiments have shown over the course of about 40 generations of fruit flies, males can increase the toxicity of their sperm.

Meanwhile, arms race, star wars defense, what are the females evolving? Things to detoxify the male toxins and once again, you have this ratcheting up in about 40 generations; females can evolve the means to detoxify the male sperm. What is going on here? This is incredibly depressing. You have drosophila trying to poison their lovers. You've got humans with their genes punching it out in the woman's uterus while they're picking out the crib for the new baby. What is all of this sort of competition about? It makes no sense at all if we're sitting there, back with Marlin Perkins, doing our behaviors for the good of the species, genetic traits even, the way sperm function and uteri, if that's the correct plural, function have evolved. What does this sort of tell us? It tells us once again, these principles of individual selection passing on copies of genes make a whole lot of sense.

Just in the same way as from the last lecture, we have that stupendously depressing scenario of a highly endangered species like the mountain gorilla where this occasional infanticide, how could they do that for the good of the species? They're not doing it for the good of the species but for individual selection. These realms, where these behaviors, and as we saw, even the physiology of how a uterus wall thickens or how a sperm functions, makes no sense outside of these principles. Okay, so these examples, tournament versus pair-bonded species, imprinted genes, sperm competition, make sense relying very heavily on that first principle of ours, individual selection, passing on as many copies of your genes as possible.

The last example here is imbedded instead, much more in that kin selection notion. Okay, so you're watching some species of primate for example, and you notice here, as shown in the diagram, there are two individuals. There's this Female A and Female B and you're sitting there watching them and suddenly, for some bizarre reason, Female A totally attacks Female B, chasing her, biting her, that sort of thing, and you sit there and say what kind of world is this one now with random acts of violence, random acts of aggression? A suddenly beats up B—what's going on here? It is only after you study these animals for awhile that you begin to find out that something much more interesting has occurred.

You look at Female A and you look at Female B, and you go back in your records. You're keeping your behavioral observations, and you will have noticed, three seconds before, or even as much as three hours before, kid of B, B's child and A's child, B's child has beaten up on A's child. B's child has bullied A's child and taken its lunch box and his bus change or whatever they're doing out in the savannah there, and suddenly an hour later, A attacks B. What do you have? You've got the McCoys and the, whoever it was, or half a Shakespearean play; you've got retribution within families. Why is A attacking B, because A knows all about kin selection or doesn't know about, but has been selected for. What you see there are patterns of aggression go very heavily along lines of inter pedigree, and this makes no sense at all until you understand this whole notion that sometimes the way to maximize the number of copies of your genes you're passing onto the next generation is taking care of relatives.

And we're back to that same realm; the female will defend her off spring against an infanticidal male, very rarely to the death, but certainly to one extent; and, again, it's that same evolutionary balancing between wanting to maximize your genes, the present kid, and nursing future ones. None of this makes sense to Marlin Perkins. All of this makes sense from the standpoint of evolution as this wind tunnel that sculpts not only optimal necks in giraffe and optimal kidneys to retain water for some dessert rodent, but optimal behaviors as well.

Okay, so this marches us through some examples here. We're applying these principles of individual selection and kin selection, and basically, this is really depressing stuff—the amount of selection for competition, competition down to the level of sperm trying to kill each other. What we've got here is nature, bloody and tooth and claw, and this seems really demoralizing; and the truism that all the evolutionary biologists bring up at this point is, there is a difference between "is" and "ought to be". What ought to be in a world of pure benevolence and peaceable kingdoms and John Lennon singing "Imagine"; and that sort of thing is, nonetheless, not what biology has selected for. You get this picture of evolutionary sculpting of huge amounts of aggression and competition and that sort of thing.

Now just as you're about to decide this is all inevitable, we come back to that third piece of our grand scheme, that reciprocal altruism stuff. Out of there comes a whole world not selecting for aggression and competition and stabbing the other guy's back and abandoning your nest and cuckoldry and things like that. There we see a whole world of evolutionary selection for cooperation, for altruism, for all sorts of things that counterbalance this, and that will be the subject of our next lecture.

Lecture Twelve
Cooperation, Competition, and Neuroeconomics

Scope:

This lecture first considers a special topic in the evolution of behavior, namely, the balance between competitive and cooperative behaviors among members of the same species. The formal analysis of such behavior, called *game theory*, is introduced and framed in both the context of the evolution of such strategizing and the sort of brains that can accomplish such strategizing. The lecture finishes this section on evolution with a brief consideration of the issues that are unique to making sense of the evolution of human social behavior and its underlying neurobiology.

Outline

I. One of the three building blocks of evolutionary biology is reciprocal altruism or cooperation, which was covered in Lecture Ten.

  A. Cooperation is evolutionarily desirable, improving conditions in many settings.

  B. The bigger advantage is gained, however, when the other individual cooperates while you cheat. However, if you both cheat, the outcome can be really bad.

  C. Thus, the question arises: When do you cooperate and when do you cheat?

  D. This question is at the heart of a relatively new field called *game theory*, which originated in the area of economics.

II. Game theory applications to evolutionary biology are manifested in a game called the *Prisoner's Dilemma*. (Figure 12a)

  A. Its basic design is one of cooperation or defection: Successfully cheating is more rewarding than mutually cooperating, which is more rewarding than no one cooperating, which is more rewarding than cooperating with a cheater.

B. Economist Robert Axelrod's famous round-robin Prisoner's Dilemma tournament led to the emergence of the tit-for-tat strategy: losing the battles but winning the war by being cooperative, clear, retributive, and forgiving.

C. The vulnerability of the tit-for-tat strategy lies in signal errors, in other words, if communication between two sides is unclear.

D. Forgiving tit-for-tat is a derived strategy that comes about when a mistake in communication is introduced into the system. After the wrong signal is given, a few rounds of cheating ensue, then one player "forgives," and cooperation is reestablished.

III. Establishing cooperation in such games as the Prisoner's Dilemma can prove challenging.

    A. The problem exists of the disadvantage for the first player to make an altruistic gesture; that player will always be one step behind.

    B. One solution is kin selection in isolated, inbred populations. (Figure 12b)

        1. A small group that has become separated from a greater group tends to inbreed, with members becoming more related to each other; in this way, cooperation begins, initially driven mostly by kin selection.

        2. When that small group, called the *founder population*, later rejoins the main population, that nucleus of cooperators influences the rest of the population to cooperate.

    C. Another solution lies in repeated interactions with the same player and the shadow of the future. In this case, players realize that, although cheating may offer a short-term advantage, it is better to cooperate in view of future rounds because the tit-for-tat strategy is about losing battles but winning the war.

    D. Another variable to consider is open-book play and reputation; that is, the ability for players to see what another's strategy has been in other games.

E. Still another variable is the interspersing of multiple games, in which the level of cooperation in one game can influence the level of cooperation in another, resulting in an equilibrium state of cooperation in both games. (Figure 12c)

F. Punishment is another great impetus for cooperation.

    1. Cooperation emerges when punishment is allowed in single-round, closed-book games.

    2. Cooperation also flourishes when there is the potential for "altruistic punishment." That is, A does something bad to B, and C, as a disinterested outsider, punishes A for doing so.

    3. Taken one step further, secondary punishment is introduced, wherein both cheaters and anyone who knowingly fails to punish a cheater are punished. Honor codes at military schools and universities engender cooperation through the threat of such secondary punishment.

G. Choice as to whom to play with out of a pool of potential partners enables players to select for cooperation.

H. Choice as to whether you play or not is another option.

IV. Other games in the repertoire of game theory include Chicken, the Ultimatum Game, and the Battle of the Sexes.

V. Intrinsic to all this behavior in games is something obvious to just about anyone: Humans do not always make rational economic choices; we are not rational in reciprocal altruistic interactions.

VI. Studying the evolution of reciprocity has culminated in the development of the field of neuroeconomics: imaging the brain during game playing and decision making. Some classic findings have come about from this imaging.

A. The outcome in a Prisoner's Dilemma game that is revealed through brain imaging to be the most powerful stimulus of the dopamine-releasing pleasure pathway is a surprise, to some, at least: cooperation between both players.

B. In another scenario, when a choice must be made between a cheap, fast payoff and a much greater reward later, the frontal cortex, which plays a central role in gratification postponement and resistance of the temptation of a quick, small payoff, is shown to be more activated.

C. The Runaway Trolley quandary in philosophy is another classic problem.

    1. You have two choices to save lives on a runaway trolley that is racing down a track about to hit and kill five people: Either you can pull a lever that will divert the trolley to another track where it will kill only one person *or* you can push one large person onto the track and that will stop the trolley before it hits the five people. With either choice, you will kill one person to save five.

    2. We tend to make completely different decisions depending on the emotional salience of how a problem is presented. In this quandary, most people choose to pull the lever.

    3. When a person is contemplating pulling the lever, the frontal cortex activates. But when the person is contemplating pushing someone off the trolley to his death, the limbic system activates. Cortical versus limbic activation is identified, depending on the emotionality with which a problem is framed.

Further Reading:

For good introductions to evolution and the neurobiology of behavior:

D. Barash, *The Survival Game: How Game Theory Explains the Biology of Cooperation and Competition*.

A. Brown, *The Darwin Wars: The Scientific Battle for the Soul of Man*.

M. Ridley, *The Origins of Virtue: Human Instincts and the Evolution of Cooperation*.

For the most magisterial book on the subject:

E. O. Wilson, *Sociobiology: The New Synthesis, Twenty-fifth Anniversary Edition*.

Questions to Consider:

1. How can it be that cooperators in the Prisoner's Dilemma lose each battle with cheaters but win the war?

2. What are the circumstances that bias toward the emergence of cooperation?

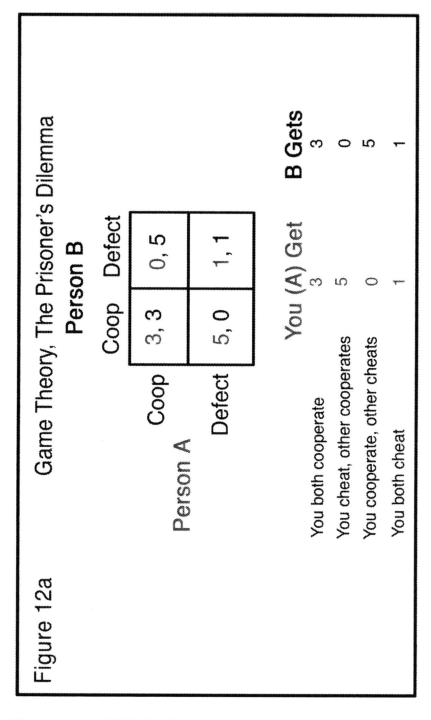

Figure 12a

Game Theory, The Prisoner's Dilemma

Person B

	Coop	Defect
Coop	3, 3	0, 5
Defect	5, 0	1, 1

Person A

	You (A) Get	B Gets
You both cooperate	3	3
You cheat, other cooperates	5	0
You cooperate, other cheats	0	5
You both cheat	1	1

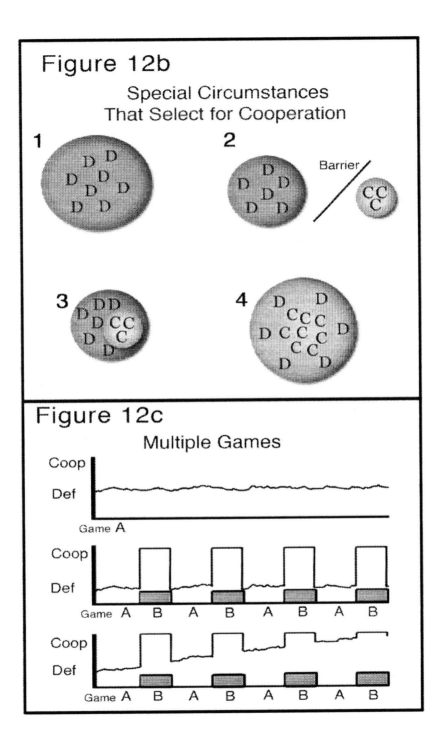

Lecture Twelve—Transcript
Cooperation, Competition, and Neuroeconomics

Welcome back, and all things considered, I'm shocked you're back again to hear more of this after how depressing the last lecture was. In fact, the only way I can still be here is I just took a very warm, soothing, bubble bath, and I assume you took the same.

Last lecture was incredibly depressing. All I did was tell you that the modern viewpoint of evolutionary biology just selects for competition and *National Enquirer* headlines; that fruit fly poisons lover and nature is just bloody and tooth and claw. Where we pick up with today is the fact that that's absolutely not the case. The same principles of evolutionary biology, which in some circumstances select for the vicious logic of competition and aggression, in other settings selects for the equally inevitable, equally sort of evolutionarily, logical aspects of cooperation, and what you see in those cases is that it makes just as much sense.

Okay, back two lectures ago, to our introduction to the building blocks of this whole field—individual selection, kin selection and our big third one was the notion of reciprocal altruism. That is, many hands make the task light; cooperation makes things better in lots of settings. With this idea suddenly you have a world where in particular circumstances it makes sense to cooperate with another individual, not out of kin selection. This could even be an individual not related to you, but in certain circumstances, cooperation is an evolutionarily desirable thing. It now helps everybody to be cooperating.

What you then have is the issue of when do you get cooperation? When does cooperation evolve simply because there are great advantages to it? But what we also saw, briefly touched on two lectures ago, is what is even better than cooperating with the other individual is having them cooperate while you cheat against them. This is selection for when do you cooperate? When do you cheat? When do you watch out particularly for the other individual cheating? What we also heard were some of the features that predict in what species you will see reciprocal altruistic systems. You've got to be smart. You've got to be social. You've got to have stable enough social groups that you could actually interact with the same individual over and over. Okay, those are logical requirements.

But then you get into this much more subtle realm—given that you're in a species where cooperation makes sense now and then—this very straightforward, horribly difficult-to-answer evolutionary question, "When is it adaptive to cooperate and when is it adaptive to cheat?," and here's where, a quarter century ago, evolutionary biologists suddenly let into their fold the most unlikely people on earth, economists and mathematicians, because what these people have often thought about within an economic realm is when it is adaptive, when it is financially to your advantages to cooperate or not. It turned out there was a whole realm derived by mathematicians beginning in the 1950s looking at this very complex math of when you cooperate and when you don't.

And this is a whole field called game theory. One of the main figures in it, straight out of *A Beautiful Mind* in the movies, was John Nash, the economist. This was a whole realm of economics, and suddenly it became clear to both the economists and the evolutionary biologists that this was a realm ripe for the same concepts of game theory applied to these issues of evolution of sociology. When does it make sense to cooperate and when not? Very quickly the poster child for game theory applications to evolutionary biology became this one game, and again the word "game" is being used in this sense in a very precise mathematical sort of setting; and this game is called the prisoner's dilemma. You cannot get three steps into the world of game theory without stumbling into the prisoner's dilemma. This is the set piece of the whole field.

Okay, here's the scenario, the imaginary scenario. There're two prisoners and they're attempting to escape; they both get caught and each one is being interrogated separately. It's not clear whether you should hold out and not tattle on the other person or if they're doing that already to you and what the punishments are. When, in that setting, do you cooperate and when do you not?

Formally the way this is described in a chart here is, you're looking at the two individuals, Person A and Person B, and each has the issue of do they cooperate or do they defect? Those are the terms used, cooperate versus defection, and the way the game is set up, there are very clear outcomes. Suppose both of you cooperate. You get three arbitrary brownie points in the math of this, and the other individual gets three as well. That's the payoff for cooperation. In contrast, you have a setting, where the other individual cooperates, and you cheat, you tattle on him. What's the outcome? You get five points, and he gets zero. Conversely in a setting where you cooperate and he cheats, you get zero, and he gets five. Or finally, if you both cheat on each other, you each only get one point.

So suddenly you have this realm where a pretty good outcome is for both to cooperate. A fabulous outcome is for the other person to cooperate and you to cheat; and the really depressing outcome is the reverse. Nonetheless, both of you cheating against each other is not a very great outcome either. Thus you get this math of when do you cooperate and when do you not.

Onto the scene, around 1980, steps this economist, a man named Robert Axelrod, who revolutionized the field with a very, very simple thing that he did. He set up a computer program that essentially did the prisoner's dilemma and could do it over and over and over again. And he wrote to all sorts of his buddies, some of whom were economists or political scientists or mathematicians or sociologists, and to each one of them he explained the prisoner's dilemma game and said, "Do me a favor; write back and tell me how you would play the game. What would be your strategy of when you cooperate and when you don't?" Some people sent back strategies where they always cheat or they always cooperate, or they do X number of times this, or they could do contingent programs if the person does this, my opponent, then I do that, otherwise I do this. He programmed each of these strategies, plunked them into the computer and ran them against each other for a gazillion generations. The use of this term here, as we will see, is probably not a random metaphor, but he begins to describe something about evolution. He ran these different programs against each other for lots and lots of computer generations, and over and over out popped this one strategy, which out-competed the others.

This was one supplied by a mathematician named Anatol Rapoport who's become this legendary figure in the field for having tossed in this program. You would think okay, what's the winning one going to be? Will it be some incredibly complex program? Of course, that is how the made-for-TV movie is supposed to go at this point, but instead, it turns out to be the wondrously simple strategy which was called "tit-for-tat." You start off cooperating. You start off taking the program of the stance of not cheating. The simple rule is, as long as your opponent keeps cooperating, you keep cooperating. If they cheat against you once, the next round you cheat back. If they continue to cheat, you continue to cheat against them, but if they go back to cooperating, you do as well—tit-for-tat—whatever they did in the previous round you do in the next one. It turned out, that tit-for-tat out competed all the other strategies. To use the evolutionary metaphor here, which is not irrelevant, tit-for-tat drove all the other strategies into extinction. It out competed all of them.

This was a landmark observation. Number one, you could use a computer to come up with a mathematically optimal behavior, and the fact that on a certain level the tit for tat strategy is kind of nice. It's nice; it's cooperative. Nonetheless, it punishes if you mess up, if you cheat against it. Amid punishing you, it's also forgiving; you go back to cooperating, and it does as well. It's perfectly straightforward. What we saw was there's a bunch of species whose patterns of social cooperation, of reciprocal altruism, match in lots of ways a tit-for-tat strategy. This was the ideal strategy in these games. What people soon realized was, there's vulnerability in the tit-for-tat strategy.

You're sitting there and saying well why should tit-for-tat win? If tit-for-tat plays against someone who cheats all the time, the very first round that individual gets more points than you. Then they cheat for the rest of the time, and as a result, you cheat for the rest of the time, and every other round has equal outcomes. Tit-for-tat is always going to lose against a strategy that cheats all the time. Why should tit-for-tat come out ahead?

The reason why is every time the cheaters interact with each other, they get hardly any points, and every time tit-for-tat interacts with another tit-for-tat, they start getting tons of points. The jargon that's always used in the field to describe this is, tit-for-tat always loses the battle but wins the war. In the long run, the cooperative strategy comes out as long as tit-for-tat can find somebody else who cooperates, and we'll see just how non-trivial that issue is.

The individual interaction may be disadvantageous, but in the long run, the cooperators out compete the cheaters with each other, but there is this one drawback, which is, what if there's a mistake? What if there's a signal error? What if the communication between the two sides is not so hot? What if somebody playing tit-for-tat inadvertently giving off a cooperation signal has somehow messed up in the wires, and instead, the opponent believes they just cheated. What if there was a signal error? That individual following the tit-for-tat strategy will cheat the next time. At which point you say what's the deal? We had this great thing going, and you cheat back and you tit-for-tat back and forth the rest of time. The tit-for-tat strategy is vulnerable to a signal error.

That was exactly what was encompassed in some thriller in the early 60s that I remember reading as a kid. They were doomsday scenarios of the United States against the Soviet Union, where there was a mistake, somebody's little fuse burned out or who knows what, and one side launched a nuclear attack on the other by accident—by accident; we didn't mean to, a signal error. At the end of the book, the only logical tit-for-tat response was to have to do it back to them. Tit-or-tat strategies are vulnerable to mistakes in the system.

Thus what you get is a derived strategy which turns out to out compete tit-for-tat as soon as you introduce the possibility of a mistake in the system, and this one is called "forgiving tit for tat." You go a certain number of rounds of this horrible back and forth, seesawing and attacking each other, and just because of the possibility there was a mistake, the rule with that one is, after a certain number of rounds, you forgive them, and that can reestablish cooperation.

Depending on the circumstance, how likely it is for an error to occur? You can have different strategies of how many rounds you need to go before forgiveness. Except there's a vulnerability to forgiving tit-for-tat, which is, if the other side has evolved a defense against that strategy, they can exploit you like crazy. They can exploit your mathematical tendency to forgive. What you see most adaptively is to start off with a pure tit-for-tat strategy, and only after umpteen rounds of the opponent proving that you can trust them; you switch over to a forgiving tit-for-tat. What is this? This is you starting to deal with somebody, a new person you're doing business with or whatever, and you've got to go a certain number of rounds before you begin to give them the benefit of the doubt. This is a mathematic variant on this.

Okay, this is all great, but the big challenge in the field, is what I blithely passed over before, tit-for-tat loses any interaction with the cheater. But as long as tit-for-tat cooperates with other tit-for-tats, they're going to lose individual battles, but win the war. Where's the other tit for tat player coming from? You start off with a world in which everybody is a cheater. There is no reciprocal altruism, and if you could only get a bunch of cooperators cooperating with each other, you're going to out-compete those folks. But what is clear is there's no mechanism to start it off with. Whoever is the first one who says, "I am the social slime mold and I've read all about Robert Axelrod, and we need a world in which we cooperate, so I'm going to make the first move," is one step behind in this game for the rest of the time and all the other slime molds snicker derisively at him.

The big challenge in the field is to understand what the circumstances are that jump start cooperation. Once it's established, that's great, but what is it that gets it going? That has been a huge issue in the field ever since; trying to understand the special circumstances that select for cooperation to begin to emerge.

Now one of the models for this is as follows, and this is one that is very familiar to evolutionary biologists. You get some population and, as shown in the chart here, it's some big old population of nothing but defectors. There is no reciprocal altruism yet. Then you get one of the things that happen often over the course of time in some species. Some land bridge comes up or some mountain collapses or something floods or whatever. You get a small subset of the population isolated by itself; isolated from the rest of the general population. The term that you have here is this is a *bio-geographic island*. You've got this little subset of population there. You have what is called founder population. Some barrier has come up, and they're separated.

Now what happens to a little population off by itself? It gets a little bit inbred. Inbreeding goes on and the second you start having some degree of inbreeding, the second these guys in this isolated population tend to be more related to each other than any given two individuals in the main population, suddenly we are transitioning back to the world of kin selection. Suddenly it is a world where you could begin to get cooperation emerging, not out of this abstract tit-for-tat, mathematics of dealing with perfect strangers, but you begin to get cooperation among relatives. You begin to select for that sort of thing.

And then, as is often the case, over time the barrier comes down. The migratory herd of whatever that cut you off from whomever for the last 30 generations—whatever it is that happens—the founder population rejoins the general one, and you've got this little nucleus of cooperators. What we saw from the math of tit-for-tat, of forgiving tit-for-tat, any variant on that is, they are going to out-compete all the defectors surrounding them, and over time, they are now selecting for the emergence of cooperation. So that's one model where this could come from, the founder population.

There are other circumstances. Now the way prisoner's dilemma was set up initially was you had only one interaction; you had only one round of strategy against another individual. That's not how the social world works. You're some elephant and you're going to be hanging out with other elephants for three quarters of a century. You're going to be having repeated interactions. This is the reality of any sort of cohesive social group. What happens is you begin to have these games played out not over one round but repeated rounds with the same individual in many cases, and what you simply begin to get is the possibility of somebody getting back at you. If you're a cheater, they're going to be far less cooperative the next round. You begin to have, and the term in the field is "a shadow the future". They are beginning to think, "Okay, I need to be a little bit more reasonable of a game player here because I'm going to be seeing this individual again in the next round," and really there's this short-term advantage to cheating right now, but in the long run, it's going to be better to cooperate as soon as you set up these games so that there's multiple rounds with the same individual. You begin to select for cooperation.

Let's look at the next variable. Suppose you're only playing one round with this individual, and then you go onto somebody else. But now what you've got is the next somebody, when they sit down to play you, they can look up what your strategy was in previous rounds. Does this person tend to cheat, or does this person tend to cooperate? And what we've now introduced is the very technical, mathematical concept of you come in there with a reputation. And as soon as you design games so that you enter with a reputation, you select for cooperation.

Now comes the next variable. Very few species sit there and only have one type of interaction with a member of their social group; in other words, with only a single type of game theory going on. Instead, the reality is, there are multiple games. Do you hunt cooperatively? Do you defend cooperative—things of that sort. The second you introduce the possibility of multiple games, things become more complex.

Okay, suppose here, in this diagram, we have a first example. We've got Game A. Some sort of prisoner's dilemma game, whatever, and it just happens that this is in a population where there's little reason to select for cooperation, and there's nothing but defect. There's no reciprocal altruism. Now you have two games going on. You switch between Game A and Game B. Suppose Game A continues to present no incentive for cooperation, whereas Game B presents an enormous incentive. You switch back and forth between the two: defection; nothing but defection in Game A; suddenly switching to cooperation in Game B. You go back and forth, back and forth.

What you wind up seeing is you begin to get in a sense, a trickle over from game B into game A. As time goes on, the level of cooperation begins to rise in Game A, and what you wind up ultimately getting is a fixation. You reach an equilibrium state of cooperation in both of the games. What you have in these mathematical models, and out in the real world as well, when you're dealing with multiple games, is that if there's one that very dominantly establishes a reciprocal trusting relationship, what you begin to select for is the same in other circumstances.

Other things that select for cooperation in this mathematical world, which makes sense the second you begin to think in terms of real life is, if you have the opportunity to punish somebody who cheats; to be willing to give up a couple of points of your own to take points away from them. What's the everyday equivalent of it? We are willing to expend some of our points, tax dollars, to fund things like police forces, criminal justice systems, things of that sort. The notion of punishment for cheating in a game theory setting selects for cooperation where you could punish the individual who's played against you—"shadow of the future"—or you could do what's called altruistic punishment; you punish somebody else in another game who is cheating in that setting. The second you introduce that, you select dramatically for what you get there, lots of cooperation.

You can take this one step further in a realm familiar to people who grew up in military academies. You introduce what's called secondary punishment. Not only can you punish somebody who cheats, but you can punish somebody who fails to punish a cheater. You can get somebody in trouble not only for an Honor Code violation in your military academy, but for failing to report somebody else, and that selects like crazy.

What the studies also show is another bit of mathematics that makes sense in real life. You select for cooperation real quickly when you begin to get to choose who you play with from a pool of potential partners—ah ha!—and as soon as you have the option of whether or not to even play.

Look at these traits. What winds up selecting for cooperation? It is multiple rounds of interactions with the same individual. Open-book play is the term that establishes a reputation—multiple games, the possibility of punishing anyone swho violates. What is this a picture of? This is traditional human society. This is a group of 60—100, gathered who've known each other for years. This is exactly the circumstances that humans have spent 99% of their evolutionary history in, small groups that know each other. Look at how more and more of us are living instead, in large anonymous urban populations. And those are precisely the settings that select against reciprocal altruism.

Now this whole approach to game theory is far more complex than that, and there are other games out there. It is not just the prisoner's dilemma, and they have all sorts of wonderful, colorful terms such as chicken game, which is the other person driving the car really fast, and who's going to swerve first. There's a whole mathematics with a different payoff structure than in prisoner's dilemma. Then there's the ultimatum game, battle of the sexes. All of these are just mathematical versions of different relationships to bring cooperation and defection, and in each case, there are patterns of optimal outcomes.

What you have running underneath the surface here is a truism that has run through branches of economics for a long time—which is, humans are perfectly rational, economic machines, and animals can't possibly do that. What we see here is—thanks to, once again, the wind tunnel of evolutionary selection—sculpting optimal patterns. You can get the same rational outcomes of social behavior in other species as well, selected for.

What we'll see in a couple of minutes is that we and the other animal species are not so rational in our reciprocal altruistic interactions. Where people have gotten insight into that is with what is the trendiest, hottest new version of thinking about the evolution of reciprocity. It is what is now called neuroeconomics. It is the whole notion of studying the brain; brain imaging of people while they are going through process of playing one of these game theory games. They put somebody in a brain imager and there will be some little computer console where they can press the "cooperate" button or the "defect" button and imaging what parts of the brain are having increases in metabolism while they're playing.

One of the first versions of this, a wondrous study, looked at people playing the grandparent of all game theory games, playing prisoner's dilemma. It looked at metabolic activity, excitement, activation, in different parts of the brain. And what they discovered was something real interesting. Remember back a gazillion lectures ago, dopamine, a neurotransmitter of pleasure and of reward and anticipation? When do those dopamine pathways activate? By all logic of humans as mindless gleaming machines of rational economic choice, when should those dopamine pleasure pathways light up? When the opponent has cooperated and you've cheated against them, you've gotten five points, they've gotten zero? That's not when the dopamine pathways lit up in this study; they became their most active when both of them were cooperating. Isn't that interesting? This part of the brain doing something wildly, economically irrational, getting most pleased in a metaphorical sense, with cooperation and not with cheating. Isn't that interesting?

Another version of this, another one that comes out is looking at the brain basis of resisting temptation. Now how can we frame this temptation? What we saw in prisoner's dilemma is there is this temptation to cheat right now. In the long run it's not worth it, but right now, it's the temptation. What's the brain basis of resisting temptation?

Here's sort of a classic economic scenario. What you've got are two choices: work versus reward. You could do one unit of work and get one unit of reward. Or a little bit later, if you're willing to do two units of work, you get three units of reward. Ah ha, if you're only disciplined enough to hold out and do the harder thing, do the two units of work, you're going to get a greater reward in the long run.

When is the brain least able to resist the temptation of going for the cheap fast payoff?

What you see in the first scenario on this chart is, suppose the cheap payoff comes four weeks from now and the more disciplined higher payoff comes four and a half weeks from now. Anybody can resist the temptation there and hold out for the tougher, harder, but better choice. And what you see is the frontal cortex—that area of the brain that does this gratification postponement stuff—it doesn't have to get very active to make that choice.

Now make things a little bit harder. Now the temptation occurs a week from now and the more disciplined big pay off is four weeks from now. In order to resist the tempter, you see the frontal cortex is a little more activated. Now the devil is dangling right in front of you the cheap payoff two minutes from now versus the more disciplined outcome four years from now. In order to resist the tempter, what you see in a study like this is massive activation of the frontal cortex. Don't do it! Don't do it! Hold out! Hold out! We're beginning to see the brain basis of don't stab the partner right in the back there in this game theory game. Hold out. It pays off in the long run. We see the brain basis of it.

Now all of this is built around, again, that model of we are rational, economic machines. We've already seen one way in which it's not. Cooperation activates more of those pleasure pathways than cheating against the cooperating opponent. Here's a fascinating study a few years ago showing not only how irrational we can be, but how an emotional settings can change the rationality of our choices.

Okay, here's a classic philosophy problem. You've got some trolley car that's rolling out of control; its brake has failed. It's barreling down the tracks and is about to hit and kill five people. You've got a choice. You can leap over and pull a lever; and by pulling the lever this diverts the trolley onto a different track where it kills one person. Do you pull the lever? In order to save five lives do you sacrifice that one person?

Here's the second scenario. The trolley is barreling out of control about to kill those five people and there's some beefy guy standing right in front of you. With your own hands, you can push him onto the track. He'll get killed, but it will stop the trolley. Do you do it? To save five people will you sacrifice one? In a formal mathematical sense, these are absolutely equivalent choices. Do you kill one in order to save five? In the first case you do nothing more emotionally soiling than pull a lever. In the second case, you use your own hands to push the person onto the track. And even though from an economic standpoint these are absolutely equivalent, people are three times more likely to choose to pull the lever than to push with their own hands. The latter case is just too emotionally salient; it's your own hands that are pushing a person to their death. What you see there is great relevance. Pushing a button and dropping some bomb from 30,000 feet up in the air is a lot easier to do than using your own bloodied hands. It's about a three-fold difference in which version people are willing to do.

So in this wonderful study they went and brain-imaged people when they were considering the two different versions of the trolley scenario. What you see is, depending on how it's framed, do you save five by sacrificing one by pulling a lever, or do you do it by pushing with your own hands? When the person is contemplating the pulling the lever scenario, what metabolically lights up? It's their cortex. And, when instead, they're contemplating, do I push someone to their death with my own hands, what part of the brain lights up? It's the limbic system.

In other words, depending on how this mathematically equivalent scenario is presented to you; depending on how much it's dripping, marinating in emotion, you engage completely different parts of the brain. And what that winds up telling you is that depending on the emotional content of things, you're using very different parts of the brain to decide what's the appropriate optimal thing to do.

So what we see here in this ending is, this is a realm where there's not only a whole lot of rationality and behavior, but it's even irrational insofar as you're using different parts of the brain to decide what to do. Now what all of these lectures have been about, these last three, is looking at the evolution of behavior. Implicit in that is the evolution of genes that do something in the nervous system; that has something to do with behavior. And it's right at this point that people often get conniptions saying, all this theorizing about the evolution of genes, what do genes actually have to do with behavior? And that's now going to be the subject of our next few lectures.

Glossary

Acetylcholine: A neurotransmitter whose functions include release from the ends of the final neurons in the parasympathetic nervous system.

Action potential: The burst of electrical excitation that shoots down the axon when a neuron is sufficiently stimulated via its dendrites. (Contrast with **resting potential**.)

Activational effects of hormones: A hormonal effect (typically in adults) that has an immediate consequence. (Contrast with **organizational effects**.)

Amino acids: The building blocks of proteins; about 20 different kinds, akin to letters, exist. Unique sequences of amino acids are strung together to form a particular protein. That sequence determines the folded shape of that protein and, thus, its function.

Amygdala: A limbic structure with a key role in aggression and fear, as well as sexual arousal in males.

Anabolic hormones: A rather imprecise term typically denoting androgenic (testosterone-related) hormones.

Androgens: A class of steroid hormones, including testosterone, with roles in aggression and sexual behavior in both sexes but most notably in males. (See also **anabolic hormones**.)

Autonomic nervous system (ANS): A series of neural pathways originating in the hypothalamus, hindbrain, and brainstem and projecting throughout the body; it regulates all sorts of nonconscious, automatic physiological changes throughout the body. The ANS consists of the sympathetic and parasympathetic nervous systems.

Axon hillock: The beginning of the axon; this is the point where small excitatory inputs from various dendrites are summated and, if of a sufficient magnitude, trigger an action potential.

Axon terminal: The part of the neuron from which neurotransmitters are released.

Axon: The part of the neuron that sends signals to other neurons. (Contrast with **dendrite**.)

Behaviorism: The school of American psychology that posited that the incidence of all behaviors can be shaped by reward and punishment and that these patterns are sufficiently universal that virtually any vertebrate species can be a stand-in for learning principles in humans. (Contrast with **ethology**.)

Benzodiazepines: Compounds that reduce anxiety. Synthetic versions include Valium and Librium; naturally occurring versions are found within the brain, but their chemical structure is poorly understood.

Central nervous system: The brain and spinal cord. (Contrast with **peripheral nervous system**.)

Chromosome: A long, continuous sequence of genes. Metaphorically, the genome is like a massive phone book of information, with each message being a single gene made up of DNA letters. Because of its size, it is broken into separate volumes—each volume being a chromosome.

Compulsion: See **obsessive-compulsive disorder**.

Congenital adrenal hyperplasia: A disorder in which female fetuses are exposed to high levels of androgens (male sex hormones).

Dendrite: The part of the neuron that receives signals from other neurons. Dendrites tend to come in the form of highly branched cables coming from the cell body of a neuron. (Contrast with **axon**.)

Deoxyribonucleic acid (DNA): the nucleic acid that carries the genetic information of the cell.

Dopamine: A neurotransmitter whose functions include a role in sequential thought (such that abnormal dopamine levels are associated with the disordered thought of schizophrenia), the anticipation of pleasure, and aspects of fine motor control.

Endocrinology: The study of hormones.

Epinephrine (a.k.a. adrenaline): Both a neurotransmitter throughout the brain and a hormone released in the adrenal gland during stress as a result of activation of the sympathetic nervous system.

Estrogen: A class of female reproductive hormones.

Ethology: The study of the behavior of animals in their natural environments. (Contrast with **behaviorism**.)

Excitatory neurotransmitter: See **neurotransmitter**.

Exon: The stretch of DNA coding for a gene can occasionally be broken into separate parts, called *exons*. The intervening stretches of DNA, which do not code for anything, are called **introns**.

Fixed action pattern: A term in ethology referring to a behavior that occurs in a fairly intact form even in the absence of experience or learning but can be further refined by experience.

Frontal cortex: A recently evolved region of the brain that plays a central role in executive cognitive function, decision making, gratification postponement, and regulation of the limbic system.

Frontotemporal dementia: A neurological disorder (most often due to a specific mutation) in which disintegration of the frontal cortex occurs.

Game theory: A field of mathematics formalizing strategies used in games of cooperation and/or competition.

Gene: A stretch of DNA that designates the construction of one protein.

Gene-environment interaction: The virtually universal phenomenon in which the effect of a gene varies as a function of the environment in which it is transcribed.

Gene transcription: The process of a gene being "read" and transcribed into RNA.

Glial cells: An accessory type of cell found in the nervous system. Glial cells support neuronal function by insulating the axons of neurons, indirectly supplying neurons with energy, scavenging dead neurons, and removing toxins from the extracellular space around neurons. (Contrast with **neurons**.)

Glucocorticoids: A class of steroid hormones secreted during stress. They include cortisol (a.k.a. hydrocortisone) and synthetic versions, such as prednisone and dexamethasone.

Glutamate: An excitatory neurotransmitter with critical roles in learning and memory. An excess of glutamate induces *excitotoxicity*, a route by which neurons are killed during various neurological insults.

Gradualism: The theory that evolutionary changes occur constantly, in small, incremental steps. (Contrast with **punctuated equilibrium**.) Gradualism produces microevolutionary changes.

Group selection: The mostly discredited notion that evolution works on groups rather than individuals and, thus, that the evolution of behavior can be understood in the context of animals behaving "for the good of the species." (Contrast with **individual selection**.)

Hippocampus: A brain region within the limbic system that plays a central role in learning and memory.

Hormones: Blood-borne chemical messengers between cells.

Hypothalamus: A limbic structure that receives heavy inputs from other parts of the limbic system; plays a central role in regulating both the autonomic nervous system and hormone release.

Imprinted genes: Genes whose function differs depending on whether they are inherited from the father or mother. Imprinting of genes in this context should not be mistaken with the ethological notion of imprinting.

Imprinting: An ethological concept in which a permanent change in behavior occurs rapidly, in the absence of experience (for example, the imprinting of newborn birds onto their mother).

Individual selection: A contemporary notion in evolutionary biology that natural selection works mostly at the level of the individual and, thus, that the evolution of behavior can be understood in the context of animals behaving to maximize the number of copies of their genes passed on to the next generation. (Contrast with **group selection**.)

Inhibitory neurotransmitter: See **neurotransmitter**.

Innate releasing mechanism (IRM): An ethological term referring to the physiological mechanisms by which a stimulus (for example, a releasing stimulus) triggers a behavior (for example, a fixed action pattern).

Intron: A stretch of DNA that does not actually code for a gene but, instead, breaks up a gene into separate parts (called **exons**).

Jumping genes: See **transposable genetic elements**.

Kin selection: A contemporary notion in evolutionary biology that an individual can maximize the number of copies of his or her genes that are passed on by aiding the reproduction of relatives.

Kluver-Bucy syndrome: A set of behavioral changes, including elevated levels of aggression, resulting from removal of large parts of the limbic system, including the amygdala.

Limbic system: A part of the brain most strikingly involved in emotion. Some major parts include the hippocampus, amygdala, hypothalamus, and septum.

Long-term potentiation (LTP): A phenomenon in which the strength of synaptic communication between two neurons is enhanced in a persistent manner; thought to be a cellular analog of learning.

Mutation: An error in the copying of a gene. Classically, mutations can take three forms: In *point mutations*, a letter in the DNA code is misread as a different letter. In *deletion mutations*, a letter is entirely lost. In *insertion mutations*, an extra letter is inserted.

Myelin sheath: The insulation, made from glial cells, that wraps around the axons of neurons. Myelin allows action potentials to travel down the axon more quickly.

Neurobiology: The study of the nervous system.

Neuroeconomics: A new field examining the brain bases of economic decision making.

Neuroendocrinology: The study of the interactions between the nervous system and hormones.

Neuroethology: The study of the neural mechanisms mediating the naturalistic behavior of animals.

Neurons: The primary cells of the nervous system. (Contrast with **glial cells**.)

Neurotransmitter: Chemical messengers released from axon terminals as a result of an action potential; these travel across the synapse and bind to specific receptors on the postsynaptic side, thereby changing the electrical excitation of the second neuron. Excitatory neurotransmitters increase the likelihood that the next

©2005 The Teaching Company Limited Partnership

neuron will have an action potential, whereas inhibitory neurotransmitters decrease the likelihood.

Nongenetic inheritance: A phenomenon in which some event in the fetus changes the function of that individual when she is an adult, and that change produces a similar change in her own eventual fetus. Thus, a trait can be passed on for generations but in a way that does not involve genes and classic inheritance.

Norepinephrine (a.k.a. noradrenaline): A neurotransmitter whose functions include release from the ends of the final neurons in the sympathetic nervous system, as well as a role in depression (with, most likely, a depletion occurring).

Obsession: See **obsessive-compulsive disorder**.

Obsessive-compulsive disorder: A neuropsychiatric disorder categorized by virtually ceaseless intrusions of distracting, disturbing, and repetitive thoughts (*obsessions*) and by irresistible urges to carry out pointless, ritualistic behaviors (*compulsions*).

Organizational effects of hormones: Hormonal effects early in life (for example, in the fetus) that do not have an immediate consequence but that cause changes in the body's response to some hormone during adult life. (Contrast with **activational effects**.)

Pair-bonding species: Species in which mating tends to be monogamous. (Contrast with **tournament species**.)

Parasympathetic nervous system (PNS): The half of the autonomic nervous system associated with calm, vegetative function. (Contrast with **sympathetic nervous system**.)

Peptide hormones: A class of hormones made from amino acids. They predominately work by changing the activity of preexisting proteins.

Peripheral nervous system: Neurons and associated glial cells that occur outside the brain or spinal cord. (Contrast with **central nervous system**.)

Pituitary: The gland underneath the hypothalamus that releases an array of hormones under the control of the brain.

Plasticity: The general notion of aspects of neural function changing over time.

Prisoner's Dilemma: A classic game theory scenario.

Progesterone: A class of female reproductive hormones.

Promoters: Stretches of DNA that do not code for a gene but serve as the on-off switch for a gene to be transcribed.

Protein: Long strings of amino acids. Unique sequences of amino acids are strung together to form a particular protein. That sequence determines the folded shape of that protein and, thus, its function.

Pseudokinship: A form of cultural manipulation by which people are led to view other individuals as more related to them than they actually are.

Pseudospeciation: A form of cultural manipulation by which people are led to view other individuals as less related to them than they actually are.

Punctuated equilibrium: The theory that evolution consists of long periods of stasis, when there are no evolutionary changes, interspersed with periods of rapid and dramatic change. (Contrast with **gradualism**.) Punctuated equilibrium produces macroevolutionary changes.

Releasing stimulus: An ethological term referring to the sensory stimulus in an environment that triggers a behavior.

Resting potential: The state of electrical excitation in a neuron when it is quiescent. (Contrast with **action potential**.)

Ribonucleic acid (RNA): An intermediate form of information. A strand of RNA is made under the direction of a single gene; that stretch of RNA, in turn, contains the information for the stringing together of amino acids into a protein.

RNA translation: The process of RNA being "read" and translated into protein.

Schizotypal personality disorder: A neuropsychiatric disorder, on a genetic continuum with schizophrenia, characterized by social withdrawal, overly concrete thought, and metamagical beliefs.

Selective serotonin reuptake inhibitors (SSRIs): Drugs such as Prozac that block the removal of serotonin from the synapse. Insofar as they lessen the symptoms of depression, this implies depression involves a shortage of dopamine.

Septum: Limbic structure with a key role in inhibiting aggression.

Serotonin: A neurotransmitter whose functions include a role in aggression, sleep onset, depression, and impulsivity.

Spatial summation: When an action potential is triggered thanks to enough separate dendritic inputs being stimulated all at once. (Contrast with **temporal summation**.)

Steroid hormones: A class of hormones made from steroid precursor molecules that include estrogens, progestins, androgens, glucocorticoids, and mineralocorticoids. They predominately work by changing genomic events in cells.

Sympathetic nervous system (SNS): The half of the autonomic nervous system associated with arousal and emergency physiological responses. (Contrast with **parasympathetic nervous system**.)

Synapse: The space between an axon terminal and the dendritic spine of the next neuron.

Synaptic plasticity: The concept of the strength of communication between two neurons changing over time.

Temporal personality disorder: A neuropsychiatric disorder associated with temporal lobe epilepsy, characterized by perseverative behavioral patterns, aversion to novelty, obsessive writing (hypergraphia), and an intense interest in religious and philosophical subjects.

Temporal summation: When an action potential is triggered thanks to the same subthreshold dendritic input being stimulated over and over. (Contrast with **spatial summation**.)

Testosterone: A subtype of androgen.

Theory of mind: The understanding that other individuals have different thoughts and knowledge than you; most frequently used as a term in child development.

Thrifty metabolism: The idea that malnutrition during the prenatal environment causes metabolic "programming" so that for the rest of the individual's life, there is more efficient storage of nutrients.

Tourette's syndrome: A neuropsychiatric disorder categorized by uncontrolled outbursts of scatology, tics, and utterances.

Tournament species: Species in which mating tends to be highly polygamous and involves high levels of male-male aggression and competition. (Contrast with **pair-bonding species**.)

Transcription factors: Messengers (often proteins) that bind to promoters and turn genes on or off.

Transposable genetic elements: Stretches of DNA that can be moved around; also called *jumping genes*.

Ventral tegmentum: A brain region that sends dopamine-releasing axons to the frontal cortex and limbic system, where that dopamine plays a central role in reward and anticipation of reward.

Biographical Notes

Axelrod, Robert (1943–). Economist who is a key figure in game theory/neuroeconomics, being the first to generate Prisoner's Dilemma round robins and showing the utility of the tit-for-tat strategy.

Cannon, Walter (1871–1945). One of the founders of stress physiology. Major figure in delineating the functions of the autonomic nervous system. Coined the term *fight-or-flight syndrome*.

Eldredge, Niles (1943–). Evolutionary biologist who, along with S. J. Gould, generated the punctuated equilibrium hypothesis.

Gage, Phineas (1823–1860). Famous neurological patient whose frontal cortex was destroyed in an accidental explosion.

Gould, Stephen Jay (1941–2002). Evolutionary biologist and science writer. One of the two scientists (along with Nils Eldredge) who generated the punctuated equilibrium hypothesis.

Guillemin, Roger (1924–). Nobel Laureate endocrinologist who, along with Andrew Schally, first identified the hormones with which the brain regulates the anterior pituitary.

Haldane, J. B. S. (1892–1964). Evolutionary biologist and leftist political writer.

Hamilton, William D. (1936–2000). Evolutionary biologist who, among other things, played a central role in the shift in the field away from group selection thinking.

Harlow, Harry (1905–1981). Psychologist who pioneered studies regarding the importance of maternal care and peer socialization on development in primates.

Hebb, Donald (1904–1985). Neuroscientist most closely associated with the idea that learning involves the strengthening of connections of preexisting synapses, rather than the formation of new synapses.

Hubel, David (1926–). Nobel Laureate who, along with Torsten Wiesel, did classic work showing how the cortex processes visual information.

Kety, Seymour (1915–2000). Psychiatrist who pioneered adoption studies for identifying genetic contributions to mental illness, beginning with his work on schizophrenia.

Kohlberg, Lawrence (1927–1987). Psychologist who has been the central figure in the study of moral development in children.

Lorenz, Konrad (1903–1989). Nobel Laureate who, along with Niko Tinbergen and Karl von Frisch, founded ethology. Was also a Nazi propagandist who was jailed for his activities after World War II.

McClintock, Barbara (1902–1992). Nobel Laureate who, amid decades of skepticism, pioneered the notion that genes could move around the genome (that is, transposable genetic elements).

Mendel, Gregor (1822–1884). Father of genetics who, in his classic breeding studies, pioneered the notion of dominant and recessive heritable traits.

Moniz, António Caetano de Abreu Freire Egas (1874–1955). Nobel Laureate neurologist who invented frontal lobotomies.

Papez, James (1883–1958). Neurologist who first conceived of the limbic system as an integrated brain region central to emotion.

Schally, Andrew (1926–). Nobel Laureate endocrinologist who, along with Roger Guillemin, first identified the hormones with which the brain regulates the anterior pituitary.

Selye, Hans (1907–1982). One of the founders of stress physiology, playing the central role in uncovering the importance of glucocorticoid hormones in the stress response.

Skinner, B. F. (1904–1990). Psychologist and writer who was a leading figure throughout the century in advocating behaviorism.

Tinbergen, Niko (1907–1988). Nobel Laureate who, along with Karl von Frisch and Konrad Lorenz, founded ethology.

Vale, Wylie (1941–). Key figure in the characterization of various hypothalamic hormones; first to do so for CRH, the initiator of the stress response.

von Frisch, Karl (1886–1982). Nobel Laureate who, along with Niko Tinbergen and Konrad Lorenz, founded ethology.

Watson, John B. (1878–1958). Psychologist generally viewed as being the founder of behaviorism.

Wiesel, Torsten (1924–). Nobel Laureate who, along with David Hubel, did classic work showing how the cortex processes visual information.

Wilson, Edward O. (1929–). Entomologist, naturalist, and writer who, among other major contributions, is viewed as one of the central figures in the field of sociobiology.

Bibliography

Introductory Readings (not necessarily easy but should be accessible to the motivated nonscientist):

Alcock, J. *Animal Behavior: An Evolutionary Approach*, 7th ed. Sunderland, MA: Sinauer, 2001. A great introduction to ethology.

Barash, D. *The Survival Game: How Game Theory Explains the Biology of Cooperation and Competition*. New York: Times Books, 2003. A good introduction to game theory.

Barondes, S. *Molecules and Mental Illness*, 2nd ed. New York: Scientific American Library, W.H. Freeman, 1999. A particularly good overview of what neurotransmitters have to do with mental illness.

Becker, J., M. Breedlove, D. Crews, and M. McCarthy. *Behavioral Endocrinology*, 2nd ed. Cambridge, MA: MIT Press, 2002. An excellent text on neuroendocrinology, including the subjects of hormones and aggression and early endocrine exposure and aggression.

Brown, A. *The Darwin Wars: The Scientific Battle for the Soul of Man*. London: Simon and Schuster, 1999. A good introduction to evolution and the neurobiology of behavior.

Coles, R. *The Moral Intelligence of Children: How to Raise a Moral Child*. New York: Penguin/Putnam, 1998. A classic in the field of moral development in children. Also covers the subject of the evolution of aggression and nonaggression.

Damasio, A. *Descartes' Error: Emotion, Reason, and the Human Brain*. New York: HarperCollins, 1994. A masterly introduction to the role of the frontal cortex in emotional regulation. Also covers the subject of the evolution of aggression and nonaggression.

Damon, W. *Moral Child: Nurturing Children's Natural Moral Growth*. New York: Free Press, 1988. A classic in the field of moral development in children. Also covers the subject of the evolution of aggression and nonaggression.

Kalat, J. *Biological Psychology*, 8th ed. Belmont, CA: Wadsworth Thomson Learning, 2003. A particularly good and accessible treatment of the autonomic nervous system.

Kohlberg, L. *The Psychology of Moral Development: The Nature and Validity of Moral Stages*. New York: Harper and Row, 1984. A summary of the work of the psychologist who has been the central figure in the study of moral development in children. Also covers the subject of the evolution of aggression and nonaggression.

Konner, M. *The Tangled Wing: Biological Constraints on the Human Spirit*. New York: Times Books/Henry Holt, 2002. Probably the most nuanced and insightful book available concerning the biology of human behavior (and beautifully written by an eminent scientist/physician). Includes in-depth coverage of aggression and the theories about the nature of aggression.

Kruuk, H. *Niko's Nature: The Life of Niko Tinbergen and His Science of Animal Behaviour*. Oxford, U.K.: Oxford University Press, 2003. A nice biography of Tinbergen, who was truly a giant of a scientist and person.

LeDoux, J. *The Emotional Brain: The Mysterious Underpinnings of Emotional Life*. New York: Simon and Schuster, 1996. A good reference on the limbic system.

———. *Synaptic Self: How Our Brains Become Who We Are*. New York: Penguin Books, 2002. As with LeDoux's 1996 publication, a fine book covering the limbic system.

Lewontin, R. *It Ain't Necessarily So: The Dream of the Human Genome and Other Illusions*. New York: New York Review of Books, 2000. A very strong critique of behavioral genetics as a field by an eminent geneticist.

MacLean, P. *The Triune Brain in Evolution: Role in Paleocerebral Functions*. New York: Plenum Press, 1990. A classic on the subject by one of the key people in the field.

Moore, D. *The Dependent Gene: The Fallacy of Nature vs. Nurture*. New York: Times Books, 2002. An excellent introduction to the subject of macroevolution of genes and the regulation of gene expression by the environment.

Nelson, R. *Handbook of Biology of Aggression*. Oxford, U.K.: Oxford University Press, 2005. An excellent introduction to the topic of aggression.

———. *An Introduction to Behavioral Endocrinology*, 2nd ed. Sunderland, MA: Sinauer, 2000. An excellent text on neuroendocrinology, including the subjects of hormones and aggression and early endocrine exposure and aggression.

Niehoff, D. *The Biology of Violence*. New York: Free Press, 1998. An excellent introduction to the topic of aggression.

Plomin, R. *Behavioral Genetics*, 3rd ed. New York: W.H. Freeman, 1997. An excellent introduction to what genes might have to do with behavior; written by a leader in the field. Includes the extraordinarily controversial subject of genetics and aggression.

Ridley, M. *Nature via Nurture: Genes, Experience, and What Makes Us Human*. New York: HarperCollins, 2003. An excellent introduction to the subject of macroevolution of genes and the regulation of gene expression by the environment.

———. *The Origins of Virtue: Human Instincts and the Evolution of Cooperation*. New York: Penguin Books, 1998. A good introduction to evolution and the neurobiology of behavior.

Sapolsky, R. *Monkeyluv and Other Essays on Our Lives as Animals*. New York: Scribner, 2005. By the course professor; contains further information about the neurobiology of our individual differences.

———. *The Trouble with Testosterone and Other Essays on the Biology of the Human Predicament*. New York: Scribner, 1997. By the course professor; contains further information about the neurobiology of our individual differences.

Squire, L. *Memory and Brain*. Oxford, U.K.: Oxford University Press, 1987. A good, although somewhat dated, introduction to the neurobiology of learning and memory, including long-term potentiation.

Whishaw, I., and B. Kolb. *Fundamentals of Human Neuropsychology*, 5th ed. New York: Worth Books, 2003. A review of the cognitive aspects of frontal function. Also covers the subject of the evolution of aggression and nonaggression.

Widmaier, E., H. Raff, and K. Strang. *Vander, Sherman, and Luciano's Human Physiology*, 9th ed. Boston, MA: McGraw Hill, 2004. A good, broad introduction to the nervous system.

Advanced Readings:

Cooper, J., F. Bloom, and R. Roth. *The Biochemical Basis of Neuropharmacology*, 8th ed. Oxford, U.K.: Oxford University Press, 2003. The best introductory book specifically about neurotransmission.

Gould, S. *The Structure of Evolutionary Theory*. Cambridge, MA: Harvard University Press, 2002. A massive overview of the idea of punctuated equilibrium.

Kandel, E., J. Schwartz, and T. Jessell. *The Foundations of Neural Science*, 4th ed. Boston, MA: McGraw Hill, 2000. The best (although quite advanced) textbook in the field of neurobiology.

Larsen, P., et al. *William's Textbook of Endocrinology*, 10th ed. Philadelphia: Saunders, 2003. The (very difficult) bible of the field of neuroendocrinology.

Nicholls, J., R. Martin, B. Wallace, and P. Fuchs. *From Neuron to Brain*, 4th ed. Sunderland, MA: Sinauer, 2001. A more advanced treatment of the nervous system.

Siegel, G., and B. Agranoff. *Basic Neurochemistry: Molecular, Cellular, and Medical Aspects*, 6th ed. Philadelphia: Lippincott-Raven, 1999. A more advanced text covering neurotransmission.

Squire, L. *Fundamental Neuroscience*, 2nd ed. London, U.K.: Academic Press, 2002. An excellent neuroscience textbook that covers long-term potentiation in some detail.

Watson, J., et al. *Molecular Biology of the Gene*, 5th ed. San Francisco: Pearson/Benjamin Cummings, 2004. A classic overview of how genes work by the co-discoverer of the structure of DNA.

Wilson, E. O. *Sociobiology: The New Synthesis, Twenty-fifth Anniversary Edition*. Cambridge, MA: Belknap Press, 2000. The most magisterial book on the subject of the evolution of behavior.

Internet Resources:

Harry Frank Guggenheim Foundation. http://www.hfg.org/. This organization funds research devoted to the understanding of violence. Once on the home page, click on "Search Research Reports."

International Brain Research Organization (IBRO). http://www.iac-usnc.org/education.html. This page contains several portals to lectures by leading neuroscientists. Some, however, are likely to be technical.

National Institute of Mental Health. http://www.nimh.nih.gov/. Home page for the main government branch devoted to research in mental health. There are numerous points on this home page that will gain entry to information relevant to this course.

Society for Neuroscience. http://web.sfn.org. Home page for the largest organization in the world devoted to the study of the brain. Once at the main site, click on "Public Resources."